The EVERYTHING
FAMILY TREE BOOK
2ND EDITION

Dear Reader:

You are about to embark on an exciting adventure. By picking up this book, you've taken the first step toward discovering more about yourself and the people and events from the past that made you what you are today.

My fascination with the past got off to a slow start. I distinctly remember, as a child, yawning through family stories. I often moaned about having to visit this or that relative, and lamented having to spend time in school learning about people who were dead. As it is for many other people, a school genealogy project was the catalyst for me. The family tree drawn out by my mother in my baby book, and the long letters full of names, dates, and places from both of my grandmothers, had me interested despite myself. Then there was the family trip to France; looking for family surnames in the old cemetery in Crespières where my maternal great-grandparents are buried was my favorite day of the entire trip. I was hooked! Twenty years later, I still am.

I appreciate this chance to introduce you to the fascinating and exhilarating challenge known as genealogy. I hope you'll soon be happily digging through the attic, searching online, hunting at the courthouse, and poking around in the cemetery. The thrill of finding that first clue to your ancestors is just the beginning, leading you eagerly to the next clue and the next. It's a lifelong journey, and I'm honored that you've chosen to begin it here.

Happy hunting,

Kimberly Powell

The EVERYTHING® Series

Editorial

Publishing Director	Gary M. Krebs
Associate Managing Editor	Laura M. Daly
Associate Copy Chief	Brett Palana-Shanahan
Acquisitions Editor	Gina Chaimanis
Development Editor	Rachel Engelson
Associate Production Editor	Casey Ebert

Production

Director of Manufacturing	Susan Beale
Associate Director of Production	Michelle Roy Kelly
Cover Design	Paul Beatrice
	Matt LeBlanc
	Erick DaCosta
Design and Layout	Colleen Cunningham
	Holly Curtis
	Sorae Lee
Series Cover Artist	Barry Littmann

Visit the entire Everything® Series at *www.everything.com*

THE

EVERYTHING®
FAMILY TREE BOOK
2ND EDITION

Research and preserve your family history

Kimberly Powell

Adams Media
Avon, Massachusetts

*To my grandparents—Granddad, Granddaddy Owens, Grandmother,
and Mama—for kindling my passion for family history with your
stories, your faith, and your love.*

An Everything® Series Book.
Everything® and everything.com® are registered trademarks of F+W Publications, Inc.

Published by Adams Media, an F+W Publications Company
57 Littlefield Street, Avon, MA 02322 U.S.A.
www.adamsmedia.com

ISBN: 1-59337-395-3
Printed in the United States of America.

J I H G F E D C B A

**Library of Congress Cataloging-in-Publication Data
is available from the publisher.**

This publication is designed to provide accurate and authoritative information with regard
to the subject matter covered. It is sold with the understanding that the publisher is not
engaged in rendering legal, accounting, or other professional advice. If legal advice or
other expert assistance is required, the services of a competent professional person should
be sought.

     —From a *Declaration of Principles* jointly adopted by a Committee of the
American Bar Association and a Committee of Publishers and Associations

Many of the designations used by manufacturers and sellers to distinguish their products
are claimed as trademarks. Where those designations appear in this book and Adams
Media was aware of a trademark claim, the designations have been printed with initial
capital letters.

*This book is available at quantity discounts for bulk purchases.
For information, please call 1-800-872-5627.*

Contents

Acknowledgments

Books are so much more than a product of the author. My heartfelt appreciation goes out to everyone at Adams Media who made this book possible, especially Gina Chaimanis for her infinite patience and insightful ideas. A special thanks goes to Barb Doyen for giving me this chance, and to my mother, Roselyne Thomas, for being my second set of eyes. I'd also like to thank the many readers of my Web site at About.com (✍*http://genealogy.about.com*) for their questions and comments, which keep me learning every day.

This book wouldn't have been possible without the love, support, and encouragement of my wonderful family. To my husband and soulmate, Albrecht, I'd like to say thanks for believing in me. Your faith is the reason this book is a reality. And to my amazing children—Kelsey, Garrett, and Kira—your help in giving Mommy time to write was the best present of all. I hope this book makes you proud.

Top Ten Beginner Mistakes to Avoid

1. Not everyone with your last name is a relative. Just because your last name is Washington doesn't mean you have a connection to America's first president.

2. Don't trust everything you see in print. Whether you find it online or in a book, confirm any information you find by going back to the original source when possible.

3. Don't neglect your living relatives. They are the single best resource for family information that can't be found elsewhere.

4. Don't do all of your searching online. The Internet is an excellent source of genealogical information, but a lot of the pieces to the puzzle of your family tree will only be found in libraries, archives, and other repositories.

5. Beware the generic family history. Those mass-produced coats of arms and family tree scrolls that you see at the mall or receive fliers for in the mail won't tell you anything about your own family tree.

6. Family legends aren't always fact. While most family stories of scandalous ancestors or famous relatives may have somebasis in fact, they often tend to be exaggerated with each retelling. Don't take them as truth, but don't ignore them, either—research them instead.

7. Genealogy isn't just name collecting. While it is fulfilling to watch your family tree grow, it is more exciting to learn about the people behind the names and dates.

8. Don't expect others to do your work for you. Genealogists are a very helpful bunch, but they are more likely to want to help you if you've obviously done your own homework first.

9. Names do change. Familiarize yourself with all the names used by your ancestors, and don't neglect to search for all alternate spellings.

10. Document every source you have searched, even if you fail to find anything helpful. Otherwise you'll waste hours re-examining documents and Web sites that you've already looked at.

Introduction

▶ HAVE YOU EVER THOUGHT you might be related to a president or a queen? Been curious about why Grandpa never spoke about his family? Hoped for a bit of scandal in your background? Wondered who your red hair and freckles came from? People have all sorts of questions about their family history, and just as many unique motivations for digging into their roots. What starts as a curiosity, however, soon grows into a passion. Some even say it's an addiction. Consider yourself warned!

Genealogy, the study of family history or descent, is now the second most popular hobby in the United States, surpassed only by gardening. As many as 73 percent of Americans are interested in discovering their family history, according to a 2005 research poll by Market Strategies, Inc., and MyFamily.com, Inc. That's up almost 30 percent from a similar poll conducted by Maritz Research just ten years earlier. It's not surprising, then, to learn that the Family History Library in Salt Lake City is one of Utah's top ten tourist attractions, or that the Ellis Island immigration records Web site topped more than 2.5 billion hits during its first year of operation.

Genealogy is a fascinating field—there's no doubt about that. The challenge and excitement alone are enough to get some people interested. Most, however, start tracing their family tree because they want to learn more about themselves and their heritage. They find themselves curious after typing their surname into a search engine, learning they have an inherited health condition, or listening to family stories over Thanksgiving dinner. Some of the most common reasons for researching a family tree include: to satisfy a curiosity about yourself and your roots; to create a legacy for future generations; to compile a family medical history; to preserve family cultural and ethnic traditions; to write and publish a family history book; to confirm a family legend or verify descent from a famous individual; or to qualify for a lineage or heritage society like the Daughters of the American Revolution.

Whatever your own personal interests, you may wonder whether tracing your family tree is really worth the time and effort. Your ancestors are dead, after all. Genealogy is about much more than the past, however. It can bring families together, re-establish and strengthen family connections, and provide a legacy for future generations. The tremendous growth of genealogy on the Internet means that you can even fit your research into a few hours a month, so time and distance are no longer the constraint they once were. Genealogy really is a hobby for anyone.

With the steps and guidance provided in this book, you'll learn how to reach out and touch the past. You'll be able to locate your ancestors' headstones, track down second cousins, discover the meaning of your surname, and actually walk on the land where your forebears once lived. You'll also learn how to leave a legacy for future generations by preserving family photos and heirlooms, and sharing your discoveries in a written family history.

The thrill of uncovering and holding that first fragile, yellowed document that your ancestors once held themselves is one you'll have to experience to understand. Once you do, however, you'll be addicted for life. Genealogy is an extremely rewarding pastime, with continual new finds and challenges to keep it exciting. Thankfully, you'll never run out of new ancestors to discover.

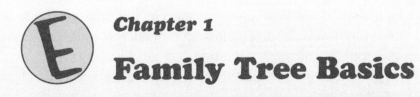

Chapter 1

Family Tree Basics

Genealogy is the study of relationships—the connections between individuals that have brought your family through history to the point at which you were born. Two parents, four grandparents, eight great-grandparents, sixteen great-great-grandparents . . . by the time you've worked your way through ten generations of your family you'll have discovered more than 1,000 ancestors! Before jumping into your past, however, you need to learn a few tools of the trade—the symbols, terms, and rules used by genealogists to collect, record, and present the relationships of a family tree.

Who Makes Up the Family Tree?

The family tree is the most recognized format for sorting out and displaying family connections. Named for its typical tree shape, a family tree refers to any type of graphical representation of the links between family members and generations. Using yourself as the trunk, the branches of the tree reaching out above you represent your ancestors (parents, grandparents, and so on), while your descendants (children, grandchildren, and so on) descend below you, forming the roots of the tree.

Family relationships are a bit more regular than are the branches on a tree, so it often makes more sense to think of your family tree as an inverted pyramid. In this layout, you are the point at the bottom. Not counting remarriages, the second generation upward on the inverted pyramid will include both of your parents; the third generation, your four grandparents (your parents' parents); the next generation, your eight great-grandparents; and so on. Thus, your ancestors form the ancestral pyramid, with each generation branching further to form an upside-down triangle.

Ancestral Pyramid
(Your Ancestors)

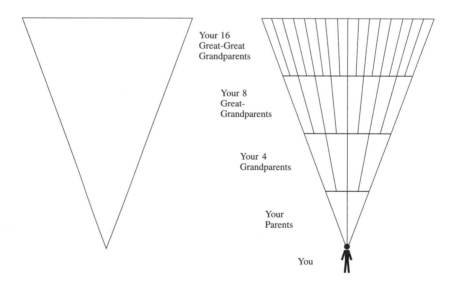

Your 16
Great-Great
Grandparents

Your 8
Great-
Grandparents

Your 4
Grandparents

Your
Parents

You

You can also use the pyramid to represent your descendants, by turning it right-side up. In this case, you are the point at the top, with your descendants—children, grandchildren, and great-grandchildren—branching out below you.

Descendants Pyramid
From a Common Ancestor Couple

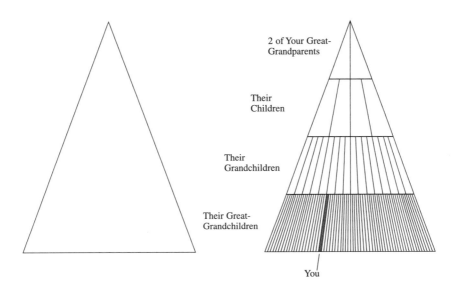

What Is an Ancestor?

Ancestors are the people from whom you are directly descended, such as your grandparents and great-grandparents. The relationship between you and your ancestors is known as a lineal relationship. Your aunts, uncles, and cousins are relatives, but they are not your ancestors. You are related because you descend from common ancestors, but you are not connected to each other in a direct (or lineal) line. You have a collateral relationship with these relatives.

Understanding Cousin Relationships

When they learn you're researching the family tree, the first thing most family members want to know is how they are related to you and each other. Siblings, aunts, uncles, and first cousins are pretty easy to figure out, but after that the relationships can get a bit tangled. When you start tossing out "you're my second cousin, twice removed," your relatives will know you mean business!

Although the general term "cousin" is usually specific enough for casual conversation, it is important when tracing the family tree to understand exactly how everyone is related to one another:

- First cousins are family members who have two of the same grandparents in common (in other words, the children of your parents' siblings are your first cousins).
- Second cousins have two great-grandparents in common, but not the same grandparents.
- Third cousins have two great-great-grandparents in common.

The term removed, when referring to cousins, means that the cousins are from different generations in the family tree. They still have ancestors in common, but are a different number of generations "removed" from those common ancestors. Once removed refers to a difference of one generation. Your father's first cousin is also your first cousin, but once removed. You share grandparents in common, which makes you first cousins, but you are one generation further down the family tree than is your father's first cousin—making him your first cousin, once removed. Twice removed refers to a two-generation difference between cousins; three times removed a three-generation difference; and so on.

FACT

Family trees can be presented in a number of layouts. They can be fan shaped, with the lines radiating out from you at the center. They can also be hourglass shaped, with you in the middle, your ancestors above you, and your descendants below. As long as the design represents the links between generations, it still can be called a family tree.

Half, Step, and Adopted Relationships

Blended families are very common these days, so most family trees contain at least a few nontraditional relationships. Half relationships, step relationships, and adoptions all have their place in the family tree. Bonds of love and family can be just as strong as bonds of blood, and should be portrayed as such in any family history. Most genealogy software programs (see Chapter 17) give you the option to specify the specific relationship between two individuals with tags such as natural, adopted, foster, married, partners, friends, or private. Unless it is a sensitive family issue, it is best to honestly identify all relationships for what they are.

Charting Your Course

As you begin to collect names, dates, places, and other details about your family, special charts can help you keep track of your data and put the pieces together. Intended primarily as research tools, genealogical charts can help you easily identify at a glance what progress you have made and where you still have more information that you need to obtain. You can create the charts with pencil and paper or on a computer—whichever method best works for you.

ALERT!

Be aware that family relationships may often be loosely defined, or have meanings that have changed over time. The terms "junior" and "senior" may refer to an uncle and nephew, or even two unrelated people, as well as to father and son. Sometimes, people may have even referred to family friends by names such as "aunt" or "uncle."

The two most common charts used by genealogists to record their research data are the pedigree chart and the family group sheet. You can download and print blank versions of these on the Internet at no cost or print them from many family tree software programs. You also can purchase them in a wide variety of formats from many genealogical companies and bookstores.

Pedigree Chart

The most commonly recognized genealogical chart is the pedigree chart. This chart begins with you and branches back through the generations, displaying the lines of your direct ancestors. This chart is sometimes referred to as an ancestry chart, lineage chart, or family tree. A standard pedigree chart covers four generations, with space to include names, plus dates and places of birth, death, and marriage for each individual. Larger pedigree charts with room for more generations also are available, but keep in mind that the more generations on the chart, the less room there is to enter data about each person.

Pedigree charts follow a standard format. The first line on the left (number 1) is where you enter your name, or the name of the person whose ancestry you are tracing. The father of individual number 1 is entered as number 2 on the upper line, while the mother is entered as number 3 on the lower line. Each time the generations branch, the male goes on top and his wife is listed below. Another easy way to remember is that men are always assigned even numbers, while the numbers for women are odd.

Pedigree charts don't usually include room for notes or source information. If you plan to share your pedigree chart with others, it helps to include a separate page with your notes and sources keyed to the information on your pedigree chart. Otherwise, people won't know the source of your facts or where to follow up if they note an inconsistency or error.

It won't take long before you run out of room on your original pedigree chart. When that happens, you'll need to create a new pedigree chart for each of the individuals included in the fourth generation on your first chart. For example, your paternal grandfather is listed as number 8 on your original pedigree chart. To add information about his parents, you will need to begin a new pedigree chart with your paternal grandfather listed as ancestor number 1. Label this new pedigree chart as Chart 2 and make a reference next to your paternal grandfather's space on chart 1 that his line is continued on Chart 2. To make it easy to connect generations, you should also make a note on Chart 2 referring back to the original chart (for example, person number 1 on Chart 2 is the same as person number 8 on Chart 1).

Alternatively, you can choose to follow a system that assigns a unique ID number to each individual in the family tree. In this case, Chart 2 would start with ancestor number 8, his father would be ancestor number 16 (twice his number) and his mother number 17 (twice his number plus one). This avoids the trouble of having to make reference notes pointing from one chart to the next. See Appendix B for a blank pedigree chart.

Family Group Sheet

A second commonly used genealogy chart is the family group sheet. This form focuses on the family unit, with room for more detail about individuals than the pedigree chart provides. Each family group sheet covers just one family—a couple and their children—with fields for recording birth, death, marriage, and burial place for each individual. Most family group sheets also include room for recording the spouse of each child. In addition, there is usually a section for notes and a place to include source reference numbers.

Pedigree charts and family group sheets work together to help you keep track of your research progress. The pedigree chart provides an overview of the family tree, while the family group sheet, which should be completed for each marriage on the pedigree chart, records further details about each individual family. See Appendix B for a family group sheet to use.

Taking Notes

Conducting interviews with relatives, sifting through photos and documents, and digging through databases on the Internet—researching a family tree quickly generates a lot of information. Even if you use a computer to enter data, note-taking with pencil and paper is still an important part of genealogy research. Good notes simplify the process of organizing and reviewing the information you find, and they protect you from having to rely on your memory for vital details.

Whenever possible, resist the temptation to scribble notes on envelopes, napkins, and other odds and ends. Such notes will get lost or end up in a big box in the back of the basement. A research notebook will keep your notes much more organized. The type of notebook isn't that important, but a three-ring binder allows you to take notes on loose-leaf paper, as well as include any photocopies that you make. If you like to type, a laptop computer also makes a good note-taking tool.

FACT

Even with a research notebook, there will be times when you scribble down notes on whatever is handy. Copying the notes into your notebook introduces the chance for transcription error, so paste, tape, or glue them into your notebook instead. Plastic sleeves inserted into a three-ring binder also make handy pouches for these little note-taking extras.

Notes are much more useful if you keep track of where and when the information was found. Label each page in your notebook with the date and place the notes were taken, as well as a complete reference, or citation, to the source of the information. If you're using a three-ring binder for note-taking, use only the front side of each page so that you can rearrange them more easily.

Whether writing down details from genealogical documents or transcribing a recorded conversation or interview, genealogical note-taking often involves copying details from an original source. This copying can take a number of forms, but the three most common are transcripts, abstracts, and extracts.

Transcribing

To transcribe, or make a transcription, is to copy a document word for word in its entirety. Everything is copied exactly as it appears in the original document, including any errors, misspellings, abbreviations, and punctuation. If something needs to be clarified, then comments can be added in square brackets—not in parentheses. This convention tells other readers that you have added the information contained within the brackets and that it was not found in the original. If you are uncertain about a particular word or phrase, then include what you can, underlining the part that is unclear.

Flag the word or phrase with a question mark enclosed in square brackets to show that the transcription is in doubt.

Abstracting

Abstracts are summaries that record all important details from a document or source, yet leave out nonessential words, punctuation, and so on. An abstract is basically a summary of the document's essential details—names, dates, places, and events. As with transcriptions, abstracts should seek to avoid personal interpretations of the data. Copy all names, dates, and abbreviations exactly as they appear, including misspellings, and record details in the same order in which they appear in the original.

ALERT!

If a name appears abbreviated in a document, copy the abbreviation rather than writing out a name in full. The Jos. may refer to Joseph, but it could also be Joshua. What looks like an *o* might turn out to be an *a*, meaning the name could also be James. If necessary, add your interpretation in square brackets after the abbreviated name.

Extracting

Extracts are similar to abstracts in that they include only portions of the original. Instead of summarizing, however, an extract is an exact word-for-word copy of selected portions of the document, set off by quotation marks. Extracts can stand alone, or be included as part of an abstract when phrases or paragraphs seem so important that they are copied word for word. When extracted portions of a document are included in an abstract, it is important to set them off with quotation marks to distinguish them from the abstracted material.

Writing It Right

Family history is meant to be shared, which is why genealogists use standard formats for entering data such as names, dates, and places. These conventions ensure that the information is as complete as possible, easy to understand, and not open to misinterpretation.

Recording Names

People's names are entered in their natural order—first name (also referred to as a forename or given name), middle name(s), and surname (last name). Married women are entered with their maiden name (surname at birth) rather than their husband's last name. If you prefer to include both last names, enclose the maiden name in parentheses prior to the married name.

While it is not necessary, most genealogists record surnames in capital letters. This makes it easy to distinguish surnames when scanning pedigree charts, family group sheets, and even message board posts.

John William BRIDGERS
Mary (Thomas) CARTER

Name recording conventions for special situations:

- When a woman has married more than once, enter the given name followed by the maiden name in parentheses, followed by the last names of her husbands in order of marriage. *Example:* Shelley Lynn (Koth) HIERS BISHOP
- Nicknames, if entered, should be included in quotes, not parentheses, following the given name. Example: Elizabeth "Mary" Rose BAKER
- If an individual is known by more than one name due to adoption, name change, or other situation, include the alternate name in parentheses following the surname. Precede the alternate name with "AKA" for "also known as." *Example:* John Roger POWELL (AKA John Roger BOATWRIGHT)
- Spellings of surnames often change over time, or may have been changed or "Americanized" at some point in history. Record the earlier surname first, followed by the more current usage. Example: Stanley Walter TOMAN/THOMAS

Most genealogy software programs allow you to choose how you want names, dates, and places to appear in your file and printed reports. This simplifies data entry because you can enter the data in any format, and the program will convert it to your chosen default setting. Last names, for example, will automatically be converted to all caps.

Recording Dates

Dates are written differently in the United States than they are in most other parts of the world. A date commonly written as July 12, 1969 (month, day, year) in the United States would be written as 12 July 1969 in most other countries. This makes little difference when the dates are written out, as in the above examples, but when you run across a date written 7/12/1969 it is hard to know whether it refers to July 12 or December 7. To avoid confusion in family histories, it is standard convention to use the day, month, and year format for all genealogical data, with the year written out in full to avoid confusion about which century it refers to. Months are generally written out in full, although standard three-letter abbreviations may be used. When in doubt about a date, record it exactly as written in the original source and include your interpretation in square brackets.

If you encounter the term *instant*, as in *the 8th instant*, in an old obituary or family letter, it refers to the current month (in other words, the eighth day of this month). A corresponding term, *ultimo*, refers to the previous month (for example, *the 16th ultimo* means the sixteenth day of the previous month).

Recording Places

The standard convention for recording locations within the United States is to list the name of the place (such as town, village, or city), followed by the county or parish in which it was located, and the state. The county or parish can be set off by commas, or included in parentheses. Examples are: Pittsburgh, Allegheny County, Pennsylvania; Tarboro (Edgecombe), North Carolina.

A similar approach is used when recording locations in other countries, though the divisions may be slightly different, including shires, parishes, and provinces. Regardless of the country, begin with the smallest jurisdiction and continue to the largest.

Because records are usually found in the place where they were originally recorded, it is essential to list the county, parish, or other geopolitical area that had jurisdiction over the place at the time the event occurred. Due to changing geographical and political boundaries, this may be a different county than the one in which the place is located today.

Dates and Calendars

Accurately recording dates is a matter of importance in genealogy. However, not all dates are as they appear at first glance. Calendar changes and archaic dating conventions mean that a date as written in an old record may have little in common with today's modern system of day, month, and calendar year.

"Old Style" Versus "New Style" Calendar

In 1582, Pope Gregory XIII ordered that ten days be dropped from the Julian calendar currently in effect. His decree also changed the beginning of the new year from March 25 to January 1. The new system, known as the Gregorian calendar, brought the calendar into synchronization with the sun, so that the vernal equinox occurred on March 21. Countries that were predominantly Catholic immediately adopted the new calendar, but many other countries took their time before making the switch. England and the British colonies, for example, held out until 1752. By this time, the discrepancy between the two calendars was eleven days, instead of ten, due to leap year. To resolve the discrepancy, the British government ordered that September 2, 1752, be followed by September 14, 1752. Some other countries waited even longer to convert to the Gregorian calendar—for example, Russia in 1918 and Greece in 1923.

Double Dating

Why is it important for genealogists to be aware of this calendar change? Events that occurred between January 1 and March 25 prior to the year 1752 may be subject to the convention of double dating. This practice assigns events that occurred during that time period two dates—one written correctly for each calendar. This entails not only taking into account the eleven-day difference between calendars, but also the fact that the years differed by one. This is because the period from January 1 to March 25 occurred at the end of the year under the old Julian calendar, but was moved to the beginning of the year under the new Gregorian calendar when the first day of the new year was moved from March 25 to January 1.

Double dating may be represented in two different formats. In some cases, the date may only indicate the difference in years; for example, 7 March 1749 would appear as 7 March 1749/50. Alternatively, it may be shown as 7 March 1749 O.S. (old style) or 18 March 1750 N.S. (new style). This practice allows for using the original date without having to convert it to fit both calendars.

FACT

George Washington was born on 11 February 1731. When the English changed the calendar two decades later, he adjusted his birthday, redating it as 22 February 1732. This adjusted birthday was the one celebrated as a national holiday until Congress moved it in 1971 to the third Monday in February and renamed it Presidents' Day in order to commemorate all past presidents.

Quaker Date-Recording Customs

Quakers typically did not use the names of the months or days of the week because most of these names were derived from those of pagan gods (for example, *Thursday* came from "Thor's Day"). Instead, they recorded dates using numbers to describe the day of the week and month of the year: 7th da 3rd mo 1733.

Converting these dates can be especially tricky because the Gregorian calendar change must be taken into account. The first month in 1751, for example, was March, while the first month in 1753 was January. When in doubt, always transcribe the date exactly as written in the original document.

Numbering the Family Tree

A family tree with only a few dozen people is fairly straightforward. Larger pedigrees, however, require a numbering system to allow the reader to easily follow lines from generation to generation within genealogy reports and family histories. Numbering systems are especially helpful for following families when the information is presented in written, rather than chart format. Without numbers to show who is related to who, most people would be lost by the end of the first page.

The trouble with numbering systems, however, is that many would-be family historians get creative and devise their own. True, doing so most likely works well for them. But most such nonstandard numbering systems take hours of time and a few aspirin to be understood by anyone else who uses the research. To avoid the difficulties caused by this inventive numbering, three basic numbering formats are widely accepted in genealogical circles: the ahnentafel system for ascending genealogies, and the Register and NGS Quarterly systems for descending genealogies.

Ahnentafel System

The ahnentafel system, used in the pedigree chart discussed previously in this chapter, is the most commonly used convention for ascending genealogies—lineages that begin from a single individual and move backward through his ancestors. The ahnentafel system is also known as the Sosa-Stradonitz system. This system was named after Jerome de Sosa, a Spanish genealogist who first used it in 1676, and Stephan Kekule von Stradonitz, who explained and popularized the numbered system in his "Ahnentafel Atlas," which he published in 1896. In the ahnentafel system, the root individual is listed as person number 1. The next generation assigns the father as person number 2 and the mother as person number 3. Continuing on, the paternal grandfather would be number 4, the paternal grandmother number 5, and so on. The number of an individual's father is always double the person's number, and his mother is double the number plus one. Other than the starting individual, males are all assigned even ID numbers, and women odd ID numbers.

Numbering Your Genealogy: Basic Systems, Complex Families, and International Kin by Joan Ferris Curran, Madilyn Coen Crane, and John H. Wray, provides an excellent discussion of the basic numbering systems that are widely accepted in the genealogical community, with easy-to-understand examples of each.

Register and NGS Quarterly Systems

Descending genealogies in the United States most often use the slightly varying Register system, named for the quarterly of the New England Historic Genealogical Society, and the NGS Quarterly system (also called the NGSQ system), developed for the quarterly journal of the National Genealogical Society. Both of these numbering systems begin with an individual (usually the immigrant ancestor or earliest known ancestor) and then follow the descendants of that person from generation to generation. Most published family histories take this approach. Both numbering systems begin with number 1, assigned to the root individual, but they differ slightly.

Register System

In the Register system, the children of ancestor number 1 are each given Roman numerals (i, ii, iii, iv, and so on) in the order of birth. Children whose lines are carried forward to the next generation are also assigned an Arabic number (1, 2, 3, 4, and so on). Children who have no known descendants are not assigned this Arabic number. A superscript number immediately following a person's name represents the person's generation of descent relative to the key individual.

NGSQ System

The NGSQ system differs from the Register system in that all individuals are assigned an Arabic number, whether or not their line is carried forward. A "+" mark in front of the Arabic numeral designates children for whom more information appears in future generations. Each child is also listed with a Roman numeral, indicating birth order within the family.

Citing Your Sources

Gathering facts about your family and assembling them into a family tree is quite an accomplishment, but it is the ability to back up these facts with sources that gives your research credibility. Great-grandpa's date of birth, for example, carries more weight if you also indicate where this information was obtained—whether from a family member, his birth certificate, a tombstone, or an online family tree. Keeping track of each and every piece of information, and its source, is important as a means of evaluating or verifying your work.

FACT

A source is the document, interview, photograph, database, or other record in which a specific fact or piece of information is found. A citation is a formal reference to that source, including all details necessary for another researcher to identify and locate the source material.

Present-day genealogical standards require that any statement of fact, whether a birth date or a maiden name, carry its own individual source citation. Citing the sources for data provides a reference, or "audit trail" for other researchers in case the information that they find appears to conflict with your data. If they don't know that your source for great-grandpa's birth date was a letter written by his mother two days after his birth, they can't judge for themselves whether your date is more likely to be correct than is the differing date they found mentioned in his obituary. You may need a source again, too—to double-check a fact, or to look up new information. You can picture that faded brown book of will abstracts in your head, but do you remember its name or in which library it was located? A proper source citation would include these details.

How to Cite Your Source

Source citations in genealogy generally follow standard bibliographic citation standards, such as those found in *The Chicago Manual of Style*. Genealogical sources can sometimes be unique, but a good rule of thumb is to work from general to specific, beginning with the author and title of the source, and following up with the specifics such as repository and page number.

Author—The one who wrote the book, compiled the data, or provided the interview.

Title—The name of the source. If it is an article or subset, then include the title of the article in quotes, followed by the title of the periodical.

Publication details—Place of publication, name of the publisher, and date of publication (place: publisher, date); volume, issue, and page number for periodicals; series and roll or item number for microfilm.

Location—Name of repository and location where the source is located. Include the Web site name and URL (the complete Web address) for online sources.

Specifics—Page number, entry number and date, the date you viewed a Web site, and any other details.

Cite What You See

Derivative sources, discussed in more detail in Chapter 18, are sources that have been created or "derived" from a previously existing source. These include such sources as online databases, printed books of abstracts, pedigree charts, and cemetery transcriptions. Most such derivative sources will include citations to the original source, but in your genealogy you must cite what you actually "see" or use—the derivative source, not the original(s) from which it was created.

If you learn the date of your ancestor's death from a published book of will abstracts, for example, you would cite the book, not the original will. The same rule would apply for a birth date gleaned from a cemetery transcription published online by the local genealogical society. In this case, you would not cite great-grandma's tombstone as your source, because you haven't actually seen her grave marker. Instead, you would cite the online transcription created by the local genealogical society. The cemetery transcription may include a typing error, or the transcriber may have misread the tombstone. If such a mistake exists and you cite the original tombstone without reference to the online transcription where you really found your information, others will assume that the error is yours.

Chapter 2

 **The Journey Begins
at Home**

No matter how excited you are about taking a leap back in time, your genealogy journey should always begin with the present. Numerous clues to your family history are most likely tucked into your memory, or squirreled away in a nook or cranny in your house or the home of a relative. Researching and documenting your own life, as well as the lives of close family members, also helps to develop the strong roots necessary to support your budding family tree.

Start with Yourself

Of course you probably already know who you are and when you were born. Still, as basic as it may sound, you should begin your family tree adventure by documenting your own life, as well as the lives of your close ancestors. Knowing the names of your parents, grandparents, or even great-grandparents isn't enough. You also need to research and record other details about your family, from birth dates to hair color to places where they lived—anything that will help to distinguish family members in records as you delve further into the mysteries of your past.

You should always focus first on the concrete facts you can establish from solid sources, approaching your family tree research from the ground up. Start with the known (the roots) and work your way backward in time to the unknown (the leaves), just the way a tree grows in real life.

You may be surprised just how many people have been bestowed with identical or similar names, even seemingly unusual ones such as Kinchen Cherry or Ezekiel Crisp, and how easy this makes it to latch onto the wrong individual as your ancestor.

Write It Down

Most people grow up knowing at least a little about their own family. But how often does any of it actually get written down? Start collecting those details now and get them on paper. Names and dates are always good, as well as memories and stories. Anything you can come up with will provide a starting point for your family tree search. Start a journal or notebook and keep it handy. New details will continue to occur to you as you're vacuuming the den, driving to work, or taking a shower. Because memories often deteriorate with time, search out documents that chronicle your own life, including your birth, childhood, education, marriage, occupations, the births of your children or grandchildren, and other important life events. If only your ancestors had done the same!

Expand the Search

Once you've finished talking to yourself (and assured everyone in the family that you aren't going crazy), it is time to tackle your home. Scour the attic, dig into boxes, and rummage through drawers for photographs, official documents, certificates, newspaper clippings, the family Bible, letters, diaries, even baby books. Think of it as a family history mystery—any clue you find may help unravel the riddles of your past. Approaching your search with imagination often reveals tidbits of family history in the most unexpected places. Your parents' wedding picture may have the marriage date and location scrawled on the back. A shoebox stuffed in the back of the hall closet may yield a clipping of Great-Aunt Thelma's obituary. The cookie jar that has been in your family for generations may have your great-great-grandmother's famous cookie recipe tucked inside. An embroidered sampler may have the artist's name or a date stitched into the design.

Next Come Mom and Dad

Once you've exhausted the contents of your home and the reaches of your memory, it is time to expand the search to living family members. If you're lucky enough to have parents and/or grandparents still living, now is the time to solicit their participation. Don't just barge in and start asking a lot of questions, however. Take the time to explain your interest in genealogy and your quest for clues to your family's past.

Be understanding if relatives have reservations about answering personal questions or allowing you to search through their possessions. You would probably feel the same if the situation was reversed. Even the most helpful family members may try to turn you away because they feel they have nothing of significance to contribute or that the past is better left in the past.

Digging in the Attic

It's amazing what people save over the course of a lifetime. Boxes stuffed with papers and greeting cards, letters tied together lovingly with ribbon, albums full of pictures and postcards—little slices of life, reduced to scraps of paper and ink. They may seem inconsequential to many of your relatives, especially after being tucked away in the attic for decades. Bring them out into the light of day, however, and the memories of those life events, important enough to record and save, will quickly come flooding back. This is why home sources often furnish the most valuable clues for your family tree. They provide not only names and dates but also a glimpse into what life was like for living family members and long-dead ancestors.

Photographs

Among the longest surviving and treasured of all home sources, photographs are a valuable resource for family historians. Truly a "snapshot in time," photographs depict people, places, and events as they existed, helping to place all of the names and dates in your family tree into historical context. Photos are a favorite source of clues for genealogists, yielding names, dates, and notes written on the backs of the pictures; the name and location of the photographer on studio photos; and details such as clothing styles or buildings pictured in the background.

Postcards and Letters

Similar to photographs, letters and postcards are another visual source of clues to your family's past. Usually filled with names (albeit first names) and dates, letters and postcards can help you sort out family relationships, pinpoint where your ancestors lived, and provide a personal glimpse into their daily lives. Aside from the clues in your ancestor's missive, you may also be able to identify an ancestor's town or track a family's movements through postmarks and addresses. Even the pictures on the postcards may be more personal than you may think. A photo of a ship may actually depict the one on which the family sailed to America, while the pretty village church pictured on another postcard could be the one in which the family worshipped.

Beware of salutations such as "Aunt Maggie" or "Dear Cousin." Family relationship terms are, and were, often used loosely. "Cousin" could really mean second cousin or just a general distant family relationship. "Aunt" could refer to a great-aunt, step-aunt, or even a family friend. The commonly used terms Sr. and Jr. may not necessarily identify father and son.

Official Records

Tucked away in dresser drawers, safe deposit boxes, scrapbooks, and closets, important family documents may be more important than they first appear. Due to such things as courthouse fires, neglect, or other damage inflicted through the years, your family's copy of the certificate may be the only surviving record. Beyond names and dates, family records also serve as a guidepost to further clues. Great-grandpa's baptismal certificate, for example, may lead you to his family's church and several generations of your family tree resting in the parish cemetery.

Family Bibles

Many families turned to the Bible as the place to keep track of births, marriages, deaths, and other important family events. Sometimes these few handwritten pages may actually be the only source for your family's vital information, especially if the Bible includes records of generations of individuals who lived prior to the time when civil records were officially maintained in the locality. Not all family Bibles are created equal, however. Bible entries are more likely to contain errors when they are all written in the same ink and handwriting, or include events that predate the Bible's publication. These clues indicate that the entries were most likely not made at the time of the actual events and, therefore, are more likely to be affected by faulty memories.

Scrapbooks and Albums

Full of newspaper clippings, funeral cards, birth announcements, award certificates, hospital bracelets, wedding invitations, and other important family mementos, scrapbooks can provide a delightful window into the lives of your ancestors. In addition to the expected names, dates, and historical references, you can also learn a lot about a family from the things they considered important enough to save.

Diaries and Journals

Among the most personal of family sources, journals and diaries bring your ancestors to life in a way nothing else can. Even something as simple as an account book for the family farm or business, filled with apparently boring notations about crop harvests, livestock inventories, the cost of supplies, or damage caused by weather, can paint a detailed picture of the family's life at the time. These types of sources are also very useful because they are typically full of easily verified accounts of current events, providing a clue to the accuracy of the remaining information.

You may also find other treasures tucked between Bible pages, such as letters, newspaper clippings, funeral cards, photographs, a lock of baby hair, greeting cards, and other items of special interest to the owner.

Ask and You May Receive

Once you have written down everything you know about your family and scoured the homes of all the relatives for clues, it is time to sit down and talk with your family. All you will need for this project are a notebook and a pencil, a tape recorder or video camera, an inquiring mind, and a sense of adventure. Gathering oral histories is a critical first step in your family tree adventure.

No matter what your excuse—too busy, too far away, or just too lazy—do not put off talking to family members. No documents or photos will ever be able to tell you as much about your family as will your living relatives. Their stories are priceless.

Where to Start?

While you should eventually talk to every uncle, aunt, cousin, and family friend that you can find, you have to start somewhere. For many, this is Mom, Dad, or a living grandparent. Alternatively, ask a few relatives which family member is generally known to be the family historian, the one who is always collecting pictures and telling stories. While it is sad to reflect on, any older relatives should also be placed high on your priority list. They won't be around forever, after all, and their increasing years may cause mental, verbal, physical, or visual impairments that can affect their speech, ability to tolerate a long interview, or capacity to remember people, places, and events.

Come Up with a Plan

Although talking to family members is usually something that comes naturally, it can get a bit more complicated when the conversation is directed toward eliciting certain facts or memories. Just the word *interview* is sometimes enough to make even the most easygoing relative shudder. To improve your chances of setting family members at ease and collecting the information you need, you should start by devising an interview plan. This can include such things as making an appointment with your family member, preparing for the interview, and creating a list of questions in advance. Face-to-face is always best, but if meeting in person means putting off the interview, don't hesitate to solicit help from distant relatives via letter, phone, or e-mail.

When writing to a distant relative, you'll increase your chances of a response if you tell her about yourself, your family, and why you are interested in the family history. Enclose a list of open-ended questions rather than a note saying "tell me everything about the family." Enclose a stamped, self-addressed envelope to further increase your chances of a helpful reply.

Ask Open-Ended Questions

Questions are less about the answers and more about prompting your family members to remember things they may not have thought about in years. When deciding which questions to ask, think about your objectives: What do you already know? What do you want to learn? About which people and events is each family member likely to be the most knowledgeable?

As you prepare your questions, keep the following important points in mind:

- Do your research. Have your family charts and notes in front of you to help you formulate questions to fill in some of the holes in your research.
- Use open-ended questions that encourage personal commentary, rather than close-ended questions that require only "yes" or "no" answers.
- Try to elicit stories as well as facts. While you should always try to get specific details such as names and dates, "facts" also include finding out what, how, where, and why something happened.

Sample Interview Questions

Though it is best to develop your own list of questions based on the personalities and history of your particular family, this can often seem a bit intimidating when you're new to genealogy. Here are a few sample questions to get the creative juices flowing:

1. What is your full name? Do you know why your parents chose that name for you? Were you named after someone? Do you have a nickname? What do you know about your family surname? Has the spelling been changed in the past?
2. When were you born, and where? Do you remember any stories that your parents shared with you about your birth? Do you have your birth and/or baptismal certificates? Baby pictures, a baby book, a lock of hair?
3. Do you have any siblings? Where and when were they born? What were they like? Do you have any favorite memories of them? Did they marry? Have families?

4. When and where did you meet your spouse? Was she/he your first love? What are your memories of the proposal, the wedding ceremony, the honeymoon?

5. Where and when were your parents born? What are their full names? What do/did they look like? What were their occupations? How did they come to meet and marry?

6. Where and when were your grandparents born (both paternal and maternal)? What do/did they look like? What were their occupations? How did they come to meet and marry? When and where were their children born?

7. Did you serve in the military? In a war? Which branch of the service were you in? Did you receive any military commendations? What are your most vivid memories of your time in the military?

8. Who was the oldest person you can remember in your family as a child? What do you remember about that person? Do you remember visiting other relatives or family friends as a child?

9. Are there any items, traditions, or customs in the family that have been handed down from generation to generation? Favorite family recipes? Naming traditions?

10. Tell me about the home you grew up in—what day-to-day life was like for you as a child. How was your home heated and lighted, what sort of household chores were you responsible for, how were Sundays and holidays celebrated?

11. How is the world different today than it was when you were a child? Which discoveries, events, and changes had the most impact on your life?

The Art of the Interview

Because most of your very special older relatives won't write down their life stories, they need your help and encouragement. Often they lack the writing skills or health, or perhaps even the energy to spend weeks putting their lives on paper. What a blessing it is, both for them and for you, to be able to capture their vivid reminiscences on audio- or videotape. Then, at the touch of a button, you and generations to come can experience the hopes, fears, joys, and disappointments of a very real life, described in person by the one who lived it.

Schedule in Advance

Getting people to share their stories, especially on tape, isn't always easy. For the best results, it is very important to respect your relative's time and privacy. Whether you plan to conduct a face-to-face or telephone interview, your best course of action is to make contact with your relative in advance and schedule a mutually convenient time for your meeting. You'll make your relative more comfortable if you also share a list of questions with her in advance or at least give her an idea of the topics you would like to cover in the interview. If she is still unsure about the whole "interview" thing, offer to give her the chance to see and approve of anything that you write before you share it with others.

Phone interviews can be tough, but can also make it easier to collect information over an extended period of time. When interviewing a relative by phone, you'll often achieve better results if you conduct the interview as a series of calls. It gives the interviewee a chance to know you and better understand your interest and motivations.

Be Prepared

To help elicit memories, bring props such as old photographs, favorite songs, and treasured items to your interview. You should also take time prior to the scheduled interview to familiarize yourself with as much as you can find out about her life and her place in the family tree. This will help you ask the best questions and make the most of your time together.

Whether you're recording the interview on tape or taking notes by hand, first record your name, the date, the place the interview is being conducted, and the name of the interviewee.

Once you have everything set up and all parties are comfortable, begin the discussion with a question or topic that you know will elicit a reply, such as a favorite story that you have heard her tell in the past. After you get the ball rolling, use your prepared questions as a guideline, but don't be afraid to let your relative go off on a tangent. She may have many things to say that you never thought to ask!

As the interview continues:

- Be an interested listener. Take an active part in the dialogue, without dominating it.
- Don't push for answers. Your relative may not wish to speak ill of the dead or may have other reasons for not wanting to share certain memories. Move on to something else.
- Don't interrupt or attempt to correct your relative, even when you know she's wrong about something. This can end an interview in a hurry!
- Keep it short. Interviews should usually not cover more than one or two hours at a stretch. It's tiring for you and for the person being interviewed.

When the interview is over, be sure to thank your relative for her time. Following up with a written thank-you letter and a transcript or written report of the interview is also a nice touch.

Clues in Family Photographs

Since Frenchman Joseph Nicephore Niépce created the first photographic image in 1827, photographs have become an increasingly popular way of capturing family memories for posterity. As such, photos play a very important part in the growth of your family tree. Even beyond the pictures on the front and the names and dates on the back, photos can provide a wealth of clues about your family. The type of photograph, the way it's mounted, the name of the photographer, the subjects' clothing and hairstyles, and the background surroundings can all help you date your photo and tell you more about the people pictured there and the life they led.

FACT

Tintypes are sometimes referred to as ferrotypes or melainotypes because of the iron backing. They were more commonly called tintypes, however, because tin shears were used to cut the photographs from the iron sheet. They look very similar to ambrotypes but, because they are made of iron, they'll attract a magnet—an easy test!

Types of Photographs

Identifying the type of photograph you are looking at is the first step in evaluating your family's photographic history. Early photography introduced a number of different prints and processes, but the ones you'll most commonly encounter are daguerreotypes, ambrotypes, tintypes, and card photographs.

Daguerreotypes

The first commercially successful photograph, known as the daguerreotype, was named after its creator, Louis Jacques Mandé Daguerre. Popular from 1839 to 1860, this type of photograph was basically an image captured on silver-clad copper plate. To protect the plate from damage, the photo was then sealed in glass with a decorative mat, and often placed in a hinged wooden case. A daguerreotype is distinguished by its shiny, reflective surface, the fact that it can appear as a negative or positive depending upon the angle of light or viewing, and frequently by its containment in a case.

Ambrotypes

Unlike the daguerreotype, the ambrotype was not named for its inventor; rather, the word combines the Greek *ambrotos*, which means "immortal," and *type*. Using a process first introduced by Frederick Scott Archer, the ambrotype was created by coating a piece of glass with collodion (a type of cottonlike cellulose dissolved in ether and alcohol). The glass plate was then either painted black on the back side or mounted on a black paper or velvet backing so that the image could be seen. Like daguerreotypes, ambrotypes were usually encased with a mat in a protective glass plate, and enclosed in a small wooden or leather case. The two types of photos look similar, but ambrotypes appear as a positive image at all viewing angles. Ambrotypes were popular from 1854 to about 1865.

Tintypes

An advancement on ambrotypes and daguerreotypes because of their lighter weight and increased durability, tintypes were created by a process patented by Hamilton Smith in 1856. The photos were actually reproduced on a thin sheet of iron, not tin, followed with a coat of black varnish for support. Early tintypes were cased like daguerreotypes and ambrotypes, but later ones were usually just presented in paper mats. Very popular in America, tintypes remained in use from 1856 until the mid-1930s.

Card Photographs

Most likely the bulk of old photos in your family's collection consist of photographic prints, mounted on stiff Bristol board or cardboard, with the photo company's name stamped on the front or back. These popular paper prints, collectively referred to as card photographs, came in several formats, including cartes de visite (2½" × 4"), cabinet cards (mostly 4½" × 6½"), and stereographs (either 3" × 7" or 4" × 7"). Because these paper prints were inexpensive to produce, durable, and available in quantity, they became the most common type of photograph in America by the end of the 1860s.

Identifying the Photographer

Many of the photos in your family collection probably have the photography studio imprint, either handwritten, embossed, scratched, or stamped somewhere on the front or back. Generally this imprint identifies the name of the photographer who took the image or the name of the studio where the photo was taken. Sometimes, especially for photos of important individuals, this imprint may refer to a publisher or distributor. Sometimes the imprints will even include the studio address. Armed with this information, you can consult sources such as old business directories, newspapers, historical societies, census records, and even the Internet in order to learn more about the particular photographer or studio. The goal is to identify the photographer's dates and places of operation to help you place your family photograph at a particular time and location.

Fashion, Hairstyles, and Other Clues

While the type of photograph and photographer may help narrow down the time period, internal clues will help you date the photo more precisely and, possibly, identify the people. It's amazing just how much little details—from facial features and hairstyles to clothing, architecture, and props—can tell you about a photo and the people in it.

ALERT!

It takes some practice, but distinctive facial characteristics can sometimes help you identify people in family photographs. Using photos of family members who have already been identified, compare features such as facial shapes, eyes, ears, noses, jaw lines, hair patterns, and moles with those of people in your unidentified photos. Older relatives can often be very helpful with facial identification.

Clothing and hairstyles can often be useful when determining a possible date for a photograph. Paying attention not only to what was worn, but how it was worn, can help you draw conclusions about the pictured individuals. Also look for the little details, such as accessories—gloves, hats, jewelry, and so on. Using a good resource book, such as Joan Severa's *Dressed for the Photographer: Ordinary Americans and Fashion, 1840–1900*, try to use these clues to narrow down the time period. You can then look at similar photographs from that time period to verify your conclusions.

With some good old-fashioned library research, you may also be able to use the details in many family photographs to date the picture within a few years' time. Look for identifiable businesses or signs, architectural styles, and technological elements such as streetlights (gas, electric), road conditions (dirt, cobblestone, paved), telegraph lines, railroad tracks, automobiles, typewriters, radios, and televisions. While one such item probably won't help you date a photograph with any precision, the sum of them all will definitely help you narrow down the time period as well as tell you more about what life was like for the individuals pictured.

Chapter 3

Growing the Family Tree

After you gather details from family members and fill in as much of your charts as you can, it's easy to see where pieces are missing from the puzzle of your family tree. You are now ready to move ahead with your research by consulting a variety of public sources and records. Before plunging in feet first, however, you have to decide which line of the family to pursue, and you also need to learn about a few more tools and techniques that will help you along your way.

Setting Goals

What do you have in mind for your family tree project? How far back in time do you want to go? What do you hope to accomplish? Some people simply want to learn more about who they are and where they came from. Others may have something more specific in mind—perhaps compiling a family medical history, or learning where their ancestors lived before crossing the ocean to America's shores. Whatever your reasons for researching your family's history, setting a goal (or two) will help to guide the course of your research.

Evaluate the Gaps

Begin by looking over your pedigree chart and identifying the gaps in your family tree. If you're still missing a lot of information, don't get over-whelmed. You'll fill it in a piece at a time. Start with the information closest to you in time and place, as it will be easiest to find. When you're new to genealogy research, you probably shouldn't start off by trying to track down your great-great-great-great-grandfather, who is rumored to have fought in the American Revolution. Instead, evaluate your information gaps, and determine which pieces you can find most efficiently. Eventually you will find all of the easy pieces of the puzzle, and in the process you will learn the research skills you need to tackle more difficult goals.

FACT

Proving that a hypothesis or fact is incorrect is every bit as important as proving that it is correct. When developing your research plan, be sure to include records that could possibly contradict your theories, as well as those that are most likely to support them.

Create a Plan

To make the most effective use of your time, create a research plan. The plan should include the various steps needed to accomplish your goal. The plan should include your objective, a listing of known facts, a working hypothesis, a list of sources to investigate, and a research strategy. If your goal is to create a digitized collection of old family photos, your research plan should include the steps necessary for acquiring photos from family members to add to your collection, obtaining any necessary software or hardware to scan in the photos, and setting aside the time necessary to physically follow through with your project. The plan may also include time needed to interview relatives in order to identify the people in the photographs, and plans to create a CD-ROM slide show or photo album with the pictures when you're done.

One Leaf at a Time

Whether you intend to concentrate on just a single family line or want to research everyone, including distant cousins and other extended family, family trees are best built leaf by leaf and branch by branch.

There will be times when it makes sense to research several different people at once, but try not to bite off more than you can chew at one time. You'll end up with a lot of little bits and pieces instead of good solid answers, which inevitably leads to frustration.

Focus on one family member at a time and learn everything you can about him or her. Look for school records, occupational records, probate records, obituaries, and the host of other records created throughout a person's life. Gather together everything you can about that individual, and evaluate what you find for credibility and accuracy. Enter the information in your notes, charts, and database, including complete source citations. Then take the time to assess what you've learned and plan where you want to go next.

Has It Already Been Done?

While it is very unlikely that you'll find your entire family tree already completed, you may be surprised at how much research has already been done that ties into your own family tree. Published information about your family may appear in a variety of resources, including computer databases, books, and periodicals. Often, if you can use your family interviews and home sources to go back just two to three generations, you'll be able to connect with research already done by others. Before jumping into original records, begin your research with a survey of what's already in print.

Computerized Family Trees

Hundreds of thousands of genealogies and family trees have been published on the Internet, including millions of names. Enter the names of a few of your ancestors in the pedigree databases at sites such as RootsWeb. com, FamilySearch.org, Ancestry.com, Genealogy.com, GenCircles.com, and OneGreatFamily.com, and you may find that some distant branch of your family has already published a family tree. You will learn more about Internet research in Chapter 15, "Walking the Web."

Books

Head to a library in the county where your ancestors lived and you're likely to find books about your family and the history of the area. You can find published family histories, local histories, and biographies by searching the card catalog. Many public libraries subscribe to WorldCat, which allows you to search library holdings in thousands of libraries at once. You can also search the Library of Congress online for published family histories. Enter your family name or the locality where your family lived as the subject of your search.

ALERT!

Many of the county histories published around the end of the nineteenth century included biographies of local residents. Affectionately referred to as "mug books," because locals paid to have their photos and biographies included, they often contain errors and exaggerations (everyone wants their family to look good). You certainly can use them, but be careful about accepting them at face value.

Thousands of family history books have also been digitized and placed in online databases, generally available by subscription. The majority of these books were published between 1880 and 1920, putting them in the public domain. HeritageQuest Online, for example, contains the full text of more than 25,000 local and family history books, and can be accessed free of charge by members of participating libraries and societies.

Periodicals

Hidden among the pages of thousands of magazines, journals, and newsletters is a treasure trove of family histories, genealogical case studies, transcribed records, biographies, and local histories. They really aren't that difficult to locate, thanks to the Periodical Source Index (PERSI). Created and maintained by the Allen County Public Library (ACPL) in Fort Wayne, Indiana, PERSI is a massive index to the articles published in nearly 10,000 genealogical and historical periodicals in the last two centuries.

FACT

It can be tempting to believe an account that apparently proves your family descends from royalty, a notorious criminal, or other famous figure, but being in print doesn't make it true. Do not take as gospel any published account of your family tree without first double-checking its facts and verifying its sources. If no references are given, then be doubly suspicious.

PERSI can be searched from within any Allen County Public Library facility. Outside of Allen County, PERSI is available at many libraries around the country on CD-ROM or through HeritageQuest Online. You can also access it at local Family History Centers, or purchase your own copy on CD-ROM. Ancestry.com also offers the index as part of its regular online subscription package.

You can search PERSI by surname, locality, or other keyword. It is not a full-text index, however, so only the names and locations that feature prominently in an article may be included. Your search will provide the title of any relevant articles, and the name, date, and publisher of the periodicals in which they appeared. Once you locate an article of interest, talk with the interlibrary loan librarian at your local library for help in locating the nearest library that has a copy of the magazine containing the article. Alternatively, for a fee, you can request photocopies of up to six articles at a time directly from the ACPL.

Do Your Homework

Once you've learned where and when your ancestors lived, it's time to hit the books. You've done the first part by reading this book and familiarizing yourself with basic genealogy research techniques. But you're not done yet! Before delving into original records, you need to learn a bit about the history of the area where your ancestors lived and the record sources available for that region.

The Church of Jesus Christ of Latter-day Saints (Mormon Church) offers a wide variety of free research guides and tutorials, including research outlines for each of the U.S. states and many countries throughout the world. Each outline provides a brief overview of research in the state, covering important topics such as boundary changes and courthouse fires. It also describes records of genealogical value, where they are located, and how they can best be used. The research outlines are available at Family History Centers and online at FamilySearch.org.

FACT

Many important genealogical records no longer exist because they have been destroyed by fire, flood, vermin, war, or neglect. Counties with significant record loss, usually due to the Civil War or a catastrophic fire, are referred to by genealogists as "burned counties." When records do survive, they are said to be "extant"—still in existence.

The Family History Library has many county records on microfilm, and its Family History Library Catalog (available online) is a good place to review what's available for your area of interest. Do a "place search" for the county name and you'll be presented with a list of available records organized by topic. County and local genealogical societies can also provide information on available records and significant historical dates in the community.

Mapping Your Course

Maps aren't usually the first thing that come to mind when researching a family tree. They can't tell you when your grandparents were born or how they died. But if you can't name the place where your ancestors lived, it is difficult to know where to start your search for records. Maps, both new and old, can show you a lot about your ancestors—where they were born, went to school, worked, and raised their families. They can help you locate the county seat, where useful records about your kin may be found. They can point the way to the old family homestead or cemetery. Maps can even help you trace the migration route of your family as they moved across the country. Don't underestimate the usefulness of modern road maps, either. How else are you going to find that rural county courthouse?

If a courthouse for a neighboring county was closer or easier to get to, then your ancestor may have applied for a marriage license or filed a record of birth there as well as in the county in which he resided. Use a map to help you determine which locations could be possible, and check the records for each.

Every genealogist should start with a detailed road map or atlas to become familiar with the area in which his ancestors lived. Look for nearby cities, towns, counties, and major geophysical features including rivers, slopes, forests, and streams. County highway maps, usually published by the state highway or transportation department, often show the locations of rural churches, cemeteries, and schools. Understanding where your ancestor lived in relation to his neighbors, workplace, school, and church may provide insight into what his daily life may have been like. How far did he have to travel to the nearest store? Did he have a lot of family living nearby? Where was the nearest county courthouse?

Types of Maps

Aside from the traditional road map, a wide variety of other maps may be useful in solving family history puzzles. Although obviously not created with genealogists in mind, the following types of maps may provide assistance with your research.

FACT

More than 55,000 topographic maps have been prepared by the U.S. Geological Survey (USGS), covering almost the entire United States. USGS maps can be ordered for a nominal fee from the USGS Web site at *www.usgs.gov* or by calling **1-888-ASK-USGS.** The most useful for the majority of genealogy purposes are the 7.5-minute, 1:24,000-scale quadrangle maps.

Topographic Maps

Topographic maps, also called relief maps, not only show the location of roads and buildings, but also graphically represent surface features such as elevations and creeks. They include a great deal of detail, identifying virtually all creeks, streams, hills, and roads, and also show more obscure features such as cemeteries, churches, railroad tracks, and mines. Once you start researching the property owned by your ancestors (discussed in further detail in Chapter 11), topographic maps can help you plot the exact location of a piece of land based on range/township divisions (in the thirty public-land states) or waterways and other surface features (in the twenty state-land states).

Historical Maps and County Atlases

Popular in the nineteenth century, historic county and town maps are useful for research in rural areas because they often include names of some property owners. Old maps can also help locate towns and villages that no longer exist, or are known in the present time by a different name.

Political Boundary Change Maps

Before you can locate records of your ancestors in a specific locality, you must first learn which county and state had jurisdiction for the time period of interest. A variety of maps have been produced which show the changes in jurisdictional boundaries over a period of time. From them you can learn how existing counties were divided to form new counties, and which county's records might contain information about your ancestors.

Survey and Plat Maps

Land maps and plat books provide a historical record of ownership of a particular piece of property. Entries will usually include the specific location and description of the property, including the name of the owner and neighbors. A physical drawing of the property's boundaries, including some details about surrounding properties, may also be included.

Tax and Assessment Maps

Sometimes called cadastral maps, these maps were created for administrative districts to aid in determining tax assessments. At a minimum, they show property boundaries and value of the land, and often include a reference to the landowners as well.

Fire Insurance Maps

Detailed maps of thousands of urban areas around the country have been created for use by insurance companies to determine the risk factors in underwriting a particular business or home. Published from the late nineteenth century to the present, fire insurance maps can provide interesting details including the outline, configuration, and function of specific buildings. They also depict property boundaries, street names, and house and block numbers.

ALERT!

Your ancestors may have lived on the same spot of land for many years, yet officially lived in several different counties. Boundary maps are also especially helpful for European research, depicting how country and political boundaries changed following times of war.

Corresponding with Confidence

Gathering information often means writing letters—a lot of them. A well-written letter can open many doors, bringing a wealth of information from faraway places and far-flung cousins. A letter can often save a trip to the courthouse, state archives, vital records bureau, library, cemetery, or church to obtain copies of records. E-mail makes it easy to collaborate with relatives or other researchers with just a few clicks of the mouse. In short, the ability to write effective letters is a must for family history researchers.

Writing Letters to Institutions

Responding to genealogical requests is not the primary function of most public offices, courthouses, and churches. Your goal should be to make it as easy as possible for your request to be handled quickly, so that the staff can return to their day-to-day business. Busy clerks will most appreciate a short letter that gets right to the point. Who wants to read a lengthy story about your Great-Grandma Mildred when they have more pressing work to do? Be clear and concise—let the institution know exactly what you are looking for and include as much *relevant* information as you can about the subject of your request, making sure to do the following:

- Clarify the specific record type – marriage certificate, military discharge paper, etc.
- Include the full name of the individual(s) involved, including maiden name for women, as well as alternate spellings or nicknames.
- Provide the date the event took place; use an approximate date if necessary.
- State your relationship to the individual whose record you are requesting.
- Sign the request.

Prior to sending the letter, be sure that you have the correct, current address for the institution, as well as knowledge of the fees that the office charges for the service you're requesting. If you're unsure, take time to give the office a quick call to verify. Payment should be sent by check or money order, not cash. Some offices will accept credit cards. Even if the organization doesn't have a specific fee schedule for genealogy requests, it is always nice to send a few dollars to cover its expenses and time. Small societies in particular often don't have room in their budget for luxuries such as postage.

Even when you're writing to a family member, it is always good practice to enclose a self-addressed stamped envelope. People are more likely to respond to your query if they don't have to waste time tracking down your address.

Many small county courthouses and genealogical societies charge only for copies and may require a two-step process for requesting records by mail. You'll begin by sending your request. Once they've looked up the records and determined the number of copies, they will send you a statement and bill. Upon receipt of your payment, they will put the copies in the mail. Some will send the copies along with the bill, trusting you for payment. Make sure that you don't let them down!

Writing Letters to Family Members

Unlike most busy public clerks, family members will generally appreciate a more personal touch. Begin your letter with some news about yourself or the family. If the people to whom you are writing are distant relatives who don't know you, take the time to introduce yourself before jumping right in with your request. If your correspondents are also interested in the family history, offer to share any information you have collected on their branch of the family. They will probably be just as interested in what you know about the family as you are in what you can learn from them.

Genealogy Queries

Queries are an effective way to find others who are researching the same surnames or in the same locations as you. Basically a short advertisement or request for contact from like-minded researchers, a query can focus on a specific individual, family, surname, location, event, or even a specific research problem. Genealogy queries may be submitted to genealogy magazines, newspapers, or Web sites.

A good genealogy query is more than just slapping together your genealogy information in the form of a question. A successful query should provide specific information without overwhelming the reader. The easier you make it for other researchers to understand what you're looking for, the more likely you are to receive a response. Details—specific names, dates, and places—are important, but don't include too many or you'll discourage people from reading what you wrote. Queries are meant to be short and to the point.

When crafting your genealogy query it pays to follow a few simple rules:

- Include only one surname or question per query.
- Be specific with your question. Most people won't respond to "Send me everything you know. . . ."
- Write surnames in CAPITAL letters for easy scanning.
- State what you've already searched, whether or not you found anything.
- Include the name, date, and location in the subject line, as well as in the body of your query.
- If you don't know the exact date, include an approximate date or date range.

An example of an effective genealogy query:

MEARES, Edgecombe Co., NC, USA; 1800–1900. I'm looking for information about the wife and parents of Willie MEARES, who was born abt. 1809 in NC and died between 1860 and 1870, probably in Edgecombe Co., NC. His wife's name was Elizabeth (maiden name unknown, but possibly PEEL). They had at least seven children according to census records: Mary Frances, Martha Jane, John W., Elizabeth, James, William, and Charles (Charley).

Keeping Track of Your Correspondence

You should always keep a copy of each letter or e-mail that you send requesting genealogical information. This helps you keep track of the information you've requested, and whether or not you've received a reply. Most genealogists use a correspondence log or correspondence calendar as a framework for logging their correspondence requests.

ALERT!

Thousands of genealogy queries posted on Internet message boards and Web sites are a dead end for researchers, because the e-mail address of the person who posted the message is no longer valid. Keep track of the queries you post online, including the URL and date, so you can go back and update them if there is a change to your contact information.

A variety of preprinted correspondence logs and forms are available from genealogical supply houses. You also may download forms from the Internet at no cost. You may also choose to develop your own system based on your personal needs. Whatever the form, a basic correspondence log should include room for these items:

- Date you sent the letter/e-mail
- Name and address of the person or institution, or URL of the Web site
- Type of information requested
- Date you received a reply
- Information received

Correspondence logs can be used in different ways. If you don't send a lot of letters, then one log may be enough to handle all of your requests. You may also choose to maintain several different correspondence logs—organized by surname, location, or even by individual. Some people maintain two correspondence logs, one for written letters and one for electronic queries.

Tracking Your Progress

In addition to tracking your correspondence, you'll also want to create a system for tracking your research progress. For someone new to family tree research, this level of organization may seem like overkill. You'll change your tune, however, when papers start piling up, and the questions right along with them.

Your family tree may start with just a few branches, but it will leaf out quickly. Keeping a research log or research notebook is a good way to keep track of what you've already learned and what you're still searching for. Use it to record your research goals and plans, discussed earlier in this chapter, as well as the process of your research.

Preprinted research logs and planners can be found at genealogical supply stores and on the Internet, but a research notebook will do just as well. A basic research log includes space to record what you plan to look for, where you plan to look for it, the date of your search, what you found, a source citation, and comments. Many genealogists prefer to use a research notebook, which allows additional room for recording the thought processes that take you from clue to clue and record to record. Think of it as a journal of your family tree search.

Chapter 4

The Name of the Game

A source of pride and curiosity, names are both a part of who we are and where we came from. We wonder about the people who carried the name before us—who they were, what they were like, where they came from. Surname meanings and origins aren't quite as obvious as most would like, however. A name isn't likely to lead directly to your ancestral pedigree. Names, however, often provide clues to your family's long-distant origins or help you make connections to a new branch in the family tree.

The Origin of Surnames

While hard to believe in the hustle and bustle of today's society, last names weren't really necessary until about 1,000 years ago. In a world that was much less crowded—a world in which most folks never ventured more than a few miles from their place of birth and every man knew his neighbors—first, or given, names were the only designations necessary. Even kings got by with a single name.

During the Middle Ages, as families got bigger and villages a bit more crowded, individual names were no longer adequate for distinguishing friends and neighbors from one another. A man named Peter might be referred to as "Peter, son of William" to distinguish him from a neighboring "Peter, the tailor." Often the nobility and wealthy landowners were the first to adopt this custom, distinguishing themselves from others through the name of their ancestral home. Over the span of several hundred years, the use of descriptive surnames spread to the towns and countryside. Such names, while used to distinguish individuals from one another, were not originally passed down from father to son. "Peter, son of William," for example, may have had a son known as "John, the carpenter."

Hereditary surnames, the last names passed down through male generations of the family, didn't come into general use until about 500 years ago (A.D. 1500). The Scandinavian countries, following their custom of using the father's name as a last name for his children, didn't begin passing down family surnames until the nineteenth century. The practice of using surnames wasn't common in Turkey until 1933, when they became required by the government. In Mongolia, where surnames were banned during the Soviet Era, residents actually chose new surnames for their families as recently as 2004.

Not all cultures follow the given name, middle name, surname pattern used in America. In some countries, most notably in parts of Asia, it is not uncommon to find the surname or family name listed first, with the given name second. In many Spanish-speaking countries people have two last names, one from their mother and one from their father.

The majority of hereditary surnames began as simple descriptive designations, such as "Richard living among the oak trees" or "James the smith" or "Walter, son of John" or "Harold with the beard." Over time those descriptions stuck and eventually evolved into full names such as Richard OAKS, James SMITH, Walter JOHNSON, and Harold BEARD. As demonstrated in these examples, surnames generally evolved from one of four general sources: a geographical location, an occupation, the name of a parent, or a nickname based on a description of physical appearance or personality.

Geographic or Local Surnames

Local or geographic surnames, which are perhaps the most common way to distinguish a man from his neighbor, derive from the individual's place of residence or the town or country from which he originated. Within a small village, geographical features such as rocks, hills, and streams were commonly used to identify one "John" from another. John EASTWOOD, for example, lived east of the woods, while John BROOKS lived by a brook, and John GREEN lived near the village green. Depending upon the country and language of origin, some local names may be hard to identify. For example, DUNLOP derives from the Scottish *dun lapach*, which means "muddy hill"; the German STEINWEG, which identifies someone who lived along a stony path, derives from *stein* (stony) + *weg* (way). Local surnames can often be identified by their endings, such as *-hill*, *-brook*, and *-dale*.

Surnames that derived from the estate, village, region, or country of an individual are interesting because they can sometimes be traced back through the generations to their exact location of origin. PARRIS designated one who came from Paris, France; NORMAN, one who came from Normandy. It is important to realize that such surnames may have developed independently in several different locations and time periods. The CALDER surname, for example, could mean one who came from the region of the Calder River in Yorkshire, England, or it could mean one who originally came from one of the many English and Scottish towns named Calder.

ALERT!

Because most occupational surnames developed during the medieval period, some of the references to specialty crafts and trades prevalent at the time are not always what one might expect. The name BARKER originated with the occupation of leather tanning, while FARMER was one who collected taxes, not a farmer in today's agricultural sense of the word.

Occupational Surnames

Chosen to reflect the occupation, vocation, or status of an individual, occupational surnames are fairly self-explanatory. The popular surname SMITH, for example, derived from the common occupation of blacksmith. A MILLER was one who ground flour from grain; SHEPHERD was one who herded sheep; BISHOP was usually an employee of a bishop; and FLETCHER was one who made arrows.

Patronymic Surnames

Referring to someone by the name of their father was common practice before the development of surnames, especially in the Scandinavian countries. Over time, the man first referred to as Tom's son eventually became known as TOMSON or THOMPSON. This practice of taking names from the father or paternal side of the family is known as *patronymics*. Such names were usually formed by adding a prefix or suffix denoting either "son of" or "daughter of" to the father's name. English and Scandinavian names ending in *-son* or *-sen* are examples of patronymic surnames, as are names beginning with the Welsh *Ap-* (AP HOWELL, which became POWELL), the Norman *Fitz-* (FITZGERALD), the Irish *O-* (O'BRIEN), and the Gaelic *Mac-* (MacARTHUR). On rare occasions a surname may also have derived from the mother, a practice known as matronymics.

Common U.S. Surnames* and Their Meanings

Name	Origin	Meaning
Smith	English	A man who works with metal; a smith or blacksmith
Johnson	English	Son of John (gift of God)
Williams	Norman	Son of William (*wil*=desire + *helm*=helmet, protection)
Jones	English, Welsh	Son of John (gift of God)
Brown	Various	One with brown hair, complexion, or clothing
Davis	English, Welsh	Son of David (beloved)
Miller	English	One who owned or worked in a grain mill
Wilson	English, Scottish	Son of Will, a nickname for William
Moore	English	One who lived at or near a moor or marshy bog
Taylor	English	A tailor; originally from the Latin *taliare*, to cut
Anderson	Various	Son of Andrew (man, manly)
Thomas	Various	Derived from the given name Thomas (twin)
Jackson	English	Son of Jack, a diminutive of the French name Jacques
White	Various	One with very light hair or complexion
Harris	English, Welsh	Son of Harry (from Henry, "home ruler")
Martin	Various	Derived from the given name Martinus (warriorlike)
Thompson	English, Scottish	Son of Thomas or Tom (twin)
Garcia	Spanish	Derived from the given name Garcia (spear, firm)
Martinez	Spanish	Son of Martin (from Mars, the Roman god of war)
Robinson	English	Son of Robin, a pet form of Robert (bright fame)
Clark	English	Cleric, clerk, or scholar
Rodriguez	Spanish	Son of Rodrigo or Roderick (famous power)
Lewis	English	Derived from the given name Lewis (renowned)
Lee	English	One who lived in or near a laye, or clearing
Walker	English, Scottish	A fuller of cloth (walked on cloth to thicken it)

*From the 1990 U.S. Federal Census

Descriptive Surnames

Making up an estimated 10 percent of all family names, descriptive names are thought to have originally evolved as nicknames during the Middle Ages, when men may have jokingly created descriptive names for their neighbors based on personality or physical appearance. Thus, tall, lanky Robert became known as Robert LONG, from the Old English *long*, meaning tall. Many descriptive surnames are obvious, such as BLACK (one with a dark complexion or hair), ARMSTRONG (one with a strong arm), and MOODY (a moody individual). Others may be a bit more obtuse, such as FOX (a sly person) and KENNEDY (helmeted; ugly head).

Name Changes and Spelling Variations

Many of us are known by names today that would surprise our immigrant ancestors. Spellings and pronunciations have changed, often many times, since the names were first brought to America by immigrants from cities, towns, villages, and countries all over the world. The surname you have today may be spelled slightly differently or even bear almost no resemblance to the name once claimed by your distant ancestor.

Surnames have changed and evolved over time for a variety of reasons, ranging from a clerk who wrote down a name the way he heard it to an immigrant's desire to assimilate into his new country. Understanding the reasons why names may have changed can better prepare you for locating your ancestors' records under variations in spelling or, possibly, determining the name's original spelling.

FACT

It is not at all uncommon to find different branches of the same family using variant spellings of the family name. As families moved apart and spread throughout the country, misspellings recorded by court clerks or other officials may have survived, or individuals may have further "Americanized" their surname to reflect the area in which they lived.

Language Barriers

Unfamiliar with the nuances of many languages, court clerks, school-teachers, clergymen, and other officials often recorded names the way they sounded. With little or no knowledge of the English language, it wasn't uncommon for a recent immigrant to accept this new spelling as the official "American" version of his name, and adopt it as his own. The surname NOEL may have become NOWELL; a name like EAKIN converted to AIKEN; or PEARCE written down as PERCE, PIERCE, or PEARSE.

ALERT!

Though many families believe that an ancestor's name was changed at Ellis Island, professional historians have found this to be rare. Ship manifests were usually prepared before departure by a ship official, who copied down the names from the emigrants' official documents. Because U.S. immigration officials generally worked directly from these ship lists, they had no reason to write down names—incorrectly, or otherwise.

Desire to Fit In

Eager to adopt his new country and assimilate into the new culture, an immigrant may have changed or "Americanized" his name in some fashion. Often this was achieved by using the English meaning for the name. German names like BRAUN and ZIMMERMAN became translated into English as BROWN and CARPENTER. Names that were hard for new neighbors to spell or pronounce may have been simplified, to more closely relate them to the language and pronunciations common in the area. Examples include the Swedish JONSSON becoming JOHNSON and the German ALBRECHT being altered to ALBRIGHT. Alternatively, a name may have been changed to a close English or American equivalent—TOMAN to THOMAS or KUNTZ to COONS.

Transliteration

Because most American typewriters and printing equipment couldn't handle characters and markings not represented in the Latin alphabet, surnames from some countries had to be transliterated, or reproduced phonetically in English, in a manner that would tell others how to pronounce the names correctly. The German surname Müller might be transliterated into English as MULLER. Because transliteration is at least partially subjective, it often resulted in many different variations of the same original surname.

Saying a surname out loud is a good way to brainstorm for alternate spellings that may appear in various records. If you have a willing child, ask her to help you with this project. Children tend to spell phonetically and will likely come up with more creative spellings than you ever could.

Fear of Discrimination

Because the move to a new country often represented a new life to many immigrants, some changed their last names to avoid association with their old country or to conceal their religious orientation. Many German-Americans changed their names during and after World War I for fear of discrimination. It also wasn't uncommon for Jews, facing anti-Semitism, to do the same. The Jewish surname COHEN might be changed to COHN or KAHN, and ROSENTHAL to RONALD.

Naming Practices and Patterns

Surnames aren't the only names that are important when researching your family tree. The selection of given names within a family may follow an unwritten but traditional pattern that can sometimes provide a link to further generations. There really are no set rules or formulas that hold true for all families, though. Naming patterns vary from country to country and from one time period to the next, and the majority of families didn't follow them.

In the eighteenth- and nineteenth-century British Isles, a popular pattern was often followed when naming children:

First son—named for the paternal grandfather
Second son—named for the maternal grandfather
Third son—named for his father
Fourth son—named for the father's eldest brother
First daughter—named for the maternal grandmother
Second daughter—named for the paternal grandmother
Third daughter—named for her mother
Fourth daughter—named for the mother's eldest sister

It is important to note that even families who followed this general pattern didn't follow it strictly. If the pattern would result in duplicate names (for example, if both grandfathers were named William), then the parents would usually skip to the next name on the list. They might also choose to switch the order of the grandparents, or choose an ancestor's middle name rather than the first name.

Another naming practice often found in families is bestowing the same name on several different siblings. Prior to the twenty-first century, parents could usually count on as many as one-third of their children not surviving to adulthood. Several sons within a family might be given the father's first name just to ensure that it would be passed on to future generations. In such cases the children were often called by their middle names, to prevent the confusion of having three sons named William. In cases in which a child died, the next child born of the same sex would often be given the deceased child's name.

ALERT!

In many cases the maiden name of the mother or grandmother was passed down as a first or middle name. Don't jump to conclusions when you see an unusual name, however. It may have been chosen for other reasons, such as to honor a friend or famous individual, or just because a parent liked the name.

Nicknames

You've found your great-grandfather's marriage license to a woman named Mary, only to find Polly listed as your great-grandfather's wife in the 1880 census. Did your great-grandfather remarry? Are the records incorrect? Not necessarily. While our ancestors sometimes appeared to change their names as often as their clothes, it is usually just a case of a nickname or middle name being recorded in official records.

The use of nicknames, especially for girls, was common practice in America during previous centuries. The confusing part for genealogists is that some nicknames don't make sense at first glance. Not everyone would suspect that Nancy was a popular nickname for Anne, and Patsy a common nickname for Martha or Matilda. Some of the most commonly encountered combinations of given name and nickname include these:

- **Ann/Anne**—Nan, Nancy
- **Dorothy**—Dolly, Dottie
- **Elizabeth**—Beth, Betsey, Bess, Lisa, Eliza
- **Helen**—Nell, Nellie, Leonora, Eleanor
- **Louise**—Alison, Eloise, Lois
- **Margaret**—Maggie, Greta, Peggy, Daisy
- **Mary**—Polly, Minnie, Mamie, May
- **Sarah**—Sally, Sallie, Sadie

While men's nicknames were usually more straightforward (such as Bill for William), men's names sometimes present their own research peculiarities. When a man you've always known as Thomas suddenly appears in the records as Howard, it can leave you wondering whether it's really the same man. As already mentioned, it was fairly common practice in early America for a man to be known by his middle name, which was used by family members and friends. When it was time for an official record, however, he may have trotted out his first name. If you suspect that two records with different names really refer to the same person, you'll need to search for further records to verify this assumption. The best proof is a record that documents both names together. Sometimes you can find corroboration from initials used on census schedules, or in formal court documents such as land records or wills.

Heraldry and Coats of Arms

Many Americans are delighted to discover objects bearing their family name and coat of arms. Mall kiosks and Internet sites cater to this interest by offering various items—wall plaques, sweatshirts, mugs, scrolls—emblazoned with a wide variety of family names, crests, and coats of arms. These items rarely have any bearing on the family's actual lineage, since they overlook or neglect legitimate, authorized hereditary rights and claims to such heraldic symbols. Nevertheless, they are fun to have and allow us to show a sense of pride in our family heritage.

What Is a Coat of Arms?

The simplest way to make sense of medieval English crests, shields, and coats of arms is to imagine a medieval warrior or knight, dressed in armor, going forth to battle. How can he be recognized in an army of knights likewise dressed in shiny metal armor? As early as A.D. 1150, a knight would incorporate four elements in his battle gear in order to identify himself:

- His coat of arms, a tunic-length surcoat that wrapped around the armor to protect it from cold, heat, and rain. This coat was decorated with a design uniquely his.
- His shield, used to block sword thrusts, arrows, and spears. On it he painted the same design as the one displayed on his coat.
- A unique crest perched atop his helmet. The helmet was most commonly made of leather or wood and decorated with feathers or other protrusions. The crest identified the knight in crowded hand-to-hand combat situations in which coats and shields were not easily visible.
- A ropelike wreath of silk, created of one to three twisted colors, that attached to the top of the helmet and the base of the crest.

Each portion of the design—symbols and colors—on the knight's coat and shield had a specific purpose that met exacting standards of the day. Among popular symbols emblazoned on the shields were variations of the Christian cross; all or parts of leaves, sheaves, and flowers; animals such as lions, leopards, horses, deer, fish, and lizards; birds such as eagles and hawks; and such mythical creatures as unicorns and monsters. Collectively, these distinctive devices, marks, and colors became referred to as an achievement of arms, or a coat of arms, for its original display on surcoats.

What Is Heraldry?

The term *heraldry* refers to the heralds, or announcers, at tournaments, who introduced the warriors and knights who were competing. In order to easily distinguish among competitors, the heralds had to know which designs belonged to whom. Hence they became the experts and arbiters of who could display which symbols—almost like granters of copyrights.

In time, central authorities emerged to approve the use of "heraldic" designs and the introduction of new ones. The English monarchy established a College of Arms to oversee the granting and registration of heraldic devices in England, Wales, and Northern Ireland. All heraldry in Scotland is governed by the Court of the Lord Lyon King of Arms, more commonly known as the Lyon Court. In the Republic of Ireland, the granting of heraldic devices is controlled by the Office of the Chief Herald of Ireland.

FACT

Because there are no legal requirements governing the granting of coats of arms in America, you can design a unique coat of arms for yourself or a parent. The American College of Heraldry can help you register the design for your own use and that of your descendants, and will even list your registration in its annual journal, *The Heraldic Register of America*.

The Granting of Arms

By custom during the Middle Ages, and later under the laws of the heraldic authorities, the design displayed on a man's armor, helmet, coat, and shield belonged to him alone, to pass down exclusively to his firstborn son. Other sons would take the father's heraldic design and alter it slightly to make it their own in a tradition known as cadency. While females could inherit arms from their fathers, they could only pass them down to their children if they had no brothers. Otherwise the changing surnames associated with a coat of arms could cause mass confusion. When families merged through marriage it was common practice to combine their respective coats of arms in some manner, a practice known as marshalling.

Essentially, a coat of arms—passed down the line from father to firstborn son—belongs by law to only one man. This is why there is no such thing as a coat of arms for a surname, and why most Americans proudly displaying those heraldic plaques and T-shirts likely have no legitimate connection with them.

Chapter 5

Where Do I Look for That?

Genealogy is like detective work, because it requires piecing together several clues to provide the solution to a mystery. Though you'll occasionally catch a lucky break, adding a new ancestor to your family tree usually entails locating several documents or sources to pinpoint the important people and events in your ancestor's life. As a genealogy detective, your job is to determine which records are most likely to provide the answers you seek, and whether it's conceivable that those records exist for the location and time period in which your ancestor lived.

Multiply Your Chances

To uniquely identify an ancestor and his place in the family tree, genealogists focus on documenting significant life events, such as birth, death, and marriage. While there may be several John Smiths born on May 3, 1821, for example, there is probably only one John Smith who was born on that date in Portsmouth, Virginia; married Anne Shipley on February 17, 1843; had three children, named John, Nancy Ann, and Charles; and died in 1867. This is why you'll need to find several different written records for each of the individuals in your family tree.

FACT

The 1900 U.S. Federal Census is the only available American census to include columns for the exact month and year of birth of every person enumerated. Earlier and later censuses include only the ages of each individual, making the 1900 census a key resource for approximating the birth date of an ancestor.

The first step toward locating the answers you seek is determining which records to use and the order in which to search them. For ancestors who lived in the twentieth century, civil records of birth, death, and marriage usually provide the best source for answers, because they are relatively easy to access and cover a large percentage of the population. As your research pushes back in time, however, you'll need to search for specific information about events that were never recorded, such as the date of death of a relative, and you'll find that many records have been lost to time, neglect, war, disaster, or disinterest. In such cases, your goal is to find as much information as possible, using the best documents available, much as a detective uses circumstantial evidence to make a case.

Order of Importance

There is no magic formula that determines the correct order in which to search different types of records for your ancestors. As a general rule, however, the basic records to search, in descending order of importance based on accuracy, completeness, and availability are:

1. Civil records
2. Church records
3. Family records
4. Specific individual record types, such as immigration, military, land, newspaper, and probate records
5. Census records
6. Published sources, such as compiled databases and previously published genealogies

ALERT!

Names really aren't as unique as you may think. To protect yourself from identifying the wrong individual as your ancestor, use multiple record sources to uniquely identify your ancestor through major events and family relationships at several different points during her life.

Some records may be more likely than others to contain the information that you seek, but also may be less accessible because they haven't been microfilmed or transcribed. Others may be easy to find, but are less reliable because they were recorded long after the event or were based on hearsay or inference.

Though it's often best to follow the guidelines in the previous list, don't be afraid to search records in any order that meets your needs. Many researchers begin their family tree by searching census records and published sources because they are so readily accessible in libraries and on the Internet. As long as you balance their greater likelihood of inaccuracy by following up clues in other records, these records make great stepping stones for filling in your family tree quickly.

Birth Date or Location

A birth certificate is the most commonly used source for identifying a birth date and location, but birth records weren't kept consistently in many U.S. states until the second decade of the twentieth century. To locate a birth certificate or other records that may yield an ancestor's birth date or location, you will first need to know:

- **Full Name**—This should include the maiden name for your female ancestors.
- **Approximate Year of Birth**—This can be estimated using your ancestor's age at various life events.
- **Approximate Place of Birth**—This can usually be found on records that were generated later in an ancestor's life, or by tracing the movements of family members and neighbors.

Once you have your ancestor's full name and approximate year and location of birth, the following records, listed in descending order of importance, are all good places to look for an actual date and location of birth, or to narrow down or confirm an approximate birth date. It is important to note that the availability of these records will vary by time period and locality.

1. **Vital records**—Birth, marriage, death, divorce
2. **Church records**—Baptism, christening, marriage
3. **Newspaper notices**—Birth announcements, marriage banns, obituaries
4. **Family sources**—Bible records, interviews, passports, driver's licenses, birth announcements, citizenship papers, and family photos
5. **Military records**—Service records, pension files, draft registrations, awards, discharge papers
6. **Census and tax records**—Age at the date of the census, country of birth
7. **Cemetery records**—Tombstones, funeral home records, sexton's records
8. **Immigration/emigration records**—Citizenship papers, ship passenger lists, port entry/exit records
9. **Land records**—Deeds, homestead applications, mortgages, and other property records may provide clues as to place of birth

10. **Wills and estate records**—Often provide the age at death, from which you can approximate the year of birth

It is important to note that the availability of these records will vary by time period and locality.

Marriage Date or Location

The best source for a marriage date or location is a marriage certificate. To locate a marriage certificate, or other records that may yield the date or location of a marriage, you need to know the full name of both individuals (including the maiden name for female ancestors) and the approximate year and place of marriage.

FACT

The 1900 U.S. Federal Census is the only available American census to record the number of years couples were married, while the 1930 census lists the age at first marriage of each individual. The 1910 U.S. Federal Census lists the number of years in the present marriage for those with multiple marriages.

Similar to the search for birth date beyond the birth certificate, marriage dates may be found in many places besides marriage records, including:

1. **Death records**—Kept in many areas long before marriage records, death records may contain a marriage date or location
2. **Church records**—Usually predating civil registration, church registers are an excellent source of information on early marriages
3. **Newspaper notices**—Marriage banns, marriage announcements, and obituaries
4. **Family sources**—Bible records, family interviews, letters, diaries, and family photographs

5. **Census records**—Census and tax records may include the number of years married, as well as ages and birth locations for children, which can help to narrow down a marriage date or location

6. **Cemetery records**—Tombstones, funeral home records, and sexton's records may include the spouse's name and/or the date of marriage

7. **Published sources**—Many early marriage records have been indexed and published in book and electronic format

8. **Pension records**—Pension application records, especially military pension records, often include marriage information

9. **Land records**—Deeds, homestead applications, mortgages, and other property records often mention the spouse

Also, you can often estimate a wedding date from the date of birth of the couple's first child and can sometimes determine the place of marriage by examining the birth location of the couple's oldest child or the place where the couple's parents lived prior to the marriage.

Death Date or Location

Because genealogy usually works its way backward through an ancestor's life, death records often provide an important foundation for further research. To locate a death certificate, or other records that may yield the date or location of a death, you will need to know:

Full Name—This should include the married name for female ancestors.

Approximate Year of Death—You can often estimate a death date using records such as wills, land deeds, and estate settlements. A death date may also be narrowed down by the omission of the individual from census or tax records in a location where she is expected to be found.

Approximate Place of Death—If you aren't sure where your ancestor died, the best place to start is her last known location. If that is unsuccessful, next check places where other family members were living at the time.

While death certificates, obituaries, and tombstone records are the most common and easily accessible sources of death information, there are many sources for death dates and locations. Listed in descending order of importance, based on quality of information and accessibility of the record:

1. **Church records**—Church registers will usually contain a date of death, as well as information about funerals and burials.
2. **Newspaper notices**—Obituaries are an obvious source for a death date, and are fairly reliable because they are usually written within a few days of the death.
3. **Cemetery records**—Tombstone inscriptions, funeral home records, and sexton's records are usually fairly accurate sources for a date of death.
4. **Family sources**—Many records found in the home can be used to locate or narrow down a date of death, including Bible records, family interviews, letters, diaries, insurance records, photos, and funeral cards.
5. **Census records**—The omission of an individual from a census or tax record, especially if the rest of his family is still listed, may indicate that he has died. Special census mortality schedules, which were compiled in some locations and time periods, are an excellent source for death information.
6. **Published sources**—Because death records aren't usually subject to as many privacy laws as are other records, many death records have been indexed and published in electronic format. Some cemetery records and obituaries have also been transcribed and published in books, CD collections, and electronic databases.
7. **Wills and estate records**—Wills and estate settlement records can be a big help in establishing an approximate date of death. Probate records often indicate the exact date of death.
8. **Military records**—Service records, pension applications and files, draft registrations, posthumous military awards, and discharge papers may all provide clues to a date or location of death.
9. **Land records**—The transfer of property that belonged to your ancestor may be an indication of his death, especially in the case of the distribution of his estate.

10. **Social Security records**—The Social Security Death Index (SSDI) is a good place to search for a date and location of death if your ancestor died in the United States after 1936.

Keep in mind that the date on a will does not usually indicate the date of death, but instead the date on which the will was written or recorded. Your ancestor's will may actually have been written dozens of years before his death, but it can at least be used to establish that he was alive prior to the date on the will.

Name of an Individual's Parents

Locating the names of an individual's parents is the key that unlocks the next generation, and it's one of the biggest challenges you'll face while building your family tree.

Depending upon the availability of records in the area in which your ancestor lived, the following records, listed in descending order of importance, are possible sources for the names of your ancestor's parents:

1. **Vital records**—Though birth records are the best source, you may also be able to find the names of one or both parents listed on a marriage record. Death records will sometimes include parents' names, but are usually a less accurate source because they rely on the personal knowledge of the informant.
2. **Church records**—Baptism, christening, marriage, and death records are all possible sources for parents' names.
3. **Census records**—If you know the name of your ancestor's siblings, census records that list all individuals in a household (1850 census and later) are one of the easiest ways to find the parents of your ancestor.
4. **Newspaper notices**—If you can pinpoint the area and date fairly accurately, wedding announcements, birth announcements, and obituaries are a very likely source for information about parents.
5. **Family sources**—Bible records, letters, diaries, wedding announcements, birth announcements, citizenship papers, family interviews, and the backs of family photographs may provide the names of your ancestor's parents.

6. **Cemetery records**—If you know where your ancestor is buried, you may find her parents in the same plot or a nearby plot.

7. **Land records**—Deeds, homestead applications, mortgages, and other property records may provide clues about a person's parents. Examples include deeds that record the sale of land to your ancestor for a token sum (such as $1), or records of land that was transferred to your ancestor as part of an estate settlement.

8. **Wills and estate records**—Because wills and other estate records often list children among the heirs, they are a good source for confirming a parent/child relationship.

For the best chance of locating a record that lists an ancestor's parents, you will need to know your ancestor's full name (including maiden name for females) and where your ancestor was living at the time the record you wish to search was created.

If you're unable to find the parents of your ancestor, consider switching your research focus. A sibling, for example, may have left a better paper trail than did your ancestor, and those records may provide the answer about the elusive parents!

Maiden Name of a Female Ancestor

For most Americans, the woman's surname is dropped in favor of her new husband's name when they marry, making it more difficult to trace the female branches of your family tree than you might expect.

Resources that might list the birth surname—maiden name—of your female ancestor include marriage records, death records, church records, newspaper records (marriage announcement), cemetery records (find an epitaph reading *nee* before a name, and you'll have the maiden name), Social Security card applications, military pension records, and land records.

Though the practice was not common in previous centuries, many women today retain their maiden name as a middle name. However, if the bride was previously married, she may be using her first marital surname instead of her birth name in this position.

When You Still Can't Find the Answers

During your quest for details about your ancestors, it is important to keep in mind that even a source that provides specific dates and names may not always be the most accurate. You also may find conflicting sources, and there may be times when you are not able to find an exact name, date, or location. In these instances, don't be afraid to qualify your information in a way that accommodates those realities, using "weasel words" (*probably, possibly, perhaps*) and "date brackets" (*before, after, between*) to clarify the imprecision of your data. As long as you have enough facts and sources to accurately identify an individual as belonging to your family tree, you have accomplished your primary goal.

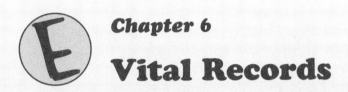

Chapter 6

Vital Records

Vital records document your ancestor's birth, marriage, and death, and they are among the most significant sources you'll use to grow your family tree. Generally referred to as "vital" because they record life's important events, these records can help establish family members in a particular location, distinguish between people of the same name, and identify the links between generations.

What's Vital?

Maintained by civil officials, vital records are a valuable source of genealogical information due to their availability, reliability, and comprehensive coverage. They also boast a fairly high accuracy rate for the event that they document.

In the United States, responsibility for registering vital events is in the hands of the individual states. As such, registration of vital statistics is not uniform across the nation, and was not a requirement in most states until the early twentieth century. Some New England towns were recording births as early as the 1600s, while in Georgia they weren't recorded in most areas prior to 1918. Many states (and non-states Washington, D.C., and Hawaii) were documenting marriages by 1880, but only Delaware, Florida, Hawaii, Iowa, Massachusetts, Michigan, New Hampshire, New Jersey, New York, Rhode Island, Vermont, Virginia, Washington, D.C., and Wisconsin had instituted registration of births and deaths by that time.

Registration of Vital Records First Required					
State	Birth	Death	State	Birth	Death
Alabama	1908	1908	Montana	1907	1907
Alaska	1913	1913	Nebraska	1905	1905
Arizona	1909	1909	Nevada	1911	1911
Arkansas	1914	1914	New Hampshire	1905	1905
California	1905	1905	New Jersey	1848	1848
Colorado	1907	1907	New Mexico	1919	1919
Connecticut	1897	1897	New York	1880	1880
Delaware	1881	1881	North Carolina	1913	1913
D.C. *	1871	1855	North Dakota	1908	1908
Florida	1899	1899	Ohio	1909	1909
Georgia	1919	1919	Oklahoma	1908	1908
Hawaii*	1896	1896	Oregon	1903	1903
Idaho	1911	1911	Pennsylvania	1906	1906
Illinois	1916	1916	Puerto Rico*	1931	1931

Indiana	1907	1900	Rhode Island	1852	1852
Iowa	1880	1880	South Carolina	1915	1915
Kansas	1911	1911	South Dakota	1905	1905
Kentucky	1911	1911	Tennessee	1914	1914
Louisiana	1914	1914	Texas	1903	1903
Maine	1892	1892	Utah	1905	1905
Maryland	1898	1898	Vermont	1857	1857
Massachusetts	1841	1841	Virginia	1912	1912
Michigan	1867	1867	Washington	1907	1907
Minnesota	1900	1900	West Virginia	1917	1917
Mississippi	1912	1912	Wisconsin	1907	1907
Missouri	1910	1910	Wyoming	1909	1909

*Table includes Hawaii, which was not made a state until 1959, Washington, D.C., which is not a state, and Puerto Rico, which is a commonwealth.

Because vital records are official government documents, local authorities usually have made a concerted effort to enforce compliance with record keeping and to preserve the records, meaning that you have a good chance of locating them.

ALERT!

In the first few years after required registration went into effect, many births, marriages, and deaths went unreported, with a compliance rate of 50 to 60 percent not uncommon. Many individuals found it inconvenient to travel to the local registrar; others were suspicious of the government's reasons for wanting such private information, ignorant of the new registration rules, or just too busy to be bothered.

How and Where to Find the Records

Begin your search for records of birth, death, or marriage by identifying which records are available for the time period and location in which your ancestor lived. Many genealogical reference books and Internet sites list origination dates and repositories for vital records in the United States (see Chapter 6: Vital Records, in Appendix A). Once you've determined the location and availability of the records you need, the next step is to contact the appropriate agency, archive, or office to obtain copies.

When requesting a copy of a vital record, be sure to ask for the long form (a full photocopy) rather than a short form (usually a transcription from the original record). This way you can make your own observations and interpretations about what information is important and what the handwriting really says, rather than leaving it up to a busy office clerk.

Whether it's called the "Bureau of Vital Statistics," "Division of Public Health," or "Vital Records Division," each state has an office in charge of the registration of vital records. Those offices are the ones to contact when you want a copy of a certificate of birth, death, marriage, or divorce. Be prepared to provide the full name of your ancestor, the approximate location and date of the event, your relationship to the person named on the certificate, and the reason for your request. Certificate fees and turnaround time will vary widely from state to state. Some states offer a lower fee for noncertified photocopies, which are perfect for genealogy research.

A search for birth, marriage, and death records prior to the onset of civil registration will take you beyond official state records and into other types of vital records at the local level. Surveys conducted in the late 1930s and early 1940s by the Works Project Administration (WPA), an agency of the federal government, include state lists of many of the available early vital records. A few states—Connecticut, Delaware, Maine, Maryland, Ohio, Pennsylvania, South Carolina, and Vermont—were not inventoried as part of this project. The *WPA List of Vital Records*, issued in 1943, shows the vital records inventories published for each of the forty participating states. Copies of the inventories are available at many larger libraries and historical societies.

FACT

While you may be tempted to begin your search with the birth record, it is better practice to start with the death record. The death record is the most recent, and therefore more likely to be available. Also, some governments allow access to birth records if you hold a copy of the death certificate to prove that the individual is deceased.

Vital records, especially birth records, are protected by privacy laws in most areas. In general, laws pertaining to birth records are more stringent than are those for marriage and death, for reasons including the fact that they can reveal illegitimacy or adoption, and also that they are sometimes misused by criminals to establish a fraudulent identity. Don't be surprised to find access to these records limited to the person named on the certificate and/or immediate family members for events that occurred anywhere from 10 years to 100 years before the present.

Birth Records

Birth records are considered to be a primary source of information for the date and place of birth because they were completed close to the time of the event by someone who was present at the birth. Birth certificates also often include the signature of the doctor or midwife who attended the birth. Privacy laws usually make birth records the most difficult of the vital records to obtain.

Birth certificates are found in three primary formats:

- **Original**—The record filed at birth
- **Amended**—A birth record that has been revised from the original to reflect corrections or new information

- **Delayed**—When a record of birth is necessary, and the birth was never officially registered, a delayed birth certificate may be issued based on other substantiated proof of the birth

The information found on a birth certificate varies widely by location and time period, but at a minimum will usually include the name, race, and gender of the child; the date and place of birth; the mother's name (often including maiden name); and the father's name. It may also contain the mother and/or father's age, race, occupation, and place of birth; the number of children in the family; and the names of witnesses to the birth.

QUESTION?

What if I can't find a birth certificate?
Evidence of birth can be found in alternative sources including baby books, baptismal or christening records, birth announcements, letters written to family members telling them of the birth, journals, dated photographs, and the family Bible.

Birth records are confidential in most states, and are usually only available to the individual named on the certificate and her direct descendants. Birth records that are more than 100 years old may have these restrictions lifted. Due to privacy concerns, very few state agencies have published their birth record indexes online. A few, such as South Dakota, do offer Internet searching of their early births. Several genealogy subscription sites also offer access to birth information for some localities.

Marriage Records

Among the oldest records maintained in many localities, marriage records can help to link the branches of your family tree. They not only offer proof that a couple was legally married, but also may provide the female's maiden name and, sometimes, the names of the couple's parents. Marriages also tend to generate a variety of documents, increasing your chances of finding a record that has survived the years.

In most cases, marriages in the United States were under the jurisdiction of towns and counties well before state registration was established. This resulted in a wide variety of marriage laws, customs, and documents. In general, however, you're likely to encounter three primary types of civil marriage records: licenses, registers, and certificates. Other types of marriage records include bonds, banns, and affidavits of consent.

- **Marriage License**—Obtained by applying to the proper civil authorities, and presented to the person who performed the marriage, marriage licenses are typically the most genealogically rich of all marriage documents. They usually include the couple's names, ages, residences, race, birth dates, and occupations; sometimes, they include the names or even the birth places of the parents.

- **Marriage Register**—On completion of the marriage ceremony, the signed marriage license was typically returned to the clerk for recording in a register or book. The details transcribed by the clerk usually include the names of the couple, the date and place of marriage, and the name of the person who performed the marriage. These bound marriage registers generally exist in both their original form and on microfilm, making them the easiest marriage records to locate.

- **Marriage Certificate**—The justice of the peace, minister, or other individual who performed the wedding usually provided the couple with a physical certificate of marriage upon completion of the ceremony. The quantity of information on such a certificate varies, but includes at least the couple's names, marriage date, and location. This certificate is usually the hardest marriage record to locate, because copies were not often kept by local officials.

- **Banns**—A church custom popular during the colonial period, marriage banns were read in church or posted in a public place on three consecutive Sundays. They announced a couple's intent to marry and gave friends, family, and neighbors the chance to voice any objections.

- **Bonds**—Common in the southern states, marriage bonds were a monetary guarantee posted by the groom and, possibly, a second person (typically a relative) to defray the costs of possible litigation if an intended marriage did not take place or was nullified. Marriage bonds, used in only some states and colonies, generally either preceded the issuance of a marriage license or replaced that step in the process.

- **Affidavits of Consent**—These affidavits granted verbal or written permission from a parent or guardian for a child to marry when the child was under the minimum legal age for marriage. The legal age of consent was usually twenty-one for males and eighteen for females, though this varies by location and time period.

While the information varies by document, locality, and time period, marriage records usually contain at least the full names of the bride and groom (including bride's maiden name or former married name), and the date and place of marriage. They may also contain some of the following information: age and birth date of bride and groom, names and places of birth for bride's and groom's parents, residences and occupations of the couple, number of previous marriages, and names and signatures of witnesses and officials.

Marriage records are most often found in the county in which the licenses were issued, usually in the jurisdiction of the county clerk or county recorder. In New York and most of New England, however, they were kept at the town level. Early marriage records, consisting mostly of scattered licenses and bonds, are available in most parts of the United States; such records were kept much earlier than were those for births and deaths. South Carolina is a notable exception—it did not maintain official marriage records prior to 1911.

Town, parish, and county officials will usually be able to provide you with copies of requested marriage records for a small fee. Searchable marriage indexes for many states and localities have also been posted online, by state vital records departments, genealogy subscription Web sites, and a number of volunteers.

ALERT!

A marriage license or bond by itself is not proof of marriage. It was not uncommon for couples to apply for a license to marry and then never follow through with the ceremony. The lack of an actual marriage date listed on the license or bond could also just be a result of poor record keeping.

CHAPTER 6: VITAL RECORDS

Death Records

Death records are especially useful for adding new generations to the family tree because they are the most recent records available for ancestors. Death records may also exist for people who were born and married before registration of births and marriages began, making the death record the only one available for those individuals.

FACT

Death records are considered a secondary source of information for anything other than the date, place, time, and cause of death. This is because other recorded information about the deceased individual, such as birth date and place and the parents' names, was provided by an informant who may not have known the individual well, may have had a faulty memory, or may have otherwise provided incorrect information.

Death certificates are most useful for simply determining the date and place of death of the deceased individual. They may also contain such details as the age at death, cause of death, exact time of death, date and place of birth, residence at time of death, occupation, parents' names and birth places, spouse's names (including maiden name for wife), marital status, place of burial, name of funeral home, name of physician or medical examiner, name of informant and his relationship to the deceased, and the names of any officials or witnesses present at the death. With some of this information you may be able to locate further records for the individual, including cemetery records, funeral home records, a marriage record, and possibly even a birth record.

Because privacy is less of a concern when dealing with deceased individuals, more and more states are posting indexes to their death records on the Internet. The Social Security Death Index (SSDI), discussed further in Chapter 13, is also a good source of death information on the Internet.

Chapter 7

Clues in the Census

Census records, rich with information about individuals, families, and communities, are one of the most valuable and widely used resources open to genealogists. They are readily available through most major libraries and on the Internet, making them an easily accessible tool for locating an individual in a specific place and time, identifying family relationships, and adding new branches to your family tree.

Understanding the U.S. Census

The Census Act of 1790, signed into law by President George Washington, established the United States as the first country in the world to undertake a regular, comprehensive count of its population. From 1790 to the present day, censuses have been conducted by the federal government every ten years; this is referred to as a decennial census. To protect the privacy of living individuals, access to the census is restricted by law for a period of seventy-two years, making the 1930 census the most recent available for family history research.

Early censuses, from 1790 to 1840, were generally a basic count of the population. Census takers documented people by household, listing only the head of household by name, and enumerating other individuals in groups by age and sex. As America grew, however, so did the need for statistics that would better reflect the status of its inhabitants. Beginning in 1850, the questions asked in the federal census were notably expanded, with census enumerators asked to obtain the name, age, sex, race, occupation, and birthplace of every individual residing in a household. Questions reflecting the needs of the rapidly expanding nation were added with each successive census—addressing topics such as citizenship, immigration, marital and educational status, property value, and occupation.

Where to Find Census Records and Indexes

Until recently, the inconsistent and incomplete indexing of census records has limited their value as a research tool. At best, census indexes included only the head of household. At worst, some census years were either never indexed, or were only partially indexed. To complicate matters, different indexing systems were used for different years, making census records a confusing tool for the novice genealogist.

Census Indexes Online

The recent rapid growth of genealogy research on the Internet has made the U.S. census a much more accessible tool for anyone researching their family tree. Thanks to the wonders of modern technology and the demand from genealogists for digitized records, all census enumerations between

1790 and 1930 can be viewed on the Internet as digital images. At minimum, a full head-of-household index is also available for every census, with "every name" indexes created for most years.

Census records are available online through three major providers: Ancestry.com, Genealogy.com, and HeritageQuest.com. Ancestry.com and Genealogy.com both offer access to census records and indexes on an individual subscription basis, while HeritageQuest is usually available at no cost to members of participating libraries and organizations. FamilySearch.org provides an "every name" index for the 1880 census at no cost.

Because the goal of the census is to account for every individual living in the United States, the chances are good that your ancestors will be included in a particular census if they resided in the country on the date the census was taken.

Published Indexes

Census indexes—both in book and CD-ROM format—have been developed and published by various private companies for the U.S. census years 1790–1870. These published indexes can be found at larger public libraries, archives, and other institutions with major genealogical collections.

Soundex and the Census

Developed in the 1930s by the Works Progress Administration (WPA) for the Social Security Administration (SSA), Soundex is a method of indexing names phonetically (in other words, grouping together surnames that sound alike, such as SMITH and SMYTH). Because names were often recorded under various spellings, this indexing method improves your chances of locating an individual.

Soundex is important for genealogists because it was used for indexing at least portions of the 1880, 1900, 1910, 1920, and 1930 censuses. A similar type of code, known as Miracode, was also used for indexing part of the 1910 census. Today, these Soundex indexes are available on microfilm, which makes it much easier to locate your ancestors, especially if you aren't sure where they were living at the time of the census. If you plan to use the microfilmed census indexes, however, you need to first understand the Soundex system.

How Soundex Works

The Soundex system basically takes a surname and turns it into a four-digit code consisting of a letter and three numbers. To determine the Soundex code for a particular surname, begin with the first letter of the surname. This is the letter that begins your Soundex code. Next, cross out any vowels in the surname (*a*, *e*, *i*, *o*, and *u*) as well as vowel-sounding consonants (*y*, *w*, and *h*). Finally, proceed in sequence through the rest of the letters in the surname, assigning a number to the next three consonants as follows:

1 B, P, F, V
2 C, S, K, G, J, Q, X, Z
3 D, T
4 L
5 M, N
6 R

Soundex Rules and Tips:

- Ignore any extra, unused letters at the end of the surname. Once you have a four-digit Soundex code, you're done. (CRISPIN would become Soundex code C621.)
- If there are not enough consonants in the name to form a four-digit code, add zeroes to the end to complete it. (POWELL would become P400.)
- When two consonants with the same value sit side-by-side, not separated by a vowel, the second letter is ignored. (For the *ck* in PACKER, only the first letter is coded; the name then becomes Soundex code P260.)

How to Use Soundex Indexes on Microfilm

Locate the correct microfilm roll for the state, year, and Soundex code of interest. Scroll through the microfilm until you reach your Soundex code. Within each code, you'll find the microfilmed index cards arranged alphabetically by the first name of the head of household, such as A266 Albert, A266 Ann, A266 Arthur, and so on.

Once you have located a Soundex index card for the person or household in which you are interested, note the following: 1) county; 2) city, town, village, or township; and 3) the four numbers located in the upper right-hand corner of the index card: volume number, enumeration district (E.D.) number, sheet number, and line number. Use the county name and enumeration district number to determine which roll of census microfilm contains the actual census record.

ALERT!

Soundex coding rules may seem a bit complicated at first, but all it really takes is a little practice. If you're feeling a bit unsure, however, Soundex codes can be automatically generated in many genealogy software programs. Several conversion tools available on the Internet also generate Soundex codes.

Soundex Census Indexes (1880–1930)

The 1880 Soundex census index—the first to use this coding method—only lists heads of households with children under the age of eleven (although everyone is listed on the actual census records). The 1900 census index, however, is more complete, listing all heads of households as well as individuals in that household who do not share that surname. Only twenty-one states are indexed for the 1910 census, some using the Soundex method and others using Miracode. These states are Alabama, Arkansas, California, Florida, Georgia, Illinois, Kansas, Kentucky, Louisiana, Michigan, Mississippi, Missouri, North Carolina, Ohio, Oklahoma, Pennsylvania, South Carolina, Tennessee, Texas, Virginia, and West Virginia.

There is a head-of-household Soundex index available for all states for the 1920 census. The Soundex index for 1930, however, is only available for the following states: Alabama, Arkansas, Florida, Georgia, Kentucky (only counties of Bell, Floyd, Harlan, Kenton, Muhlenberg, Perry, and Pike), Louisiana, Mississippi, North Carolina, South Carolina, Tennessee, Virginia, and West Virginia (only counties of Fayette, Harrison, Kanawha, Logan, McDowell, Mercer, and Raleigh).

Be Sure to Record

Whether you're searching on microfilm or on the Internet, once you find your ancestor in the census, record everything that you find, including:

- Census year (for example, 1870)
- State and county, plus township, post office, etc., when applicable
- Page number
- House or dwelling number and family number
- Microfilm series number and roll number (for example, T624, roll 112), or details about the CD, book, or Web site where you found the census information

Census data should then be transcribed (copied) exactly as you find it, even if you know it to be incorrect. Take down the details in every column for every individual listed in the household where you find your ancestor, even if they have different last names. The likelihood that they'll turn out to be related somehow is high.

Consider recording at least one or two families listed on either side of your ancestor. Otherwise you'll find yourself coming back to this same census again when you later learn the wife's maiden name and realize that her family lived right next door!

Researching the Individual Censuses

When did Great-Grandpa arrive in America? How many children did Grandma have? What were their names? Was Grandpa a banker or a farmer? Did Great-Grandma know how to read and write? Depending upon the year, census records can help answer a multitude of questions about your ancestors, including approximate dates of birth and marriage, children's names, social status, occupation, citizenship status, country of origin, educational status, and more.

1790–1830 U.S. Census

Official Census Date: First Monday in August for 1790–1820; June 1 for 1830

Although the first five federal decennial censuses (1790 through 1830) contain less detail than do those taken later, they still provide useful clues for genealogists. During these years, generally only the head of each household was identified by name, with ages of other household members reported in age categories. It takes a bit of detective work, but by tracking individuals of various ages listed in the household through these years, you can estimate the general composition of the family and its members.

1840 U.S. Census

Official Census Date: June 1

This census lists the head of each household by name. It also reports the name and exact age of Revolutionary War pensioners (including both veterans and widows). Researchers who believe that there are Revolutionary War veterans in their family trees may be able to support this through the 1840 census.

1850 U.S. Census

Official Census Date: June 1

The first federal census to list each individual by name, the 1850 census is a significant resource for genealogists whose ancestors were in America at or before that time. Five new states (Florida, Texas, Iowa, Wisconsin, and California) and four new territories (Oregon, Minnesota, New Mexico, and Utah) were added for the 1850 census.

These questions were asked in the 1850 census:

- Name, age, and sex of each individual in the household
- Color or race of each individual (white, black, or mulatto)
- Profession, occupation, or trade of each individual over age fifteen
- Value of real estate
- Place of birth (state, territory, or country)
- Whether married within the year
- Whether attended school within the year

- Whether able to read and write, if over twenty years old
- Whether deaf and dumb, blind, insane, idiotic, a pauper or a convict

ALERT!

Although all individuals are listed by name in the 1850 census, it was not until 1880 that relationships of everyone in the household to the head of the household were given. This means that, while probable family relationships can be determined for the 1850, 1860, and 1870 censuses, these connections, without further proof, are only guesswork.

1860 U.S. Census

Official Census Date: June 1

The 1860 census added a column for the value of personal property, which provides some insight into the financial status of your ancestors.

1870 U.S. Census

Official Census Date: June 1

The first census to indicate parents of foreign birth, the 1870 census is useful for identifying immigrant ancestors. It also lists the month of birth and/or marriage for individuals born or married within the previous year.

New questions added in 1870:

- Race (Indian and Chinese were added)
- Whether parents were of "foreign birth"
- Whether a male citizen over the age of twenty-one
- Whether a male citizen over the age of twenty-one and the right to vote had been denied on grounds other than rebellion or other crime

1880 U.S. Census

Official Census Date: June 1

Significant for being the first census to identify the relationship of each person to the head of household, the 1880 census also added questions about the birthplace of the mother and father of each individual. This census was the first to identify marital status, unemployment, and illness or disability and to provide the name of the street and house number for urban households.

New questions added in 1880:

- Relationship of each individual to head of household
- Whether single, married, widowed, or divorced
- Father's state, territory, or country of birth
- Mother's state, territory, or country of birth
- Number of months unemployed within the past census year
- Whether sick or temporarily disabled and, if so, nature of illness
- Whether deaf and dumb, blind, crippled, maimed, idiotic, insane, bedridden, or otherwise permanently disabled
- Street name and house number in urban areas

1890 U.S. Census

Official Census Date: First Monday in June

Returns from the 1890 federal census were all either destroyed or badly damaged in a fire in Washington, D.C., in 1921—a major loss for genealogists. Less than 1 percent of the census returns, totaling just 6,160 names, survived. There are some surviving records from a special Union Veterans and Widows schedule taken in 1890, covering half of Kentucky and all of Louisiana alphabetically through Wyoming, as well as the District of Columbia.

1900 U.S. Census

Official Census Date: June 1

Of special interest to genealogists, the 1900 U.S. census is the only available federal census to report the month and year of birth for each individual. The 1900 census is also the first census to record the number of years couples were married, the number of children born to the mother, and how many were still living at the time of the census. Immigration, citizenship, and home ownership statistics also were entered in 1900.

New questions added in 1900:

- Month and year of birth, and age at last birthday
- Number of years married

- If a mother, the number of children born and number of those children still living
- Year of immigration to the United States
- Number of years resided in the United States
- Whether or not a naturalized citizen
- Whether able to speak English
- Whether home was owned or rented, and if mortgaged
- If home was a house or a farm

1910 U.S. Census

Official Census Date: April 15

In general, the 1910 U.S. census questions followed the same format as 1900. For people researching Civil War veterans, the 1910 census is especially useful because it reports whether males were Union or Confederate veterans—a potential lead to military records. More detail concerning the naturalization status of immigrants is also provided.

New questions added in 1910:

- Number of years in present marriage
- Whether naturalized (*na*), alien (*al*), or have started the naturalization process (*pa*=papers)
- Language spoken
- Type of industry or business employed in
- Whether employee, employer, or self-employed
- Whether or not currently employed and number of weeks out of work during census year
- Whether a survivor of the Union or Confederate army or navy
- Whether blind, deaf, or dumb

1920 U.S. Census

Official Census Date: January 1

Helpful for researching immigrant ancestors, the 1920 census is the only available federal census to ask the exact year of naturalization for immigrants who became American citizens.

New questions added in 1920:

- Street or road name; house number or farm
- If naturalized, the year of naturalization
- Father's native tongue
- Mother's native tongue

1930 U.S. Census

Official Census Date: April 1

Highlighting the country's move into the technology age, the 1930 census asked residents about radio ownership. Other new questions included which war a man fought in (useful for identifying veterans' records) and the value of the individual's home or the amount of rent paid each month.

New questions added in 1930:

- Value of home or monthly mortgage or rental payment
- Whether own a radio set
- Age at first marriage
- Language spoken in home prior to coming to United States
- Whether worked yesterday
- Whether a veteran and, if so, of what war

Non-Population Schedules and Special Censuses

Did you know that the federal government also counted more than people in some years? These non-population schedules, which include mortality, agricultural, and manufacturing statistics, are an often untapped gold mine for genealogists. There were also several special censuses conducted in some years along with the regular decennial population census. While not created for such purposes, these special census schedules provide researchers with further details on certain populations, including slaves, military pensioners, and Native Americans.

FACT

The 1900 and 1910 agricultural schedules were eliminated when Congress authorized the destruction of the original census schedules (because it takes a lot of money and space to store that many documents) but only population schedules had been microfilmed—not special schedules such as the agricultural schedule.

Mortality Schedules

Mortality schedules—surviving for the federal census years of 1850, 1860, 1870, and 1880—list the name of every person who died during the twelve months prior to that census. If the census was taken on June 1, 1850, for example, the enumerator would ask who in the household had died between June 1, 1849 and May 31, 1850. Information collected about these deceased individuals includes name, age, gender, race, marital status, place of birth, occupation, and month and cause of death. The 1880 schedule also lists the birthplace of the decedent's parents. Mortality schedules are an important source for death information, because many states did not maintain official records of deaths until the early twentieth century.

Agricultural Schedules

Federal agricultural censuses were taken each decade from 1850 through 1910, but only 1850–1880 are available for research. The 1890 schedules were destroyed by fire in 1921, and the 1900 and 1910 schedules were destroyed by an act of Congress.

While not largely significant in the process of researching your family tree, agricultural schedules can provide interesting information about your ancestors' lives and occupations. Agricultural schedules typically include such information as how much acreage a farmer owned or leased, quantity and type of livestock, and wages paid to hired help. These schedules typically are not indexed, but a notation provided on the regular census population schedule for the same year will lead you to the right entry on the agricultural schedule.

ALERT!

Not all farms were included on the agricultural schedules. In 1850, for example, small farms that produced less than $100 worth of goods were omitted. By 1870, farms having fewer than three acres or producing less than $500 worth of goods were not included. Small manufacturing operations that produced less than $500 worth of goods were also not reported on the manufacturing schedules.

Manufacturing Schedules

Like agricultural schedules, manufacturing schedules do not contain a lot of personal data about your ancestors. In 1820, and again from 1850 through 1880, manufacturing and industrial census schedules collected information about manufacturing, mining, and fishery businesses, including the type of product, the amount of capital invested, the number of people employed, and the average monthly wages paid to employees. In 1880, supplemental schedules were also used for specific industries, such as lumber mills, sawmills, flour mills, gristmills, and boot- and shoemakers. Of interest to researchers with farming ancestors, manufacturing schedules are a good place to find individuals with significant "sideline" businesses, such as tanning, milling, coopering, or cheese-making.

Slave Schedules

Slave schedules list slaves in the Southern states for the years 1850 and 1860. These schedules provide only basic information, such as the owners' names, and the sexes and ages of the slaves.

Special 1885 Federal Census

Five states and territories—Colorado, Florida, Nebraska, Dakota Territory, and New Mexico Territory—conducted an 1885 census partly funded by the federal government. These records can be found at the National Archives in Washington, D.C. Colorado's and Nebraska's records have also been microfilmed. The 1885 Dakota Territory census is available for searching online (see Chapter 7: Clues in the Census in Appendix A).

1890 Special Census of Union Civil War Veterans and Their Widows

This special schedule, conducted in 1890, recorded Union veterans and widows of Union veterans of the American Civil War. A few Confederate veterans slipped in as well. Information includes the name of the veteran (or, if he did not survive, the names of both the widow and her deceased husband); the veteran's rank, company, regiment, or vessel; date of enlistment, date of discharge, and length of service; post office and address of each person listed; disability incurred by the veteran; and remarks necessary to a complete statement of his term of service. Unfortunately, almost all of the schedules for the states of Alabama alphabetically through Kansas and approximately half of those for Kentucky are unaccounted for, and believed destroyed.

State and Local Censuses

Availability of state census records varies widely by state and time period, and most remain unindexed, making them an often underutilized resource. State censuses not only stand as substitutes for some of the missing federal census schedules (most notably the 1890 federal census), but also as valuable resources for time periods between federal census years. They often include questions not asked in the federal census.

While not all states took their own censuses, and some of these enumerations have not survived, state and local census records can be found in many locations. Most states that took censuses usually did so every ten years, on the five-year mark (1855, 1865, and so on), to complement the U.S. federal census. These records are most often found at state archives or state libraries. Many state census records are also available on microfilm through local Family History Centers of the Church of Jesus Christ of Latter-day Saints.

Many cities, towns, counties, and other localities also conducted special censuses for a myriad of reasons. Like their state counterparts, most of the local censuses are unindexed. Most of them have been microfilmed and, like state census records, are available through local Family History Center locations.

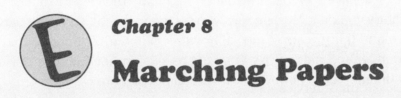

Chapter 8

Marching Papers

Nearly every generation of Americans has had its war—some more than one. From the patriots and loyalists of the American Revolution to the 16 million American veterans of World War II, chances are that at least one of your ancestors served in the military. Military records, enlightening for their insight into the lives of veterans as well as their families, are a valuable resource that you should not overlook.

Identifying Military Ancestors

Even if you have never heard stories of an ancestor's military career, it is still worth checking to see if male ancestors who lived during wartime did, in fact, serve in some capacity. To determine whether any of your ancestors were likely to have served in the military, compare their ages to a timeline of U.S. military conflicts. Most people who served in the military were between eighteen and thirty years of age, although it is not uncommon to find men both younger and older. Boys as young as sixteen, for example, served in the Continental Army during the American Revolution.

Timeline of Major U.S. Military Conflicts	
Dates	**Conflict**
1754–1763	French and Indian War
1775–1783	American Revolution
1812–1815	War of 1812
1846–1848	Mexican-American War
1861–1865	American Civil War (War Between the States)
1898	Spanish-American War
1917–1918	World War I (First World War)
1941–1945	World War II (Second World War)
1950–1953	Korean War
1965–1975	Vietnam War (Second Indochina War)
1991	Gulf War

Once you have identified ancestors of the right age, establish where they lived at the time. Narrowing your search to a particular area and time period focuses your search for clues that may confirm that your ancestor was indeed in the military. Records and sources that provide this type of evidence include family stories, tombstone inscriptions or markers, photographs in uniform, absence from a census taken during wartime, death records and obituaries, newspaper articles, and local histories.

Types of Military Records

Military records, as they apply to genealogy, refer to two general classes of records: 1) enlistment and service records and 2) records of veterans' benefits. These records are applicable to all branches of the armed services—Army, Navy, Air Force, Coast Guard, and Marines. The quantity and quality of the information varies by record and time period, but may provide such useful details as the place of birth, age at enlistment, occupation, physical description, and the name of parents, spouse, or other immediate family members.

Military Service Records

Officers and enlisted personnel who are deceased or have been discharged from the Army, Navy, Air Force, Marines, and Coast Guard can be researched through military service records. Depending upon the time period and branch of service, the majority of these records are under the jurisdiction of the National Archives and Records Administration (NARA) in Washington, D.C., or the National Personnel Records Center (NPRC) in St. Louis, Missouri. Unfortunately, a large percentage of these one-of-a-kind records were destroyed in a fire at the NPRC on July 12, 1973.

QUESTION?

Should I look first to NARA or the NPRC for my ancestor's military records?
In general, NARA holds the earlier military service records, while the NPRC has the more recent records. The availability of military service records varies by branch of service.

U.S. Army

Records of enlisted personnel who served between 1789 and October 31, 1912, and officers who served between 1789 and June 30, 1917, are held by NARA. Records of servicemen who separated from the Army after those dates are available from the NPRC, with the exception of almost 80 percent of the records of veterans discharged between November 1912 and January 1960, which were lost in the fire at the records center.

U.S. Navy

The National Archives oversees the records of enlisted personnel who served between 1798 and 1885, and officers from 1798 to 1902. Records of servicemen who left the Navy after those dates are held by the NPRC in St. Louis.

U.S. Air Force

Records of officers and enlisted personnel separated after September 24, 1947, are available from the NPRC. About 75 percent of the records for individuals (alphabetically through Hubbard, James E.) discharged between September 1947, and January 1964, were destroyed in the NPRC fire.

U.S. Marine Corps

Contact NARA for records of enlisted personnel who served from 1789 to 1904, and officers who served from 1789 to 1895. The NPRC serves as the repository for records of Marine Corps veterans discharged after these dates.

U.S. Coast Guard

NARA maintains the records of agencies that predated the Coast Guard, including the Revenue Cutter Service (Revenue Marine), the Life-Saving Service, and the Lighthouse Service, from 1791 to 1919. the NPRC has jurisdiction over records of Coast Guard officers separated after 1897, and enlisted personnel separated after 1905.

Compiled Service Records

In 1903, the U.S. War Department began a project to collect and abstract existing military documents in an effort to preserve deteriorating original records and find alternative sources for important military records lost in fires in 1800 and 1814. Information found for a soldier was entered on an index card. These efforts resulted in a collection of index cards known as the Compiled Service Record or, sometimes, the Carded Service Record (CSR). The CSR envelope, or jacket, contains abstracts of an individual's service record compiled from muster rolls, hospital records, enlistment and discharge documents, prison records, payrolls, and the like. CSRs are primarily available for veterans of the American Revolution, War of 1812, and the American Civil War.

Enlistment and Draft Registration Records

Records that relate to the enlistment or conscription of military personnel are an often overlooked gem among military documents. These records customarily include such details as name and address; date and location of birth; name of parents, spouse, or other relatives; occupation; and a physical description of the individual. All draft registration records for World War I and some of the records for World War II are open for viewing by the public.

Pension Records

Because they often contain supporting documents such as marriage certificates, birth records, personal narratives, and pages taken from the family Bible, pension records are often the most genealogically valuable records for researching military ancestors.

FACT

In general, pension benefits could be sought by a soldier who served in the U.S. armed forces between 1775 and 1916, or by his widow or heirs, for assistance due to age, sickness, incapacitation, injury, or death.

Pension records often provide the veteran's date and place of birth and death, the name of his spouse (sometimes including maiden name), and details about parents, children, and other living relatives. The National Archives has the pension applications, as well as records of pension payments.

Bounty Land Warrants

The federal government provided bounty land as a reward for citizens who served in the nation's wars between 1775 and 1855. Veterans or their heirs could claim this free land by filing an application, known as a bounty land warrant application, at a nearby courthouse. Approved applicants received a warrant, which could then be used to apply for a land patent (grant).

Aside from federal land, many states—most notably, Virginia—also offered bounty land in return for military service.

The land patent, not the warrant, is the document that actually granted the veteran ownership of the land. Warrants could be assigned or sold to other individuals, and the majority of veterans chose this option rather than taking possession of the land themselves.

Colonial Wars and the American Revolution

Because the United States as a country did not exist prior to the American Revolution, no official government records exist of the colonial wars. Outside of a few scattered rolls and rosters, little has survived. Most of the extant lists have been published and can be located at libraries that have large genealogical collections.

No one knows for certain how many individuals fought in the American Revolution, but many genealogists with ties to early America can claim an ancestor who participated. Most existing records related to the American Revolution are in the keeping of the National Archives.

Once you have determined that your ancestor most likely served, look for him in the *General Index to Compiled Military Service Records of Revolutionary War Soldiers.* Available on microfilm through the National Archives, Family History Centers, and many larger genealogical libraries, this index will provide your ancestor's name and unit, enabling you to access further details in your ancestor's compiled military service record, which is available on microfilm or through a written request to the National Archives. Revolutionary War pension files and bounty land warrant application files are also available on microfilm and, for a fee, from the National Archives.

FACT

If you aren't sure whether or not your ancestor served in the American Revolution, you may want to start by checking with the National Society Daughters of the American Revolution (DAR). Provided with a name, they will search their database of proven Revolutionary patriots free of charge (*www.dar.org*).

The American Civil War

From the initial attack on Fort Sumter in Charleston Harbor on April 12, 1861, to the surrender by General Robert E. Lee at Appomattox Courthouse on April 9, 1865, the American Civil War literally tore America apart. North fought against South. Brother fought against brother. Families were divided. Hundreds of thousands of people lost their lives. If you had ancestors living in America at the time, you'll most likely notice the war's devastating impacts in your own family tree.

Confederate Ancestors

If your ancestor served in the Confederate Army, begin your search in the NARA microfilm publication *Consolidated Index to Compiled Service Records of Confederate Soldiers*. This index will provide you with the details you need to find his record, including state, regiment, and so on. Alternatively, you can search the free online index available through the Civil War Soldiers and Sailors System or the more detailed subscription-based American Civil War Research Database (*www.civilwardata.com*). Once you have this information you can then view your ancestor's entire file in the microfilmed Confederate Compiled Service records.

Taken from the Compiled Military Service Records in the National Archives, the Civil War Soldiers and Sailors (CWSS) database indexes more than 6.3 million soldiers' names, both Union and Confederate, from 44 states and territories. You can search the database free of charge at *www.itd.nps.gov/cwss/soldiers.htm*.

Although Confederate soldiers were obviously not eligible for federal pensions, many states granted their own pensions to their Confederate veterans and widows of veterans. Generally, applicants were only eligible for a pension if they were indigent or disabled. A veteran was eligible to apply for a pension to the state in which he lived, regardless of the state in which he actually served. If you aren't sure where your ancestor lived at the time of the Civil War, try locating him in the index to the 1860 Federal Census. Confederate pension records can usually be found in the state archives or state historical society of the state issuing the pension.

Union Ancestors

Although there is no printed consolidated index to the Compiled Military Service Records for Union veterans, the soldiers' names can be searched online through the Civil War Soldiers and Sailors System. Alternatively, if you know where your ancestor served, you can search the state indexes to the records, which are available on microfilm. Depending on the state and unit, the compiled service records also may be available on microfilm. If not, you'll have to visit the National Archives in person to view the original record, or submit a written request on National Archives Trust Fund (NATF) Form 86.

The majority of Union army soldiers (or their widows, minor children, or dependent parents) applied for a federal pension in the years following the Civil War. The pension files have been indexed in the microfilm publication *General Index to Pension Files, 1861–1934*, available through the National Archives and Family History Centers. This index is also available at many major libraries and online at Ancestry.com for paying subscribers.

The pension records provide more information than do the compiled military records, including details on the soldier's service. If a widow applied for the pension, she had to provide proof of marriage, which will be in the pension file. Applications made on behalf of minor children will include both the proof of marriage and proof of birth for each of the children.

FACT

Using the information from the *General Index to Pension Files, 1861–1934*, you can now order copies of the pension records from the National Archives on NATF Form 85 or via its online request service.

Twentieth-Century Military Records

Because many soldiers who fought in twentieth-century conflicts are still living, some military records from this time period are protected by the

Privacy Act of 1974. Many of the records from WWI and some from WWII are available for research, however. Military records of deceased twentieth-century veterans can also be consulted by their next of kin—widow, parents, and children. Among the most valuable of the available twentieth-century military sources are the draft registration records of the Selective Service.

WWI Draft Registration Records

WWI draft registration records for more than 24 million men born between 1873 and 1900 are available at the National Archives Southeast Region branch in Morrow, Georgia. The WWI draft registration records have also been microfilmed and are available at some larger genealogical libraries and through Family History Centers. A partial index to these records is available online at RootsWeb.com (*www.rootsweb.com/~rwguide/WWIdraft.html*), while a partial index linked to actual digitized images of the cards is part of the subscription offerings at Ancestry.com. Both sites plan eventually to make the entire collection available.

WWII Draft Registration Records

More than 10 million men registered in six different registration sessions between 1940 and 1942. Although most of these registrations are still protected by the Privacy Act, the records of those individuals who participated in the Fourth Registration (men ages 45–65 in 1942) have been opened to the public because the participants were all born prior to 1897.

These records are available from the Selective Service System in Arlington, Virginia (*www.sss.gov/records2.htm*).

ALERT!

In order to obtain a copy of the draft registration card, you'll need to know the county or state where the registrant was living. Cards for deceased individuals (including in the five registrations still covered by the Privacy Act) registrations can be obtained by showing proof of death.

WWII Enlistment Records

Enlistment records for more than 9 million Army soldiers who served in WWII, including 130,000 women who enlisted in the Women's Army Auxiliary Corps, are available for searching online through the Access to Archival Databases (AAD) of the National Archives (✍*www.archives.gov/aad*). About 1.5 million records could not be scanned because of aging microfilm, but the remaining records provide helpful genealogical details such as the enlistee's serial number and name, state and county of residence, place and date of enlistment, grade, branch, term of enlistment, place and year of birth, race, education, civilian occupation, and marital status.

How to Order Copies of Military Records

As mentioned previously, the two main repositories of U.S. military records are the National Archives and the National Personnel Records Center. Both centers allow you to order military records online, as well as through postal mail.

The National Archives, Washington, D.C.

Military service records, including compiled service records, can be ordered online from the National Archives, or by mail using NATF Form 86. Copies of military pension claim files for military service from the American Revolution up to just before World War I, and bounty land warrant applications for federal military service prior to 1856, can also be ordered online or by mail using NATF Form 85.

National Archives—Obtaining Copies of Records
✍*www.archives.gov/research/order*

The National Personnel Records Center, St. Louis, Missouri

The National Personnel Records Center is the repository for the bulk of all U.S. military records dating from 1900 to the present. Access to many of these records is limited by privacy laws. If you are a veteran or next-of-kin of a deceased veteran, you can order records online through eVetRecs, or by mail on form SF-180. All other requests must be submitted on SF-180.

FACT

For veterans requesting their own records, there is usually no charge. All other requests will incur a fee to cover the cost of locating, copying, and mailing the record.

eVetRecs—Order Military Records Online
✍*www.archives.gov/research_room/vetrecs*

NPRC Form SF-180
✍*www.archives.gov/facilities/mo/st_louis/military_personnel_records/standard_form_180.html*

The National Archives Southeast Region, Morrow, Georgia

Original copies of the World War I Draft Registration Cards can be obtained through the Southeast Region branch of the National Archives. These cards can only be obtained via a written request.

WWI Draft Registration Card Request Form
✍*www.friendsnas.org/pdf_files/WWIDraftRequest.pdf*

Military Lineage and Historical Societies

There are probably more military-related lineage societies than any other type, providing an often untapped resource for locating previously researched information on American veterans. Lineage societies such as the National Society Daughters of the American Revolution (DAR), Sons of Confederate Veterans (SCV), and General Society of the War of 1812 require members to prove their lineage from a veteran of the war. Thus, their files are rich with records that prove the military service of thousands of our nation's military heroes, as well as family trees that trace the descendants of those military veterans.

The DAR Patriot Index lists all of the Revolutionary War patriots who have been identified to qualify individuals for membership, along with details that may include dates and places of birth and death, spouse's name, type of service, and the names of members who descend from the patriot.

Most military and patriotic lineage societies allow access to their membership applications. These can be especially useful when researching military connections because they contain the names, dates, locations, and supporting sources for the direct descent from the military ancestor to the person who submitted the application. If you can connect yourself to a society member, either past or present, that person's membership application may provide a big boost to your family tree research. Permission may be required to access the applications of living members.

The libraries and collections of military lineage and historical societies encompass a wide variety of books, microfilms, family histories, military histories, unit rosters, journals, and other collected resources. Most such collections are noncirculating, meaning that you need to visit the library in person. If you can't get to the library yourself, contact the society for a list of individuals you may engage for genealogical research in the library. You may also be able to order photocopies of microfilms or book pages if you write to the library with a specific request. Even if these firsthand accounts of men who may have served with your ancestors don't mention your ancestor personally, they can help "flesh out" the story of your ancestor's military life.

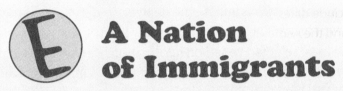

Chapter 9

A Nation of Immigrants

No matter how long your family has been in America, your ancestors came to this country from somewhere—England, Africa, Poland, China. Even the ancestors of Native Americans immigrated here, across the land bridge from Asia in the long-distant past. Imagine how scary this must have been for our ancestors—leaving their home, possessions, family, and friends for a new land and an uncertain future. Where did they come from? What made them decide to move? What did they give up by leaving their homeland? When did they first arrive on America's shores?

Why Do People Migrate?

According to a U.S. Census Bureau report, 43.4 million Americans moved between March 1999 and March 2000. Most of us today think nothing of moving across town, or even across the country. The decision to pack up and leave home, especially for a new country, wasn't nearly as easy for our ancestors. The journey—both across land to the nearest port and across the ocean by ship—was expensive. The mode and route of travel, as well as the final destination, had to be selected based on information from secondhand, often unreliable, sources. Then there was the uncertainty of finding housing and employment for the family in the New World. Given all of the expense and insecurity, what made so many people choose to immigrate to America?

FACT

While *immigration* and *emigration* both refer to the movement of people from one country to another, the terms are not synonymous. Immigration refers to moving *to* a country. Emigration means moving *from* one's native country. It's basically just a matter of perspective—Great-grandmother emigrated from Germany and immigrated to America.

People move from one place to another for a variety of reasons today. Our ancestors weren't much different. Many of the original settlers of America came to this country in the pursuit of freedom, the desire to live their lives and practice their religious beliefs without fear of reprisal or persecution. War and political turmoil were another big catalyst for emigration, as people moved to escape the resulting conflict, instability, and destruction. Natural disasters such as earthquakes, floods, drought, and fires often forced people from their homes in search of safer locations. Famine, caused by wars or crop failures, was another major incentive for emigration. The Irish potato famine of the mid-1800s sent almost a million Irish immigrants to Canada and America in search of a better life.

Locating and Using Immigration Records

Immigrant arrival records are the official documentation of an immigrant's entry into the United States. More than just a name on a list, however, these records and the voyage and decisions they represent often provide the vital link from America to the old country. For this reason, many genealogists spend a lot of time searching for an ancestor's immigration record—a task that often isn't as easy as expected. If you're about to embark on a hunt for your immigrant ancestor, be prepared to do some digging!

Consisting primarily of ship passenger lists, the format, content, and quality of available immigrant records varies greatly from one time period to another. When researching American passenger lists, there are three major time frames to consider: pre-1820, 1820–1890, and 1891–1957.

Pre-1820

Prior to 1820, the American colonies put little effort into collecting lists of passengers arriving from foreign ports, primarily because the colonies were British colonies and the majority of the white immigrants coming to the New World prior to 1790 were British subjects. Colonial officials were more concerned with documenting and taxing incoming and outgoing goods than they were with documenting a few extra colonists.

One major exception to the lack of pre-1820 U.S. passenger arrival records is the colony of Pennsylvania, which required non-British immigrants, primarily Germans, to be identified and recorded. These early Philadelphia ship lists from 1727 to 1808 are available at the Pennsylvania State Archives and have also been published in book form.

While never required by law, some pre-1820 ship manifests were created and have survived. Most can be found scattered among the holdings of archives, museums, and other agencies. Luckily for modern-day researchers, almost all existing pre-1820 lists have been discovered and published in some format—in genealogical books, historical society quarterlies, and even on the Internet. The majority of these published lists have also been indexed in a number of major works, most notably the multivolume *Passenger and Immigration Lists Index* (see the Filby entry in Chapter 9: A Nation of Immigrants in Appendix A), making them easier for researchers to locate.

Other lists of early immigrants to America have also been compiled from a variety of pre-federal records, including colonial land grants, oaths of allegiance, lists of indentured servants, and early naturalizations. Like the extant passenger lists, most of these compiled "alternative" sources of immigrant information have been published and can be located by searching the various indexes to published arrival records for the time period.

1820–1890

Following the passage of the Steerage Act by Congress in 1819, U.S. officials began formally tracking all passengers arriving in America on vessels from foreign ports. These passenger arrival records were kept on large sheets called Customs Manifests or Customs Passenger Lists. Information collected during this time period is fairly basic, generally including only this information:

- Name of the ship
- Name of the captain
- Port of embarkation
- Date and port of arrival
- Each passenger's name, age, sex, occupation, and nationality

The surviving Customs Passenger Lists are available for research on microfilm at the National Archives, arranged chronologically by port of arrival. The LDS Family History Library has copies of all of these microfilm publications, which means they can be borrowed and viewed at any Family History Center worldwide. Major genealogical libraries also provide access to at least some of these passenger list microfilms.

1891–1957

In 1891, the U.S. Office of the Superintendent of Immigration was created by law, and the federal government assumed full control of immigration at all

U.S. ports. The law also provided for the creation of immigrant receiving stations and required steamship companies to bear responsibility for transporting back to their homelands all passengers who were refused admittance to the United States. This encouraged ship officials to be more meticulous about checking immigrant paperwork and making sure the passenger manifests were complete and accurate.

ALERT!

Though not required by law, many Customs Passenger Lists included a section recording births and deaths at sea. This information may have been entered in a separate column, or may be found at the end of the passenger manifest, following the regular list of passengers. Stowaways discovered on board during the ocean passage also may have been noted.

Passenger lists created by ship officials after 1891 are called Immigration Manifests or Immigration Passenger Lists. Beginning in 1893, standard federal forms were printed and supplied to various ports of embarkation around the world to aid with collecting accurate and complete information about all passengers bound to the United States. These forms required much more information about each passenger than did previous records. In addition to name, age, sex, occupation, and nationality, each passenger was also asked to provide such details as:

- Marital status
- Last residence
- Final destination in the United States
- If ever in the United States before, when, where, and for how long
- If going to join a relative, the relative's name, address, and relationship
- The amount of money the passenger was carrying

1906, which is a pivotal year for immigrant research, saw even more questions added, including a personal description of the immigrant (complexion, eye and hair color, height, and identifying marks) as well as the city, town, or village of birth. This is the first year in which you're likely to find the exact place of birth included on a passenger list. In 1907 another useful question was added, asking for the name and address of the closest living relative in the native country.

If you aren't sure when your ancestor immigrated to this country, the 1900, 1910, 1920, and 1930 federal censuses each asked for the year of immigration and naturalization status of individuals born outside of the United States. The 1920 U.S. Census also asked for the exact year of naturalization.

As with the Customs Manifests, Immigration Passenger Lists for most ports and years have been microfilmed and can be accessed through the National Archives, the Family History Library, Family History Centers, and some major genealogical libraries. The records of more than 17 million passenger arrivals at Ellis Island, New York, between 1892 and 1924 can also be accessed at the American Family Immigration Center at Ellis Island, as well as its Web site (see Chapter 9: A Nation of Immigrants in Appendix A). The free, searchable database includes transcriptions, as well as digitized images of the original handwritten passenger lists and historic photos of many of the ships.

Strategies for Locating Your Ancestor's Ship

Most genealogists will tell you that it is a huge thrill to find your ancestors included on a ship's passenger manifest. What they may not tell you is how hard it can sometimes be to get to that point in your research. When you get lucky, you find a record or source that provides the exact date, port, and ship of arrival. The search isn't usually that easy, however. It takes intuition, perseverance, and good old-fashioned research to achieve a successful outcome.

Which Port?

Philadelphia was the major port of the Colonial era, but New York City later emerged as the primary port of entry to the United States, admitting almost 24 million immigrants between 1820 and 1920. The other major ports accepting immigrant traffic were Baltimore, Boston, and New Orleans. Passenger lists also exist for a number of smaller ports including Detroit, Michigan; Galveston, Texas; Gloucester and New Bedford in Massachusetts; Key West, Florida; Portland, Maine; Port Townsend, Tacoma, and Seattle in Washington; Providence, Rhode Island; San Francisco, California; and Skagway and Eagle in Alaska. A few entries also were recorded at locations in the southeast, such as Charleston, South Carolina; Savannah, Georgia; and Mobile, Alabama. More than 100 U.S. ports actually accepted immigrants at some point during the country's history, but the majority of these saw very few passenger arrivals or were open for only a short period of time.

FACT

Not everyone who sailed into the port of New York came through Ellis Island. From 1855 to 1890, more than 8 million immigrants were welcomed through Castle Garden, America's first official immigrant receiving center. Following its closure, immigrants were processed at a barge office in Manhattan, until Ellis Island opened on January 1, 1892.

So how do you know which port is the one that welcomed your ancestor? This can often present a difficult puzzle for genealogists. Begin by checking with family members to find out whether any stories have been passed down that may provide a clue. If your ancestor became a naturalized U.S. citizen, naturalization records created after September 25, 1906, usually contain the date and port of arrival. If all else fails, consider the location where your ancestors first settled. If they lived in or near a major port city, then you may have an easy answer. Otherwise you'll need to consider how they may have most easily traveled from the port to their new home.

Immigrants who settled in the mid-Atlantic states of Pennsylvania, Maryland, and Virginia often arrived via Philadelphia or Baltimore. Immigrants arriving at these ports may also have traveled over land to Pittsburgh, where they could catch a boat heading down the Ohio River for locations in Kentucky, Indiana, Ohio, and West Virginia. Immigrants who settled in states along the Mississippi River prior to the Civil War often chose to land at New Orleans and then travel by riverboat up the Mississippi. New York was usually the port of choice for immigrants headed to New York, New Jersey, and some of the New England states, as well as for people who traveled west via the Erie Canal to settle in the Great Lakes region. Boston was also a big port of entry for the New England states. Immigrants to the Western states may have entered through Galveston, San Francisco, or Seattle, but could have just as easily entered through New York or other East Coast ports and traveled by train, wagon, or other means across the United States.

If you're researching immigrants of German origin, the series *Germans to America* indexes German passenger arrivals at all five major U.S. ports for the years 1850–1897. Encompassing a series of 67 volumes, it is best consulted at a major genealogical library. Portions of the index are also available on CD-ROM, and through subscription to some online immigration databases.

Indexes to Passenger Lists

If you don't know the exact date and port of immigration for your ancestor, the Works Progress Administration (WPA), under the authority of the federal government, prepared indexes for most passenger arrivals at the five major ports. There are some ports and years that weren't indexed, however, most notably the busy immigration periods at New York from 1847 to 1897 and Boston from 1892 to 1901. The available indexes and the periods they cover include:

- **Baltimore:** 1820–1897, 1833–1866, and 1897–1952
- **Boston:** 1848–1891, 1902–1906, and 1906–1920
- **New Orleans:** 1853–1899 and 1900–1952
- **New York:** 1820–1846, 1897–1902, 1902–1943, and 1944–1948
- **Philadelphia:** 1800–1906 and 1883–1948

Individual indexes for many minor ports were also prepared by the WPA. Of significant interest is National Archives microfilm publication M334, *Supplemental Index to Passenger Lists of Vessels Arriving at Atlantic and Gulf*

Coast Ports (excluding New York), 1820–1874. This index covers passengers arriving at 71 U.S. ports, both major and minor, including *some* arrivals at the major ports of Baltimore, Boston, New Orleans, and Philadelphia. While the *Supplemental Index* does not include all passenger arrivals for the time period, it is definitely worth checking if you have ancestors who came to America between 1820 and 1874—especially if you aren't sure at which port they arrived.

All of these indexes, like the ship passenger lists themselves, can be found on microfilm at the National Archives, through your local Family History Center, and at many public libraries with large genealogical collections. A variety of other published indexes for various ports are also available, in book format, on CD-ROM, and in online databases. See Chapter 9: A Nation of Immigrants in Appendix A for further resources.

FACT

The Works Progress Administration (WPA) was created in 1935 to provide jobs for the millions of people left unemployed by the Depression. The Historical Records Survey, one of many projects funded by the WPA, was responsible for creating many of the indexes that genealogists have come to rely on, including indexes to immigration records, vital statistics, cemetery interments, military records, and the federal census.

Checking the Port of Embarkation

If you're not able to find a record of your ancestor's arrival in the United States, it is possible that you may learn something from his port of departure. You'll need to do some research to determine his likely port of departure based on his residence prior to coming to America. Then it is time to do some further research to learn whether emigration lists exist for that port. Some of the largest European ports of embarkation during the nineteenth and early twentieth centuries were Bremen, Germany; Hamburg, Germany, Le Havre, France; and Liverpool, England.

Bremen, Germany

Most Bremen emigration lists have been destroyed, some through routine government housekeeping and others through Allied bombing raids during WWII. Departure manifests from 1920 through 1939 have survived, however, and are available for research at the Handelskammer Archive in Bremen. Many have been transcribed and placed online by the Bremen Chamber of Commerce and the Bremen Society for Genealogical Investigation, Die Maus.

Hamburg, Germany

Lists of passengers departing the port of Hamburg between 1850 and 1934 have survived, and are available at the state archives in Hamburg. You can access these passenger lists and indexes to them on microfilm through your local Family History Center. They also are being transcribed and placed online by the Hamburg State Archives.

Le Havre, France

While no surviving passenger ship lists from Le Havre are known to exist, the Family History Library has microfilmed lists of passengers who sailed from Le Havre aboard freight vessels between 1750 and 1886. This microfilm is in French and is not indexed.

Liverpool, England

No original passenger lists for Liverpool have been preserved for years prior to 1890. Emigrant lists after that date are held by the U.K. National Archives in Record Series BT 27, *Passenger Lists Outwards, 1890–1960*. The series is also available on microfilm from the Family History Library and local Family History Centers.

Lists of emigrants from Liverpool for the years 1697–1707 have also been published in the *New England Historical and Genealogical Register*.

The recorded passenger lists for emigrants leaving Liverpool after 1890 are not indexed, so a search requires the year, month, and port of departure. If you only know the name of the ship, you'll need to consult the *Registers of Passenger Lists* (Record Series BT 32 in the U.K. National Archives).

Border Entries from Canada and Mexico

Not all immigrants to the United States came by sea. Many made their way here by land, crossing the border from Canada or Mexico. Keeping statistics on arrivals at U.S. land borders was not required by early immigration acts, however, so records weren't kept at the Canadian border until 1895 and at the border with Mexico until about 1903.

Unlike traditional ship passenger lists, these border crossing records were kept on cards—one card per person—often referred to as card manifests. The type of information recorded on these cards is very similar to what is found on passenger lists, including name of the immigrant, age, sex, marital status, occupation, and final destination in the United States.

Canadian Border Crossings

Prior to 1894, people were able to move freely across the border from Canada into the United States. This allowed many to bypass U.S. inspectors by sailing from Europe to Canadian ports, then crossing the border into the United States. Beginning in 1895, U.S. inspectors, with the cooperation of Canada, required that immigrants destined for the United States be inspected and recorded at Canadian ports of entry, and issued a Certificate of Admission. Immigrant inspectors stationed at posts along the U.S.–Canadian border then collected these inspection certificates from people as they crossed into the United States via ship, train, and on foot.

It is important to note that prior to October 1, 1906, Canadian-born immigrants crossing into the United States from Canada and Mexican nationals crossing into the United States from Mexico were not tracked by U.S. immigration officials or included on border crossing lists.

Until 1917, the records from all Canadian land border ports and seaports were filed in a group often referred to as the St. Albans Lists because they were stored at the entry port of Saint Albans, Vermont. After 1917, immigrant entries at land border ports west of the Montana/North Dakota state line were filed in Seattle. Border crossing records after June 30, 1929, are found among the records of each individual port of entry along the U.S.–Canadian border. These "Canadian Border Crossing" records, covering the years 1985–1954, are available on microfilm from the National Archives and any Family History Center.

Mexican Border Crossings

Records of immigrants crossing into the United States from Mexico begin about 1903. The National Archives and Records Administration is currently microfilming these Mexican border crossing records for land ports in Arizona, New Mexico, California, and Texas, from about 1903 to 1955.

Finding Your Ancestor's Town of Origin

Once you've located your immigrant ancestor and, possibly, found her listed on a ship passenger list, it is time to take the next step back—learning her town of birth or origin in the old country.

Although U.S. census records ask only for the country of origin, they are still worth looking at when researching immigrant ancestors. There have been occasions when a hard-working census enumerator took the time to record a specific town or county, as well as the country.

To research records overseas, you almost always need to know the specific town or village of origin because countrywide indexed records are usually rare or incomplete. As discussed earlier in this chapter, immigration records from 1906 forward usually contain this information. For earlier arrivals, however, it's time to start researching again.

Although the U.S. census required that only the country of origin be recorded for immigrants, census records are still worth looking at in the hopes of discovering an ancestor's town of birth. There have been occasions when a hard-working census enumerator took the time to record a specific town or county, in addition to the country of origin.

Records created around the time of an immigrant's death are another good source for birthplace information. While containing second-hand information, sources such as obituaries, death certificates, and burial records should all be checked for the birthplace of an ancestor. Civil marriage records, when available, can also occasionally yield a town of origin.

Becoming a Citizen

Naturalization is the process that confers U.S. citizenship upon foreign nationals after they have met the requirements of citizenship as established by Congress. Millions of immigrants to the United States have filed for citizenship or become naturalized citizens. In the process, they created a paper trail of records that contain useful genealogical information regarding immigrant origins.

FACT

Later naturalization records may also include a photograph (after 1940) and/or physical description of the applicant (after 1906).

Understanding the Naturalization Process

Until 1952, an immigrant seeking citizenship appeared before a judge and declared his intent to become a U.S. citizen. For many years, any court (federal, state, county, or local) could handle these naturalizations. The multistep naturalization process may have even started in one state, and been completed in another. Some immigrants also started the process and never finished. As a result, the records can be scattered and difficult to find.

So what makes naturalization records worth the time to search out? Aside from their sentimental value, naturalization records can also provide a possible clue to the town of an immigrant's birth when other sources fail to produce this important information.

To understand what you can learn from naturalization records, it is important to first understand the naturalization process and the documents it creates.

Declaration of Intention

Sometimes referred to as first papers, this is a document signed by immigrants declaring their intent to become U.S. citizens and renouncing their allegiance to a foreign government. Prior to the formation of the Immigration and Naturalization Service in 1906, the Declaration generally provides little useful information for genealogists—usually only the name of the immigrant and his country of birth or allegiance (not town or city). A few give the date and port of arrival. After September 25, 1906, Declarations of Intention generally include both the place of birth and the port and date of arrival.

Petition for Naturalization

After filing the Declaration of Intent and meeting the residency requirements, immigrants then filed a Petition for Naturalization verifying that they had met the requirements for citizenship. These documents are sometimes referred to as final papers. Over the years, America's requirements for citizenship status have changed, but in general an individual had to prove residency in the United States for a prescribed period of time (usually two to five years) and demonstrate good moral character through the submission of affidavits and statements by witnesses. Immigrants who entered the United States after June 29, 1906, also had to bring to court a Certificate of Arrival, showing when, where, and how they entered America. Like the Declaration of Intent, naturalization petitions prior to 1906 contain very little biographical information. After that date they usually include quite a bit of information about the immigrant including the date of emigration, date of entry, name of ship, and place of birth, as well as the name and ages of spouse and children.

Oath of Allegiance

After filing the petition for naturalization, an individual then had to take an oath of allegiance to the United States and sign the document. This record may or may not be filed with the rest of the naturalization papers.

Certificate of Naturalization

Once an individual met all requirements for naturalization and signed the oath of allegiance, the court issued an order of citizenship and gave the applicant a formal document certifying that he had been naturalized as a citizen of the United States. Naturalization certificates were given to the new citizen, and so are not found filed with the rest of the naturalization documents. They are the type of documentation that may have been passed down to someone in your family, however.

Not all foreign-born individuals had to go through the naturalization process to become U.S. citizens. After 1824, foreign-born children of aliens were naturalized upon attaining the age of twenty-one if they had lived in the United States for at least five years.

Where to Search for Naturalization Documents

The laws and requirements governing naturalization have changed frequently during the course of United States history. When researching for older naturalization records, start by looking in court records for the county or city in which your ancestor resided. If you can't locate a naturalization record there, try courts in nearby counties, or look for naturalization records at state archives or another state-level repository.

Millions of early naturalization records from counties all over the United States have also been microfilmed by the Genealogical Society of Utah. These microfilmed copies are available for research at the LDS Family History Library and Family History Centers around the world.

FACT

Between 1855 and 1922, alien women were automatically considered to be U.S. citizens by marriage to a U.S. citizen or through an alien husband's naturalization.

Since 1907, almost 10 million people have gained U.S. citizenship through naturalization. U.S. Citizenship and Immigration Services (formerly known as Immigration and Naturalization Service, or INS) holds copies of all naturalizations that took place in the United States between 1906 and 1956. The agency often charges more for copies than do county courts, but this search can save time because you don't need to know the exact court at which the naturalization was granted.

Migration Trails Across America

Once immigrants arrived on America's shores, they rarely stayed put for long. While early settlements were concentrated on the East Coast, the promise of new, cheap land quickly had people moving south and west. Other incentives for migration included the gold rushes in California and, later, Alaska; the oil boom in Texas; the promise of new jobs; natural and economic disasters such as plagues, floods, and crop failures; and a desire to explore the new frontier.

Understanding the most common migration trails for the time period and area where your ancestors lived may help you to trace them back to their previous place of residence. Some of the major U.S. migration routes include the National Road, which extended from Maryland to Illinois; the Erie Canal, which linked the Hudson River with Lake Erie, encouraging westward migration; and the Boston Post Road, which extended from New England down the East Coast into the Southern states. There were hundreds of smaller, less widely traveled migration routes in different areas and different time periods, however. Check with the genealogical society in the area in which your ancestor lived for suggestions about common migration routes for that specific area. The USGenWeb Internet site for the county may also include maps or information on common migration routes.

Chapter 10

Clues in the Cemetery

From joyous births and loving marriages to lives cut short and family tragedies, cemeteries tell the story of your ancestors. Beyond the expected names and dates of birth and death inscribed in the stones, clues can also be uncovered in less obvious locations, including gravestone verses, plot arrangements, and sextons' records. Rich in history and steeped in memories, cemeteries link you to your ancestors in a way nothing else can.

THE EVERYTHING FAMILY TREE BOOK

Why Cemeteries?

Other than a few photos and documents, tombstones are usually the only physical sign that your ancestors ever walked the earth. With their names carved carefully into stone and their remains lying just beneath your feet, it's almost as if your ancestors are speaking to you from the grave. A visit to the cemetery is a restful way to commune with your forebears and walk in their footsteps, and can physically connect you to your roots.

ALERT!

In addition to providing birth and death dates for your ancestor, cemeteries can offer useful clues about your other relatives. Surrounding tombstones and nearby plots can indicate family relationships, while fresh flowers on a grave may mean that a surviving relative lives nearby.

While not always as accurate as you may think, tombstones are a rich source for dates, birthplaces, marriages, parents' names, and other substantial details for your family tree. Ceremonial markers or inscribed symbols may provide evidence of military service, religious affiliation, or membership in a specific organization or society.

Locating Your Ancestor's Final Resting Place

A visit to the cemetery begins with learning where your ancestors are buried. Ideally, your family interviews have already provided this information, but if not, there are several other research avenues available. To determine your ancestor's burial location, you will need to begin with an educated assumption about the place and date of death (see Chapter 5).

Death Certificates and Obituaries

The location where your ancestor is interred (buried) can often be found noted on the death certificate. Death certificates, however, are typically only available for twentieth-century ancestors. If you're unable to locate a death certificate, check again with living relatives. The library serving the area in which your ancestor lived may also be able to help you find an old obituary notice, which will often name at least the funeral home, if not the cemetery itself.

Funeral Home Records

Morticians can be great allies in helping you identify an ancestor's burial location. Funeral homes may have information about your ancestor in their records, including burial location, surviving relatives, and date of death. Funeral directors are also very knowledgeable about cemeteries in their area, and may be able to put you in touch with living relatives. It is important to realize that funeral homes are not in the archive business, however, and their employees are under no obligation to assist you with your quest. The best way to obtain information from funeral home records is to write a letter to the manager of the funeral home, asking for specific information about a specific individual, including as much detail as you can.

To improve your chances of a response from a funeral home manager, offer to pay for any copying expenses and enclose a stamped, self-addressed envelope with your request.

Published Cemetery Surveys

If you know the approximate location, but really aren't very sure about the year of death, published cemetery surveys can be a great place to start your research. In an effort to preserve valuable details from aging and deteriorating cemeteries, many local genealogical and historical societies have compiled cemetery indexes or offer published books of cemetery surveys from their town or county. In addition, many gravestone transcriptions are available on the Internet.

Religious Records

If you know your ancestor's religious affiliation, the church, synagogue, or other house of worship that she attended may be able to provide burial information. Religious institutions often maintain attached cemeteries and also keep records for their members who are buried elsewhere.

FACT

The Internet is a wonderful source for free topographic map searches. The U.S. Geographic Names Information System (☞*http://geonames.usgs.gov*) and Topozone (☞*www.topozone.com*), for example, allow you to search for cemeteries within a particular county by selecting "cemetery" as the feature type. Though these databases don't include most small church and family cemeteries, they usually identify most larger ones.

Narrowing It Down

If you know the general area where your ancestor is most likely buried, but aren't sure of the specific cemetery, turn to maps and the knowledge of local residents. Members of the local historical or genealogical society can be a wonderful source of information about lesser-known burial locations, especially private family cemeteries. If you suspect that a cemetery has been moved or renamed, published local or county histories can sometimes help identify the former name and location.

Topographic maps or locality maps often show cemeteries, in addition to roads, houses, and farms. When searching for possible cemeteries on the map, even small details such as the elevation can be useful, because cemeteries were often established on high ground. If you have access to a Global Positioning System (GPS) device, whether it's part of your car's equipment or a handheld model, you can even input the geographic coordinates of the cemetery from the map to obtain directions to the cemetery.

Burial and Plot Records

Even when you've located the cemetery where your ancestor is buried, your work is not yet complete—you still need to find the actual gravestone. Large public cemeteries contain so many graves that you could walk for days without finding your ancestor's tombstone. Small, rural cemeteries can be just as much of a problem because they may sit neglected, with tombstones either broken or buried in the brush.

Most cemeteries are owned or managed by an individual or organization that is responsible for administration and upkeep. Check with the local office responsible for issuing burial permits, the official that records land sales or tax payments, or a nearby funeral home or mortician. These resources may be able to put you in touch with the right person. Larger cemeteries may have a sexton's office right on the grounds. Church cemeteries are easier—the church is often located nearby, or the cemetery may be named after the church. For small, older family cemeteries try the current landowner, nearby funeral home, or the local historical or genealogical society.

QUESTION?

What is a sexton?
A sexton is a caretaker responsible for burials and cemetery maintenance. In a small cemetery the sexton may do everything, from selling plots and maintaining the records to digging graves and mowing the grass. Larger cemeteries are more likely to have a maintenance crew and office staff, with the sexton taking on more of an overseer role.

Contacting the sexton, or person responsible for the cemetery, may yield access to a number of different documents, including:

- **Burial registers**—Chronological list of interments (burials)
- **Cemetery plats**—Map of the individual plots in a cemetery
- **Plot records**—Usually include the name of the plot owner, date of purchase, and names and dates of burials within the plot

- **Deed records**—Copies of actual deeds issued to owners of cemetery plots
- **Grave opening records**—Signed authorization to dig graves
- **Burial permits**—Official governmental permission to inter an individual

When you visit the cemetery you should check with the office or sexton to see what records are available. These vary widely from cemetery to cemetery, but will usually include at least the burial register, plat map and, possibly, the plot records.

Planning Your Visit

A little advance planning before you hop in the car for a cemetery visit can go a long way toward making your visit more pleasant and productive. If you have the option, early spring or late fall are the best times to visit the cemetery, especially if it is one that is neglected and overgrown. This means fewer weeds to wade through, and fewer ticks, bees, and other bugs to worry about.

It doesn't hurt to bring along a cell phone and a friend or fellow researcher for safety. At the very least, make sure someone knows where you are and when to expect you back. Cemeteries are generally safe places, but it's better to be safe than sorry.

The season in which you plan your visit can have an impact on whether you'll be able to locate the cemetery at all. It's not uncommon, especially in rural areas, to find small family cemeteries situated in the middle of cornfields. Needless to say, it is nearly impossible to find such cemeteries when the corn is taller than you are!

To make sure you have everything you need, it helps to assemble a tool kit in advance. A tote bag or duffle with shoulder strap makes a good container. If possible, choose one that's waterproof to protect your items from damp ground, and brightly colored so you can find it after you set it down and walk away. Stock it with the following items:

- Paper, notebook, and pen or pencils
- Camera and plenty of film (or extra memory card if it is digital)
- Optional items such as video camera, tape recorder, or a handheld computer
- Extra batteries for anything that needs them
- Spray bottle of plain water and a soft nylon brush for cleaning stones
- Clippers for clearing away grass and brush
- Sunscreen and bug repellent
- Map for marking the cemetery's location

If you are planning to visit a large cemetery, you may want to call ahead to learn the hours and find out how to get a map of the cemetery. If you haven't called before your visit, look for a sign outside of the cemetery that tells you where to find the caretaker. Many public cemeteries that are still in operation also post visitor information online. If the cemetery is private, or you have to cross private land to reach it, be sure to get permission from the landowner before visiting.

Stories in Stone

It's finally time for what you've been waiting for—visiting your ancestor's tombstone. But wait! Once you've taken that irresistible quick peek for his headstone, take some time to explore and enjoy the cemetery. You'll never be closer to your ancestor than you are during this visit.

ALERT!

As you walk through a cemetery, watch for uneven ground, because graves have a tendency to sink over time. Some graves, especially older ones, may have small foot markers, and plots may be outlined by small stones or bricks—all potential stumbling spots.

If the cemetery is not too large, and you have enough time, it can be very helpful to make a transcription of all gravestones in the cemetery. At the very least, take some time to visit the gravestones immediately surrounding your ancestor's plot. Chances are you'll end up learning down the road that some of the other people buried in the same cemetery are related to you as well. Spending a little extra time now could save you a return visit.

Transcribing the Stones

You can learn a lot more in the cemetery than just names and dates. From artwork to grave placement, cemeteries have plenty of stories to tell. Since you never know what may be important in the future, it's best to take good notes on everything:

- Note the tombstone's location in relationship to the cemetery entrance, so you (or someone else) will be able to find it again. Also note the shape of the marker and the type of stone (if you can identify it).
- Write down names, dates, and inscriptions exactly as they appear on the stone. An accurate record will help keep you from making assumptions in the excitement of the moment. Be sure to check all sides, because inscriptions may appear in more than one place.
- Sketch any symbols, emblems, and other gravestone art. These may provide valuable clues to membership in an organization that may have records about your ancestor.
- Make a note of the relationship between your ancestor's tombstone and the surrounding graves on both sides, as well as in front and in back. Family members will often be buried together in the same plot. Nearby graves may also belong to parents or other relatives. Small, unmarked stones may indicate children who died in their infancy.

Another good way to record cemetery information is to use a tape recorder or a video camera as you move around the cemetery. You can read off names, dates, and inscriptions easily, and make note of new information, such as when you start a new row. You should still take time to make written transcriptions of any important tombstones, but the recorded version will serve as a backup, as well as help you quickly gather information from other parts of the cemetery.

Gently cleaning a tombstone is generally okay. Use grass clippers on tall weeds so as not to disturb the marker. Use plain water and a nylon (not wire) bristle brush to gently clean away lichen or dirt. Never use harsh cleaning products, shaving cream, or anything abrasive on a tombstone, and do not do anything to stones that are unstable or crumbling. Damage could be irreparable!

Tombstone Symbolism and Art

From the shape of the tombstones to the artwork chiseled in stone, the symbols found in cemeteries are often a source of curiosity, such as when you find great-grandma buried under a headstone that looks like a tree stump! Do the designs and motifs have special meaning? Can they tell you anything about your ancestor's life?

The tree-stump tombstone, popular from about 1870 to 1930, depicts a cut-down tree, suggesting that the individual had been cut down in the prime of life. Occasionally, these tombstones depict entire families, with branches representing children. If W.O.W. or an ax, maul, and wedge are incorporated into the design, this signifies that the deceased was a member of the fraternal organization Woodmen of the World.

Take a walk among the tombstones of an older cemetery and you're likely to encounter a wide variety of shapes, epitaphs, and symbols. The design and composition of the markers may vary from simple sandstone tablets or granite obelisks to fancier monuments in shapes including open books, tree stumps, and beds complete with pillows. Symbols such as angels, crosses, flowers, doves, and hands usually are prevalent, but you may also see others, ranging from an inverted torch to draperies or chains. Both the type of tombstone and the symbols can help provide clues to the time period and life of your ancestor—especially useful when weather and time have worn away the epitaph.

Some of the most commonly seen cemetery symbols include:

- **Angels**—Messengers of God, angels symbolize spirituality and deliverance of the soul to heaven. An angel weeping or with bowed head symbolizes grief and mourning, possibly an untimely death.
- **Birds and Insects**—Birds in flight represent the winged soul rising to heaven, while the dove embodies purity, peace, and the Holy Spirit. Butterflies and bees are typically symbolic of resurrection.
- **Books and Scrolls**—Typically representing the book of life, a book might be portrayed either open or closed and may be held in the hand of an angel or accompanied by a quill. Books and scrolls may also represent learning and scholarship, or the Holy Bible or other religious gospel or work.
- **Crosses and Crowns**—Commonly found on tombstones, these religious symbols depict the individual's faith in God and eternal life. Each denomination has its own distinct representation of the cross. The crown typically embodies the resurrection.
- **Doors and Gates**—Usually portrayed in the open position, doors and gateways are an entrance to heaven or the afterlife.
- **Draperies and Curtains**—Especially popular during the Victorian period, draperies are a touch of home, meant to make the deceased comfortable during the trip to the afterlife. Curtains are usually carved partially lowered or closed, representing mortal life coming to an end.
- **Flowers**—Palm leaves and lilies are symbols of resurrection. Roses represent love and beauty, with a rose in full bloom indicating a full life, and a rosebud a life that hadn't fully bloomed. A broken stem indicates a life cut short. Daisies are common on children's graves to show the innocence and purity of youth.
- **Hands**—Clasped hands or handshakes represent God's welcome into heaven. If there are sleeves on each hand, especially one male and one female, they represent marriage. A single hand with the forefinger pointing upward signifies a soul that has risen to heaven. The forefinger pointing down represents God reaching down for the soul.
- **Lambs**—Usually depicted lying down, the lamb is a symbol of innocence and often graces the graves of children.

- **Torches**—An upright or lit torch represents life, while an inverted or extinguished torch may mean the end of a family line (no more male heirs to carry on the surname).
- **Trees**—The dogwood is a common symbol of resurrection and eternal life. The oak characterizes honor, strength, and endurance. Sadness and mourning are commonly illustrated with a willow tree.

While the symbols commonly found in cemeteries do have traditional textbook meanings, this may have nothing to do with the reason a particular symbol was chosen for your ancestor's tombstone. A motif may have been chosen because someone applied her own meaning to it, or just because she liked the design. Cemeteries also follow their own fashion trends, especially in terms of gravestone shape and composition. While a tombstone shaped like a sawed-off tree stump may have traditionally meant a life cut short, your great-grandma who lived to be ninety-eight may have just liked the folk-art look.

ALERT!

Like everything else in genealogy research, you should use tombstone symbols only as clues to the lives of your ancestors. Be careful not to read too much into their interpretation.

Preserving the Memories

It has been said over and over, but it bears repeating: A picture is worth a thousand words. Also, in the case of cemeteries, pictures are much better for tombstones than are chalk, shaving cream, or rubbings. Using a camera with good quality flash, plus a few other tools, you can create memories to last a lifetime.

What Time of Day Is Best?

You may not get a second chance to visit your ancestor's final resting place, so it is worth taking a little extra time to capture the best pictures possible. In order to properly highlight a carved inscription, good lighting is essential. In many cemeteries, individuals are buried facing east, with their feet pointing to the rising sun. If the tombstone inscription also faces east, then midmorning sun provides the best light. Sometimes inscriptions would be placed on the west side of the stone, however, so that people wouldn't have to stand on the grave to read it. In this case, late-afternoon sun is best. Midday, when the sun is directly overhead, sometimes provides the best compromise. The lack of shadows at that time of day can leave inscriptions flat and difficult to read, however. If the sun's not out, you actually may be better off. Outdoor photos usually turn out best on a slightly overcast day.

To help bring out the letters in a badly eroded inscription, try wetting down the tombstone with a spray bottle of plain water. As the face of the tombstone dries, the letters will stay damp, making them appear to pop out at you. This trick is especially useful for granite or sandstone markers.

Enhancing the Inscription

When optimal lighting is not possible, there are several tools you can use to reflect sunlight diagonally across the face of a tombstone. This will light the face of the stone while casting shadows in indentations, which makes inscriptions more visible and easier to read. Most of these techniques require the help of a partner:

- **Flash**—Depending upon the lighting conditions, a camera with a good fill flash may be all you need for great tombstone photos. An off-camera flash, if available, offers a better option.
- **Mirror**—This is a common tool for reflecting sunlight onto shadowy tombstones. Mylar (plastic) mirrors, available at most home stores, are lightest and not as easily broken as glass. Mirrors have to be fairly large to be effective, however, and can cast a harsh light.
- **Collapsible Reflector**—Used by many photographers, collapsible light reflectors typically fold up into a small 4"- to 6"-package, handy for traveling. The shiny, silver reflectors commonly used inside car windshields also work fairly well.

- **Aluminum Foil**—A low-budget alternative and handy for travel, a piece of cardboard wrapped in aluminum foil (shiny side out) makes a good light reflector.

Keep in mind that upright tombstones are best photographed at tombstone level, rather than at an angle from above, to help reduce distortion. This means you need to be prepared to get down on your knees and, sometimes, on your belly to get the best shot.

How to Create a Gravestone Rubbing

A favorite project for many genealogists and historians, tombstone rubbings provide a lasting "impression" of your cemetery visit. Just be absolutely sure, before you start, that the tombstone is sturdy and stable. *Do not* do a tombstone rubbing on any stone that is wobbly, flaking, chipping, or crumbling, or you could cause permanent damage. Tombstones are historical treasures and should always be treated with respect and care.

Begin your rubbing by cutting a piece of nonfusible interfacing material (Pellon) or plain craft or rice paper slightly larger than the face of the stone. You can obtain rice paper from art supply stores, and interfacing material from craft and fabric shops. Use masking tape to secure the paper or material to the stone, making sure that it covers the entire surface and won't slip as you work.

ALERT!

Tombstone rubbings have been banned in some states and in many cemeteries, especially Colonial graveyards, due to the damage it can cause to the stone. Other cemeteries require permits before allowing you to do rubbings. To be safe, it's always best to first ask for permission from the cemetery sexton or caretaker.

Using rubbing wax, a large crayon, charcoal, or chalk, rub gently but firmly over the inscription until you have a good impression of the entire tombstone face (wax works best for interfacing material).

When the rubbing is completed to your satisfaction, carefully remove it from the stone. If you used chalk for your tombstone rubbing, carefully spray the paper with a chalk spray such as Krylon. Hairspray also works. Be very careful not to get any on the tombstone. If you used interfacing and a wax crayon for your tombstone rubbing, place the material face-up on an ironing board with an old towel over it when you get back home. Press down gently with a warm iron (don't use a back-and-forth motion) to permanently set the wax into the fabric and preserve it indefinitely.

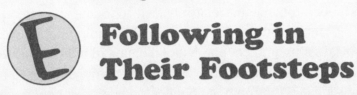

Chapter 11

Following in Their Footsteps

Land was one of the most important assets of our ancestors. It provided a home, supported the family, and indicated wealth and social status. The promise of unclaimed land was the primary force behind immigration to America and migration across the country. About 90 percent of white males in America prior to 1850 owned land, making land records the most comprehensive, commonly available records for Colonial and pioneer ancestors. Land records can help track family migration, prove relationships, and tell us about the day-to-day lives of our ancestors.

Digging for Deeds

The first land record you will typically encounter for an ancestor is a deed, which records a legal transfer of land from one individual to another. Deeds are the most prevalent and widely used of the U.S. land records, and can provide a fairly reliable method of tracking ancestors when no other record can be found. Deed records are relatively easy to locate and often provide a wealth of information about your ancestors, including family members, neighbors, social status, and occupation of the named individuals. Because land deeds often predate most other available records, they are an important potential source of information about colonial and pioneer ancestors.

Why Land Deeds?

Because deeds often involve more people than do other genealogical sources, they are a potential source for information about family members, neighbors, and even friends. They can also help locate a person in a particular location at a particular time, establish an approximate immigration date, distinguish between two men with identical names, identify wives' names, and reconstruct a neighborhood. Used in conjunction with estate, census, and other records, land records can also occasionally be used to prove a family connection in cases where no single record of relationship exists.

Laws in much of early America provided a widow with a one-third lifetime interest in the real property of her husband. To protect this right, any sale of property by the husband required the wife to separately sign a dower release in which she relinquished her right to the dower portion of her husband's land.

Locating Land Deeds

Though the original copy of the deed was retained by the landowner, a full copy of the deed was recorded by the clerk into the deed book for the locality. Deeds are almost always recorded at the county level and can usually be found under the jurisdiction of the Register of Deeds at the county court-house. Exceptions include Alaska, where land transactions are recorded at the judicial district level; Louisiana, where deeds are recorded at the parish level (the state's county equivalent); and Connecticut, Rhode Island, and Vermont, where deeds are recorded at the town level. In order to search for your ancestor's deeds, you'll need to learn which authority had jurisdiction over the area in which your ancestors lived and whether the deed records are still in its custody or have been transferred to some other location.

Searching the Deed Index

Because deeds are arranged in the deed books chronologically by the date of registration, rather than the date of the transaction, they have generally been indexed to aid in the location of specific deeds. Most deed indexes have not been computerized (although more Register of Deeds offices are putting their indexes online all the time), so a trip to the county courthouse is often necessary. Deed indexes for most locations have, however, been microfilmed by the Church of Jesus Christ of Latter-day Saints, and are available for rental from your local Family History Center (see Chapter 16). Microfilmed deed indexes may also be found at the local library, state archives, or other repositories.

FACT

Land deeds are not always registered in the courts at the time of the actual transaction. A deed of gift to a minor child, for example, would not usually be officially registered until the child reached the age of majority, which might be many years after the actual date on the deed.

Most counties have produced a grantor index of their deeds. Also known as a seller index or direct index, this indexes the deeds by the seller's last name. Most also maintain a grantee index, or buyer index, which lists deeds by the surname of the person purchasing the land. The grantee index may also be referred to as an indirect index. In some areas these two indexes may have been combined into what is referred to as a cross-index of deeds.

Once you've located the deed indexes for your locality, the next step is to search for your ancestor's name. As with other courthouse records, not all deed indexes are alphabetical. Depending upon the locality, you may encounter any one of several different indexing systems. The easiest are lists alphabetized by surname that cover, in chronological order, all deeds recorded within a particular county or locality. Other index systems, including the Russell Index, Cott Index, and Campbell Index, may also be in use. You will read more about courthouse indexes in Chapter 16.

When searching the deed index or reading a deed, look for the common Latin terms *et al* (meaning "and others") and *et ux* or *et uxor* (meaning "and wife") after the grantor or grantee's name, as these may indicate important family relationships.

From Index to Deed

Once you've located your ancestor's name in the deed index, you'll find that the index itself provides a substantial amount of helpful information. This includes the date of the deed transaction, the type of deed, the names of the grantor and grantee, and the book and page number where the deed entry can be found in the deed books. Finding the actual deed is fairly simple. Armed with the book and page numbers you found in the index, you can visit the Register of Deeds at the courthouse, send in a written request for the records, or browse the microfilm copies of the deed books at an area library, archive, or Family History Center.

Organization of State and Federal Lands

The neat thing about land purchases is that someone always had to be first. As you trace your way back through deed records, you'll eventually uncover references to the original grant of land. Prior to the Revolutionary War, most land along America's eastern shore was under the authority of the British government. The first transfer of this land into the hands of individuals began with charters granted by the King of England to colonies headed by men known as "proprietors." Depending upon the time period and area, proprietors and colonies used this land to establish towns, designate portions for public use (roads, schools, and so on), or encourage new settlers through grants of land known as "headrights."

In addition to headright and other outright grants, all proprietors and colonies eventually offered land for sale to individuals. Upon payment of the purchase price, a warrant was issued for a specified amount of land in a particular location. The individual then hired a surveyor—each area usually had its own designated surveyor—to survey the land. The drawing and written description of the land prepared by the surveyor, known as a "plat," was then returned to the proprietor's office, where a grant was issued.

Following the Revolutionary War, the states ceded control of their unsettled western lands (the original colony charters stretched from the Atlantic to Pacific) to the U.S. government. As the country grew, additional lands were added to the public domain through war or treaty, purchases from other governments (for example, the Louisiana Purchase), and the taking of Indian lands. Most land acquired by American citizens was, therefore, originally under the control of the federal government.

QUESTION?

What is a "headright"?
A headright is a grant of a specific number of acres for each "head" or settler transported to the new colony by the proprietor.

State-Land States

Lands that were initially granted or dispersed by the state (or Colonial) government are referred to as state lands. States that transferred land to individuals in this manner were primarily a part of the original thirteen colonies, or were derived from one of the colonies. Texas and Hawaii are the notable exceptions, because they were controlled by other foreign governments. The state-land states are Connecticut, Delaware, Georgia, Hawaii, Kentucky, Maine, Maryland, Massachusetts, New Hampshire, New Jersey, New York,

North Carolina, Pennsylvania, Rhode Island, South Carolina, Tennessee, Texas, Vermont, Virginia, and West Virginia.

When the Revolutionary War ended, the colonies officially became states, with each state retaining the right to disperse land within its own boundaries. In most cases, land originally granted under the authority of the crown remained in the hands of the individual to which it belonged, while the state took control of all ungranted lands. When Texas and Hawaii were added to the United States, they followed this same model—retaining the right to manage land distribution and sales within their own borders.

ALERT!

Whenever land is first distributed by a government or proprietor, the process is referred to as a *patent* or *grant* (the two terms are basically interchangeable). Despite the way it sounds, the term *grant* does not necessarily imply that the land was provided without payment—just that it was the first transfer of a piece of property from government to individual.

With a few exceptions, most land in the state-land states was surveyed using a method known as the indiscriminate-survey system, more commonly referred to as "metes and bounds." In this type of survey, land is first described in terms of its general location, often identifying nearby towns, waterways, and other physical features. Beginning at a starting corner, measurements and directions are then determined for each property line. Boundaries may be expressed using natural land features such as trees, streams, large boulders, or stone fences, as well as adjoining neighbors or properties.

A typical land description from a metes and bounds deed may read as follows:

"One Certain Tract or parcel of Land lying and being in the County of Edgecombe Beginning at three white Oaks on Persimon Tree Meadow on the head of Stirrup Iron Branch then West 220 poles to a pine then 240 pole to a sweet gum in the Harrican [Hurricane] Branch then East 220 pole to a pine then S° 240 pole to the first station containing three Hundred and thirty acres of Land and plantation. . . ."

The sixty-six-foot-long Gunter's chain, constructed of 100 linked pieces of steel or iron, was usually used to measure distance in the metes and bounds survey system. Distances between survey points were referred to in measurements of poles, rods, or perches—interchangeable units equaling 16½ feet, or twenty-five links on a Gunter's chain.

In most cases, original land grants and patents in the state-land states can be found in each state's archives. Many of these original land grants have been microfilmed and can be viewed at Family History Centers, state libraries, and other institutions with large genealogical collections.

Section, Township, and Range

Public lands in the United States consist of all land ceded to the federal government by the original colonies following the American Revolution, plus most additional land acquired through the years by purchase, treaty, and war. Land under the control of the federal government is referred to as the public domain. Thirty states, known as public-land states, were created from this public domain land: Alabama, Alaska, Arizona, Arkansas, California, Colorado, Florida, Idaho, Illinois, Indiana, Iowa, Kansas, Louisiana, Michigan, Minnesota, Mississippi, Missouri, Montana, Nebraska, Nevada, New Mexico, North Dakota, Ohio, Oklahoma, Oregon, South Dakota, Utah, Washington, Wisconsin, and Wyoming.

Rectangular Survey System

As the U.S. government prepared to sell its newly acquired land, it handled things a bit differently than did the state-land states: 1) it surveyed the land prior to making it available for purchase or homesteading, and 2) it used a more regular, explicit method of survey known as the rectangular survey system, otherwise referred to as township and range. When a survey was done on new public land, two imaginary lines were run at right angles to each other through the territory—a base line running east and west and a meridian line running north and south. The land was then subdivided from the point of this intersection into townships, sections, and subsections.

FACT

Because different areas of the United States were surveyed at different times, more than a dozen different base lines and meridians were established in the public-land states.

Townships and Ranges

Townships, a major subdivision of public lands under the rectangular survey system, typically measure six miles on a side, or thirty-six square miles. A township is identified by its relationship to a base line and a principal meridian, numbered from the base line north and south (township), and then from the meridian line east and west (range). These surveyed townships, sometimes referred to as congressional townships, should not be confused with civil (governmental) townships.

Example: *Township 3 North, Range 9 West, 5th Principal Meridian* identifies a specific township, or thirty-six-square-mile block of land, that is three tiers (or townships) north from the base line and nine tiers to the west of the 5th Principal Meridian.

Sections

Townships were then further broken down into thirty-six units of 640 acres each (one square mile), called sections. These sections were then numbered within the township, starting in the northeast corner and moving across the rows in a zigzag fashion.

Subsections

Because most individuals couldn't afford to purchase 640 acres at once, sections were usually further subdivided into a variety of sizes, though still generally square or rectangular in shape. These subdivisions could be halves (320 acres), fourths (160 acres), eighths (80 acres), sixteenths (40 acres), and so on.

How Public Land Was Distributed

Since the Northwest Ordinance of 1787, the United States government has sold or otherwise distributed public domain land through field offices of the General Land Office (GLO). Contrary to popular belief, homesteading wasn't the only way of acquiring land "out west." Some people purchased land for cash, and others on a credit or installment basis. In the early 1800s, land sections as large as 640 acres could be purchased for just $1.25 per acre. Aside from cash and credit sales, other ways in which public lands were distributed to individuals included:

- **Private Claims and Pre-emptions**—When a settler was physically on a piece of property before the GLO acquired, surveyed, or sold the tract, he was given a pre-emptive right to acquire the land from the United States—basically, a fancy way to say "squatter's rights."
- **Donation Lands**—In order to attract settlers to the remote territories of Florida, New Mexico, Oregon, and Washington during the 1850s, the federal government offered donation land grants to individuals who agreed to settle there for a minimum specified period.
- **Homesteads**—Under the Homestead Act of 1862, settlers were given 160 acres of land in the public domain in return for building a home on the land, cultivating the land, and residing there for a minimum of five years. This land did not require purchase by the acre, but the settler did pay a filing fee.

Once you've found a description of your ancestor's land, it is easy to locate a section of land in a public-land state on a map. USGS quadrangle maps have the townships and ranges marked with red lines running across the map, and numbers noted in the margin. Sections are also outlined and numbered in red.

Types of Federal Land Records

Because the federal government originally sold or otherwise transferred public land to individuals, it was also the entity responsible for creating and maintaining the records. From 1787 through 1907, every aspect of a land sale, including the patent, was handled by the local GLO office. Beginning in 1908, all land patents were issued from Washington, D.C.

Various records were created as public land was surveyed and sold. Depending upon the location and time period, these records include survey notes and plats, land entry case files, tract books, and serial patents.

Survey Notes and Plats

Beginning in the late 1700s in Ohio and progressing westward, the federal government continually surveyed new land in order to open new territories for settlement. The records generated from these land surveys generally include land descriptions, but may mention people who were already living on the land at the time it was surveyed. Survey plats are drawings of the land's boundaries or property lines, while survey field notes describe the actual survey and may include descriptions of the land. The National Archives and Records Administration maintains the original survey plats and field notes for Illinois, Indiana, Iowa, Kansas, Missouri, and Ohio. Original or duplicate survey plats and field notes for all other public land states are housed at the Bureau of Land Management (BLM).

FACT

Thirteen of the thirty public-land states are under the jurisdiction of the Eastern States' Office of the Bureau of Land Management. Referred to as the "Eastern land states," these states lie east of or border the Mississippi River and include Alabama, Arkansas, Florida, Illinois, Indiana, Iowa, Louisiana, Michigan, Minnesota, Mississippi, Missouri, Ohio, and Wisconsin. The other seventeen public-land states are referred to as the "Western states."

Land Entry Case Files

Before the homesteaders, soldiers, and other individuals received their patents, much paperwork had to be completed. Those purchasing land from the government were given receipts for payments, while those who obtained land through military bounty land warrants, pre-emption entries, or homesteading filed applications and provided proof of their claim and right to the land. These application files and other paperwork have been compiled into records known as land entry case files, which are generally the most genealogically valuable of the federal land records. Land entry case files are in the custody of the National Archives and Records Administration.

Tract Books

When a settler filed a land claim with the federal government, the entry was recorded in a tract book. Grouped by state, land office, and legal land description, tract books at a minimum include the name of the applicant and a brief description of the land. Tract books for the Eastern public land states are in the custody of the Bureau of Land Management. For the Western states they are held by the National Archives.

ALERT!

Just as with the state-land states, the federal government had nothing to do with land sales following the initial transfer (patent or grant) of land. Subsequent sales of the land between individuals, businesses, or companies are usually found in the county records.

Final Certificates and Patents

Once a settler fulfilled the requirements for his piece of land, he received a numbered final certificate indicating that he had done so. Based on this certificate, a patent for the land was then issued. A large number of these serial patents have been made available online in digitized format. The Bureau of Land Management Web site (✐*www.glorecords.blm.gov*) provides searchable access to a database of more than two million federal land patents issued between 1820 and 1908 in the thirteen Eastern public-land states. The pre-1908 patents from the Western public-land states are filed in the BLM office, which had jurisdiction over the land, and are not available online. The BLM is also in the process of digitizing the post-1908 serial patents and making them available online.

Metes, Bounds, and Meanders

As you become more experienced with genealogy research, you may wish to spend some time platting the land of your ancestors. Platting refers to drawing the shape of a piece of property from its physical description. Creating such a visual representation of your ancestor's property can help you locate his land on a map and follow how the property grew as he acquired more land, or was divided as he sold the land. This technique, although a bit advanced for the novice researcher, can be especially useful for solving tough genealogical problems that aren't easily answered through standard records.

FACT

Surveyors often used the word *meander* to indicate a property boundary that followed the courses of a waterway. This was often easier than attempting to pinpoint all of the directional changes of the creek, river, or stream. Technically, meander can describe any property line noted in a survey that does not provide both distance and direction, even if there isn't any water involved.

Metes and bounds descriptions usually follow a general pattern of alternating corners and lines, referred to as calls. Corners are points or locations where the property line changes direction, and are often found described by physical or geographical markers such as trees (for example, a black oak) or the name of an adjoining landowner (such as "Henry Gay's corner"). Lines are used to describe the distance and direction from one corner to the next, using either a compass direction and measurement or physical markers such as a waterway (for example, "down the meanders of the creek") or the name of an adjoining landowner.

Plotting a metes and bounds deed from its description is much like following in the footsteps of the original surveyor. In very basic terms, you mark a starting location or corner on your paper and then use a pencil, ruler, and round surveyor's compass or semicircular protractor to draw a line representing the property border of the length and direction defined in the deed until you reach another corner. You then draw another line to the next corner and so on until you arrive back at your starting point and the property area is fully defined. It's when you start tossing in rivers, trees, neighbors, and a variety of different measurement formats that platting starts to get complicated.

QUESTION?

Is there an easier way to plat a deed?
If you'd rather have a computer do the hard part for you, use one of several land platting software programs to convert the trees, creeks, poles, perches, degrees, and directions of the written land description into a graphical plat or outline drawing of the land.

Unless you're a trigonometry whiz and are familiar with land descriptions and the surveyor's compass, land platting can be a bit confusing at first. It's not really that hard to master—it's just a skill that takes a little practice and is beyond the scope of this book. One of the best ways to learn is to sign up for a land-platting workshop, often offered at larger genealogical conferences or, sometimes, through your local genealogical society.

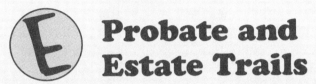

Chapter 12

Probate and Estate Trails

Wills and other estate-related documents are often among the most interesting, genealogically rich records you can locate for your ancestor. Because they have to be presented and proven in court, wills and probate records tend to be well-documented, relatively accurate, and packed with details. Estate records can also provide insight into family relationships, an inventory of your ancestor's possessions and real estate, and glimpses of personal dealings with friends and neighbors—about as close as you can get to a window into the life of your ancestor and his family.

With or Without a Will

Even today, the majority of Americans die without leaving a will. It wasn't much different for our ancestors; maybe they felt they didn't have any property worth worrying about, or maybe they died before they expected to, or, like so many of us, maybe they just didn't get around to it. Whatever the reason, the courts still usually stepped in to help with the distribution of their property in a process known as probate, from the Latin *probare*, meaning "to prove." Therefore, whether or not your ancestor left a will, you may find records pertaining to the settlement of his estate in the county probate court, in a collection of documents known as the probate packet.

Testate Estates

When an individual left a will before he died he was said to have died testate, and the person who makes the will is called the testator. A will can be as short as a single-page document leaving "everything to my spouse and children," or a complex, multipage document detailing every specific family relationship and bequest. A more typical will names the spouse and children, and specifies the distribution of land and important personal possessions. For legal purposes, there are three different types of wills:

- Attested wills are the most common type of will. An attested will may be handwritten or typed, and is signed by the testator in the presence of witnesses. The witnesses also sign, and later go to court to attest to the validity of the will.
- Holographic wills are less formal than an attested will. They are entirely handwritten by the person making the will, and must be signed and dated. Witnesses are not necessary for a holographic will.
- Nuncupative wills are oral wills dictated by the testator before witnesses, usually while on his deathbed. A nuncupative will is converted into writing at the earliest possible moment, and attested to in court by the witnesses.

Attested wills are the only wills that are valid in all jurisdictions and time periods, and will likely make up the bulk of the wills you run across during your research.

If a testator wishes to make changes to a will after it is created and signed, he can have a new will drawn up that specifically revokes all previous wills. If the intended modifications are minor, he can instead add a supplement or appendix to the will, known as a codicil. The codicil needs to be dated, signed, witnessed, and proven valid in court, just like the original will. Codicils were often used to add or change specific dispositions for heirs who had died, remarried, or otherwise changed in status since the original will was written.

FACT

A will is a legal document in which an individual specifies the disposition of his property and possessions after his death. Formally called a Last Will and Testament, the will portion originally referred to the distribution of real estate and buildings, while the testament bequeathed personal property, including money, personal possessions, and debts.

Intestate Estates

Those who died without leaving a legal will were said to have died intestate. If a will does exist but is later proven by the court to be invalid, the estate is also considered intestate.

In most states, if the deceased was a married man, the wife received one-third of his personal estate and, usually, a one-third lifetime interest—a dower right—in his real estate (land and property). The rest was divided equally among the children. If a child had previously died, his share was divided among his own legal heirs, if any. If an individual died without issue (children), then his property went to his spouse.

Dower rights did not apply in the community property states, and no longer apply in any states today. While most states still operate under rules based on English common law, the community property states—Arizona, California, Idaho, Louisiana, Nevada, New Mexico, Texas, and Washington—derive their property laws from Spanish-Mexican or Spanish-French colonial law (Wisconsin became a community property state in 1986). In community property jurisdictions, the property that a husband and wife own prior to the marriage, or inherit after the death of the spouse or end of the marriage, remains separate property. The property acquired during the marriage is considered joint or community property and each spouse is entitled to one-half interest. When the spouse dies without a will, the joint property automatically goes to the surviving spouse.

These common estate distributions are only generalities. When researching in probate records it is useful to know what laws were in effect in a state at the time of your ancestor's death, in order to understand how the court determined the estate's distribution.

QUESTION?

What happens when someone dies without a will?
When an individual dies intestate, the distribution of assets is determined according to formulas governed by the laws of the time and area. Basically, the law makes his will for him.

Understanding the Probate Process

Probate is the legal process by which a will is proven valid or, when an individual did not leave a will, the distribution of assets is determined according to the inheritance and property laws in effect at the time. Understanding the general steps involved in the probate process can help you understand the types of documents you may find for your ancestor.

1. The probate process generally begins when an heir, creditor, or other interested party petitions the court for the right to settle the estate. If the deceased left a will, it is presented to the court at this time.
2. The court clerk schedules a hearing date when the will is to be read. Anyone who contests the will may appear at the hearing. The witnesses to the will also appear at this hearing to testify to the authenticity of the will. Once the will is proven, it is recorded in the county will book.
3. The court appoints the executor named in the will or, in the case of intestate cases, an administrator, to oversee the settlement of the estate.

The court then issues a document known as Letters Testamentary or Letters of Administration, which authorizes the executor/administrator to act on behalf of the estate.

4. An inventory and appraisal of the estate is conducted, often by relatives (appointed by the court) who don't stand to benefit from the estate. They provide a written list of all assets of the estate to the court.

5. Beneficiaries named in the will are identified and contacted. Announcements are posted at the town hall and/or published in local newspapers, giving notice to people who have claims against or owe money to the estate.

6. When an estate involves minor children, a guardian is appointed to protect their interests.

7. The court also sets aside an allowance from the estate for the support of the widow or dependents until the estate is settled. If there is not enough cash available to cover this support, a sale of some of the estate's property (usually perishables or livestock) may be authorized by the court.

8. The executor/administrator pays all outstanding bills and debts owed by the estate, and prepares an adjusted inventory for the court.

9. Once the court deems all of the paperwork complete and all interested parties are in agreement, the property is divided and distributed among the heirs. Each heir signs a receipt confirming the receipt of his or her share of the estate.

10. The probate court rules that the estate is closed, and all remaining documents and receipts are filed with the court and added to the probate packet.

Each of these steps in the probate process generates paperwork and provides a source of potential clues for your research. Be sure to read every paper in the file, no matter how insignificant it may appear at first glance.

What You Can Learn from Probate Records

The documents and information contained in a probate packet can vary greatly, ranging from a single-page will to an entire box full of letters, documents, and receipts. Some of the records that may be found in a probate file include:

- Will and codicil
- Inventory or appraisal of the estate
- Appointments of executors or administrators
- Documentation of the administration or distribution of the estate
- Petitions for guardianship of minor children
- List of heirs
- Records of sale or auction of property
- Accounting of debts and/or creditors
- Assorted loose papers, including deeds, receipts, notices, and invoices

Each of these items is a source of potential clues to the life of your ancestor. The inventory, for example, may provide insight into the occupation or trade of your ancestor. People with the same surname who bought property sold at auction may have been relatives. Guardians appointed by the court for minor children are often relatives of the deceased or the spouse. A guardian with a different surname could indicate a possible clue to the widow's maiden name. Witnesses, while they couldn't be heirs, may still be relatives.

Wills also are great sources for married names of daughters as well as the names of their spouses. Children are often, though not always, listed in birth order; sons may be listed first, followed by daughters. Do not automatically assume, however, that a wife named in the will is the mother of the named children. Grandchildren who are singled out may indicate that a child died. Beneficiaries living outside the area can sometimes provide a clue to the family's prior origins. Wills can also provide personal insight into your ancestor as a person—the books he read, the hobbies he enjoyed, and even the way he felt toward his spouse and children.

Sometimes family members are omitted from a will, or left a token amount, because they were previously provided for. Sons were often given their share of the property when they married or reached the age of majority. Daughters may have been given their portion of the estate when they married. When this situation arises, check the deed records for the county for prior transfers of land from parent to child.

While useful in almost all family tree research situations, wills and probate records are an especially good source for information about ancestors who lived and died in this country prior to the federal census and vital records registration. Along with land records, estate records may be the only documents you can find that provide clues to family relationships and previous generations for those individuals.

In most states, when the father died, children were considered "orphans," even with their mother still living. A guardian was appointed to manage the orphans' share of the estate, as well as the children's maintenance and education. Records related to guardianship and estate management for these minor children are usually found in Orphan's Court, and may not be in the probate packet.

Where to Find Probate and Estate Records

In the United States, wills and probate records are generally found among the court records of the county where the deceased was living at the time of his death. Keep in mind that the boundaries and names of counties may have changed. In some states, the original documents may have been transferred to the state archives or other state-level agency. In this case, the county may or may not have retained a copy.

Where can I find my ancestor's original will?
When a will was accepted by the court, a copy was recorded in a will book maintained by the clerk of court. Usually retained by the court, the original can often be found among the estate papers in the probate packet (but some repositories have original wills filed separately). The LDS Family History Library has microfilmed many early original wills.

Once you locate the archive or courthouse that holds the probate records, check the index for the name of the deceased. You may also want to make a note of entries for the relatives of the deceased, as well as entries for others with the same surname. Make a list of all files that you want to see and give these to the clerk, archivist, or librarian, who will retrieve the records for you. While you have that person's attention, you may also want to ask whether wills, guardianships, or other related documents are filed with the probates or if they are maintained in separate files.

Many indexes to wills and estates have been published, such as *North Carolina Wills: A Testator Index, 1665–1900*, by Thorton W. Mitchell, and *Virginia Wills and Administrations, 1632–1800*, by Clayton Torrence. Statewide indexes such as these can be especially helpful when you aren't sure exactly where your ancestor died, or can't locate estate records in the county where you expected to find them. These books can usually be found at libraries with genealogical collections that cover the area in which you're interested.

Increasingly, digitized copies of wills are being placed online. Early North Carolina wills, for example, can be viewed on the Web site of the North Carolina State Archives. Other online database collections such as "Scottish wills and testaments from 1500-1901"; "Prerogative Court of Canterbury Wills for England and Wales, 1384 to 1858"; and probate indexes for Texas also provide almost instant access to wills and estate records. Some require a fee for access, but so does having the papers photocopied at the courthouse or archives.

Examine each and every paper included in the probate packet, all the way down to the smallest receipt. Make notes or have photocopies made if you can afford it. Be sure to include your source on the notes or copies, including the name of the record group, name and address of the archive, and date.

When You Can't Find a Will

There will be times when you may have trouble locating a will or probate proceeding for your ancestor. It could be that he owned no real property at the time of his death, so there was no need to go to court to settle the estate. It could be that the records were destroyed by fire, flood, or negligence. Or it could be that you're just looking in the wrong place.

Because land and real estate was usually the most expensive property owned by individuals, a good place to search for clues is in the deed index for the county where he lived. You may find a deed or deeds granting the property to his children, or a survey of the land allotted to a widow for her dower.

ALERT!

Although most wills are handled in court within a few months of an individual's death, this isn't always the case. Estates may be settled many years after the individual's death, especially in cases with minor children who need to reach the age of majority before receiving their inheritance. A contested will or other complications could also hold up the probate process.

Check court minutes for evidence of the estate proceedings. They may indicate various steps in the probate process, including the inventory of the estate, the auction of property, the granting of the wife's dower, the appointment of guardians, and the final distribution to the heirs.

When all else fails, circumvent the problem. Search for probate records for your ancestor's siblings, spouse, children, and other relatives. Depending upon what you are looking for, they may provide just as much or more information than would your ancestor's will.

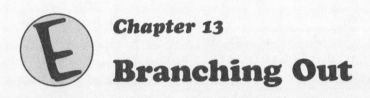

Chapter 13

Branching Out

Y ou've learned a great deal about your family so far, building a foundation for your family tree through home sources and a variety of public records and documents. These "tried and true" records usually allow you to fill in big portions of your family tree, but still may leave a few unanswered questions. This is where nontraditional records come in. Religious records, newspapers, obituaries, Social Security records, occupational records, and school records are examples of alternative records that can fill in missing gaps or verify information that you've already found.

Church and Religious Records

America has a diverse religious background. Over the centuries, its residents have belonged to hundreds of different churches, synagogues, and religious organizations. No matter what your current beliefs, religion most likely played an important role in the lives of your ancestors. Churches and synagogues often served as the community gathering spot in smaller localities, and were the site of baptisms, christenings, weddings, and funerals.

What do you do when you can't find a marriage certificate for your great-grandmother because she married twenty years before the state started keeping records? Look for church records. If you can locate your ancestor's place of worship, you open the doors to a potential wealth of genealogical data, including registers of births, baptisms, marriages, and burials. This is an especially important source for times when civil records were not maintained. Very often, religious records are the only source you can find for birth and marriage information in early American communities.

Determining Your Ancestor's Religion

To locate church records, you must first determine the place where your ancestor worshiped. Don't assume that your ancestors belonged to the same religious denomination that your family does today. With so many branches and individuals in your family tree, you are likely to have many religious affiliations represented. You'll need to do some homework to discover the religion of each of your ancestors in order to locate the church, synagogue, or other place where they worshiped.

Obituaries, cemetery records, and even death records are a good place to search for mentions of an ancestor's religious affiliation. Civil marriage records may mention the name of the minister, rabbi, or priest who conducted the marriage ceremony. Don't overlook land and probate records, since many people bequeath money or land to their church. Pick the brains of your eldest family members as well, and be sure to investigate all family sources, including Bibles, prayer cards, and newspaper announcements of marriages, births, and funerals. The church or synagogue may even appear in the background of old family photos. Knowing where your ancestors came from can also provide a clue to their religious preference. For example, most immigrants from France or Poland were Roman Catholic, most Scots were Presbyterian, and most Norwegians were Lutheran.

Once you know the religion of your ancestor, maps and city directories can often help pin down the church closest to where the family lived.

FACT

It wasn't uncommon, especially in rural areas, for people to attend a church that was not of their denomination because there wasn't a church of their particular religious affiliation nearby. They may also have converted to another religion to appease a spouse or escape religious persecution. Also, members of the same family may have not belonged to the same church.

Where Are the Records?

Once you've located the church, you next need to learn where the records are kept. Often the records are still in the possession of the local church. In this case, a letter or phone call to the church office may provide assistance with obtaining specific records. Be sure to state that you would like a photocopy of the actual record, when possible, or a full transcription. In some cases the earlier records of the church may have been transferred to a central archive. The local minister may be able to tell you where they are stored and who to contact there.

But what if the church no longer exists? The regional denominational head-quarters may know where the records can be found. Contact information for more than 1,000 denominations can be found in J. Gordon Melton's *The Encyclopedia of American Religions*. Alternatively, try contacting other churches of the same denomination in the area, or the local genealogical/historical society, to determine whether the old records survive and where they are kept.

The Church of Jesus Christ of Latter-day Saints (LDS) has microfilmed the early records of many denominations. These can be found by searching the Family History Library (FHL) catalog at your local Family History Center or online at FamilySearch.org. Do a place search for the county or city of interest, and then click on "church records" to see what is available. Church record abstracts, indexes, and other religious records are often available at public libraries and in the collections of local historical and genealogical societies. The *National Union Catalog of Manuscript Collections* may be useful in locating these records (see Chapter 13: Branching Out in Appendix A).

ALERT!

It is customary to include a donation when writing to a church for assistance with records. This helps cover the cost of the staff's time and any copies they provide. Remember, churches are private organizations and are under no obligation to grant access to their records, though many do it as a courtesy.

Newspapers and Obituaries

Newspapers are a wonderful source of history. They provide cities, towns, and other communities with a way to stay in touch with the world around them—both with major news stories and local happenings and gossip. Besides the news, newspapers are crammed with fascinating items and stories detailing the lives of our ancestors—a sort of day-to-day diary of the times. Obituaries, marriage announcements, and birth notices are especially useful to genealogists, but most of the rest is interesting too. Even the advertisements and editorial comments provide charming insight into what was important to readers at the time. There is just something neat about knowing how much your ancestors paid for butter and eggs.

Some of the useful genealogical information found in newspapers includes:

- **Birth announcements, baptisms, and christenings**—Birth announcements became popular, especially in small, local newspapers, in the early 1900s.
- **Funeral notices and obituaries**—Usually placed by the family, these notices may include a variety of details about family members (surviving and deceased), dates of birth and death, and the location of the church or burial. These may appear up to several weeks after the date of death.

- **Wedding and anniversary announcements**—Newspapers, both large and small, often include weekly columns of nuptials and weddings. Major wedding anniversaries in small communities often warrant a brief newspaper article.
- **Gossip and society news**—Even large newspapers have a section for local items of interest. These may include birthday announcements, stories of travels or visiting relatives, job promotions, illnesses, and other news of a personal nature.
- **Real estate transfers**—Small, local newspapers often include notices of comings and goings in the neighborhood. More current newspapers include brief details on property sales and purchases.
- **Police blotter**—Crime always makes the news, and daily or weekly police blotters include lists of people arrested and accounts of other local mischief.
- **Public announcements and classified ads**—Public estate and farm sales are often listed in small classified advertisements. Announcements of forced land sales, runaway slaves, missing relatives, and probate proceedings also are of interest.
- **School and military news**—Graduation ceremonies, class lists, honor rolls, special achievements, and tales of local heroes going off to war often make the newspaper.

Historic newspapers have been preserved in many areas around the world. The majority in the United States are from the nineteenth and twentieth centuries, though a few earlier newspapers exist. Libraries contain guides to newspapers in the various states. These guides are organized by location. They list the newspapers that were published during a given period of time, and then they show where surviving copies of those newspapers are kept. One of the most complete is the *U.S. Newspaper Program National Union List*. Because the original newspapers are bulky and fragile, many states have microfilmed collections of their communities' newspapers. Generally these microfilms are available at the state's library, archive, or historical society. Local newspapers may also be available at the library serving the community. If you're unable to visit the area in person, microfilmed newspapers can generally be viewed at your own local library through interlibrary loan.

Modern newspapers can be a good genealogy tool. Some researchers have had success with putting an ad in a newspaper in the place where their family had ties, asking for information or for the names of people to contact about the family. This approach often turns up information from unexpected sources, such as friends, schoolmates, or other acquaintances.

In recent years, a large number of historic newspapers have been digitized and placed online or made available on computer in major libraries. Some of the largest include *Early American Newspapers, Series I, 1690–1876* (newspapers published in the American Colonies and United States), the *New York Times* digital archive (1851–2001), the *Wall Street Journal* collection (1889–1985), and *The London Times* digital archive (1785–1985). A collaborative between the National Endowment for the Humanities and the Library of Congress is assembling an online database of 30 million digitized pages from papers published from 1836 through 1922. A wide variety of local historic newspapers are also available online through free and subscription databases (see Chapter 13: Branching Out in Appendix A). Most modern newspapers also maintain some sort of presence online, and many include archives of news articles and obituaries dating back several years.

Social Security Records

An excellent resource for researching contemporary ancestors, U.S. Social Security records contain details about the majority of Americans who have died since 1962. These records can help fill in valuable vital facts and some of the specific details about your ancestors that family members may not have been able to provide, such as date and place of birth, date of death, occupation, and parents' names.

President Franklin D. Roosevelt signed the Social Security Act into law on August 14, 1935, during the depths of the Great Depression. The new Act created a national social insurance program, designed to ensure retired workers aged sixty-five and older a continuing income. Records of the Social

Security Administration (SSA) of potential benefit to genealogists include the application for a Social Security card, and information from the "claims folder" for past recipients of benefits.

The Social Security Death Index

The SSA maintains a Death Master File, often referred to as the Social Security Death Index (SSDI), of deaths that have been reported to the SSA. The SSDI is one of the largest and most useful databases available for researching twentieth-century Americans, because it contains names, birthdates, death dates, Social Security numbers, and other useful information about more than 74 million people (primarily Americans). The majority of the records included in this index date from the present back to 1962, the year the SSA implemented a computer database for processing benefit requests, although some go back as far as 1936. It is not a database of all Americans who have died during that time period, however, just those who had a Social Security number and whose deaths have been reported to the SSA.

QUESTION?

What do the numbers in the Social Security number mean?
In most cases, the first three numbers indicate the state in which the Social Security number (SSN) was issued (usually the individual's home state). The SSA lists the geographical number assignments at *www. socialsecurity.gov/foia/stateweb.html*. The remaining six digits are more or less randomly assigned, organized to facilitate the early bookkeeping operations of the SSA, and are not useful to genealogists.

The Social Security Death Index is most easily searched on the Internet; there are several free versions available. RootsWeb.com, Ancestry.com, and NewEnglandAncestors.org usually offer the most current version, but a search for "SSDI" in a search engine will also turn up many others. The SSDI is also available at many libraries and at local Family History Centers, or bundled on CD with some family tree software programs.

If you're unable to locate a deceased individual in the SSDI, don't immediately assume that he's not included. As with all databases, there are misspellings, data entry errors, and other stumbling blocks. If you can't find a listing for your ancestor, try these techniques:

- Try all possible spellings of the names, including Soundex for the last name if available (see Chapter 7).
- Check the instructions for the particular SSDI you are searching to see if it permits the use of wildcards (Pat* would find Pat, Patrick, Patricia, and so on).
- Try switching the first and last names.
- Search for the maiden name of a married woman.
- Use middle name, nickname, or first initial in place of the first name.
- Try alternate dates—switch years around (1948 to 1984) or swap the day and month (switch April 11, 1968 [4/11/1968] to November 4, 1968 [11/4/1968]).
- Search with less information and try various combinations of detail. For example, omit the first name, but enter the year of birth, or omit the name entirely, searching only for the date of death.
- Don't enter the Zip Code; this information isn't included for the earlier records.

Locating an ancestor in the SSDI can be informative, but even more can be gleaned from his original Social Security Application Form. This is easily requested from the SSA with the name and Social Security number obtained from the SSDI.

The Social Security Application Form (SS-5)

SS-5 is the form used by individuals to apply for a Social Security number. This form can often extend your family tree search back another generation because it may contain the full names of both parents, including the mother's maiden name. Other details included on the SS-5 include the full name of the applicant, his address at the time of application, name of employer, date and place of birth, and age at the time of application. It provides much of the same information you would find on a death certificate, but is often more accurate. This is because people usually filled out their own application for Social Security, while someone else who may not have known the person as well would have completed the death certificate.

A copy of the Social Security Application Form (SS-5) of a deceased individual is available from the Social Security Administration through a Freedom of Information Act (FOIA) request. The fee is $27 if you include a Social Security number, and $29 if not. A computer extract of the information is available for a bit less, but is not suggested for genealogy purposes because mistakes or omissions could occur during the extraction.

There is a form available (✐*www.socialsecurity.gov/foia*) to request copies of the SS-5, but it is not required. Just send a letter including the individual's name, Social Security number (if known), and any other identifying details to:

Social Security Administration
OEO FOIA Workgroup
300 N. Green Street
P.O. Box 33022
Baltimore, Maryland 21290-3022

Mark both the envelope and its contents: "FREEDOM OF INFORMATION REQUEST." The wait time may be as long as six to eight weeks, so prepare to be patient!

FACT

The first Social Security number was issued to John D. Sweeney Jr. of New York. The lowest number issued (001-01-0001) was to Grace Dorothy Owen of New Hampshire. The first applicant for Social Security benefits was a retired Cleveland motorman named Ernest Ackerman, who received a lump-sum payment of seventeen cents upon retiring one day after the Social Security program began.

Occupational Records

Not much different from today, the occupations of our ancestors defined a big chunk of their lives—what time they got up in the morning, how they supported their family, and the contributions they made to the community. An ancestor's chosen occupation can often tell you much more about him than just how he earned his keep. It may also provide insight into social status, interests, passions, skills, and abilities. Employment and other occupational records can sometimes include useful genealogical information as well, including date of birth and names of family members.

ALERT!

If you find that your ancestor's listed occupation is an outdated, confusing term, turn to a glossary of old occupational terms for the meaning of job titles that have fallen into disuse through the years, such as a ripper (seller of fish), hosteler (innkeeper), slopseller (merchant of ready-made clothes), or pettifogger (unscrupulous lawyer). See Chapter 13: Branching Out in Appendix A.

Learning what your ancestor did for a living is usually pretty easy. Occupation can often be found listed in census records, Social Security records, city directories, death certificates, marriage certificates, military records, naturalization petitions, and a number of other genealogical records. Follow your ancestor's occupation through a wide variety of records from different time periods, because he may have changed jobs at least once or twice, or even suffered through periods of unemployment.

Employment Records

If you can associate your ancestor with a specific company or business, you may be able to locate records of the company in a corporate or society archive. Employment, payroll, pension, and other company records may provide some useful genealogical information. In some cases these records are considered confidential and access is restricted. In other cases there may be no records at all. When you contact the company for information, be prepared to show proof of your relationship to the individual in question.

Apprenticeship Records

From Colonial America through to the twentieth century, some teenage girls and boys were indentured to a skilled craftsman for the purpose of learning a trade. In many cases the apprentice was an orphan, bound into apprenticeship by the court. These apprenticeship agreements can often be found among the records of the local, county, or state courts. State archives and historical societies may have collections on microfilm.

Trades, Associations, and Unions

As America grew, more and more of our ancestors became lawyers, ministers, doctors, blacksmiths, lumberjacks, printers, and tailors—plus a host of other professions and trades necessary for the country's expansion. Members of most vocations tended to band together, forming professional organizations, trade associations, and unions for the purpose of exchanging information and providing referrals. These associations often generated valuable records, including directories and employment rolls.

Railroad employees are a special situation, given America's dependence on the construction of railroads for its westward expansion. As many as 2.25 million people worked for the railroad companies at the industry's peak, around 1920. Tracking down these railroad company records is highly dependent upon learning the history of the particular railroad company. You need to learn which railroads operated in that geographical area at the time, including the routes they took, stations served, and affiliations they may have had with other railroad lines. An ancestor who received a pension from any of the railroad companies after 1936 should be on record at the Railroad Retirement Board. They will search their records for a fee, as long as you can provide the Social Security number or the employee's name, the railroad worked for, and where and when the person was employed.

The *Encyclopedia of Associations*, published biannually by Gale Research Company, includes contact information and details about published journals and newsletters for trade associations that are still in existence. Many of these associations have been in continuous existence since the mid-nineteenth century, providing a rich source of historical information.

You can often identify twentieth-century railroad employees by checking their Social Security numbers. The Social Security Administration issued special numbers that began with 700 through 728 to railroad employees from 1937 to 1963. After 1963, railroad employees were assigned numbers based on their geographical location, just like the rest of the population.

Researching the Self-Employed

If your ancestor was self-employed, perhaps a farmer, blacksmith, or tavern owner, look to his own personal records for details about his occupation. Estate records can be especially telling, as the inventory of items will often provide clues to his occupation. An abundance of a particular item or items, in excess of normal household usage, may suggest a specific profession or business. If your ancestor owned a small business, there may be a record of the business license still in existence with the city or county. Special agricultural and manufacturing census schedules (see Chapter 7) can provide contextual information on the business, such as its size, inventory, and net worth. Property and tax records are also a potential source of information about family-owned farms and businesses.

School Records

Yearbooks, enrollment lists, class photos, and report cards—records from your ancestor's school days provide a fascinating glimpse into her early life. Other than birth certificates, individuals under the age of sixteen don't usually generate many official records, making school records an invaluable resource. Even in rural areas, most children received at least a few years of formal education, so school records also potentially cover a large percentage of the population.

Educational institutions, by their very nature, generate and keep a lot of records. College and university records are generally the easiest to locate, because many of these institutions have been around for a long time. High school and grade school records can be a bit more challenging to unearth, but not always as difficult as people may expect. If the school is still in existence, the records usually are still in the school's possession. In the case of long-closed schools, records may still be housed in local libraries, with historical or genealogical societies, in the city or state archives, or in private collections. The local school board may be able to tell you whether such records exist, and where they are kept.

A number of school records have been microfilmed by the Genealogical Society of Utah and can be found in the Family History Library Catalog. Search by state or county, and then under the subject heading "Schools." The Internet is another potential source for school lists, yearbook photos, and other school records. These are most often found on county-specific genealogy Web sites, such as those at USGenWeb.com.

FACT

School attendance in early America was spotty at best. Less than 10 percent of nineteenth-century students stayed in school past the eighth grade, dropping out to work alongside their parents on the family farm or in the family business. It wasn't until 1918 that all states had passed laws requiring children to attend school through at least the elementary years.

A variety of school records may be of interest to genealogists, including enrollment and registration lists, student transcripts, admission applications, and school board minutes. Schools were also required to conduct regular censuses of the students, teachers, and staff to plan for future school enrollment and needs. These school censuses are sometimes the only surviving record of students who attended long-closed, rural schools. These schedules count the children of school age living in the district, and list the names and ages of the children, along with the names of the parents.

School alumni associations are a good source for locating copies of alumni directories, copies of old yearbooks, photos, and information about the present whereabouts of former students. Many alumni groups maintain newsletters, which are full of news items and event announcements of their members. Some also compile biographies and histories of some of the school's more prominent alumni. Commemorative class reunion booklets from former reunions may also be found among their files, and may include photos and short biographical sketches of the people who attended. Class reunion Web sites often include contact information for the school's alumni association, as well as information about former students.

ALERT!

School memorabilia, including class photos, yearbooks, graduation and reunion booklets, and sports-related items, can sometimes be found for sale at local antiques stores, and on Internet auction sites such as eBay®.

Fraternities and sororities have a long history in America, and are generally excellent record keepers. If your ancestor was a member of a sorority or fraternity, contact the school, state, or national chapter for information about the organization's history and details about records that may have been kept and how they can be accessed.

The "History" in Family History

Genealogy is a personalized journey back in time—a chance to relive history through the eyes of your ancestors. Understanding what happened in the past can breathe life into what might otherwise be a dull recitation of names, dates, and other facts. You can find valuable clues to the lives and personalities of your ancestors by researching the history of the time and place where they lived.

By using historical records and timelines to bring your ancestors to life, your family tree will become so much more than a plain diagram. The individuals on your family tree will become real people. You'll be able to describe their physical characteristics and whether they were farmers, doctors, tailors, or teachers. You'll discover what their daily life was like, from household chores to fashion to newsworthy events of the time.

Create a Timeline for Your Ancestors

One of the first, most important steps in family history research is to gain an understanding of the history of the location and time period in which your ancestors lived. A timeline visually brings together elements of time, history, and community in small, easy-to-understand chunks. It can show you, at a glance, which major local or world events may have influenced your ancestor's actions or movements.

FACT

A timeline can help you answer questions such as whether an epidemic was a possible cause of the deaths of so many of your ancestors in 1901, or whether an ancestor was old enough to have served in a particular war.

A good timeline should include major events from your ancestor's life mixed in with historical events and important observations from the location in which she lived. This can also point out resources that might be available for a particular ancestor, and where to look for them. If you know that the county your ancestor lived in was formed in 1885, then you won't waste time writing to the county for her marriage record from 1862.

It's easy to create your own timeline from scratch, or you can use the timeline function available in many family tree software programs. Genelines, a standalone timeline charting program by Progeny Software, includes numerous timeline charts, as well as a database of major historical events. A variety of online historical timelines can provide you with facts ranging from military conflicts to epidemics. Encyclopedias, county histories, and online historical resources are other good sources of facts for your timeline.

Add Some Social History

You can research historical newspapers, photographs, local histories, fashion histories, old magazines, cookbooks, maps, specialized museums, and estate and census records to learn more about the time period and place in which your ancestors lived. Resources such as these provide details about ethnic customs, religious practices, fashion trends, occupational hazards, the price of butter and eggs, and even local gossip.

Outside of the names and dates these resources can provide, it is important to also realize what they can tell you about the everyday life of your ancestors. This brings you closer to your past and provides narrative for your family history. Get to know your ancestors the way you know your own family—because that's what they are.

Chapter 14

Special Situations in Family Trees

The wide variety of cultural and ethnic lineages in America sometimes presents distinctive genealogy problems requiring special, tailored approaches. As with any family history, your special ethnic or adoptive heritage begins with you and your parents. Just because your ancestors were adoptees, slaves, religious prisoners, or American Indians, this doesn't mean that you cannot trace their family trees as you would any other. You may need to familiarize yourself with a wider variety of unique records and history, but this just makes the search more interesting!

Adoption

It is estimated that as many as one in eight Americans are directly touched by adoption, as an adoptee, biological parent, adoptive parent, or sibling. This can add a special, but emotional dimension to a family tree search. Some adoptees have no desire to know their birth parents, accepting their adoptive parents as their only parents. Both law and love make them a family, with ties at least as strong as a family related by blood, so they take their adoptive parents' family lines and research genealogy along those. Others pursue an abiding curiosity about their biological parents and the generations before them. It is also not uncommon for adoptees to be curious about the genealogy of both their adoptive parents and their birth parents.

Adoptions make genealogy research difficult, and often require special research skills and strategies to solve the puzzle. The task is even further complicated in cases in which the adoption took place several generations back in the family tree, or was not legally handled through the court system. Formidable barriers of sealed records, altered birth certificates, and uncooperative officials and family members often hinder the search for the truth of an adoptee's past. Then there is the emotional impact. Not everyone welcomes a reunion. Some birth parents absolutely do not want to be found. Fears of discovering unpleasant facts or facing rejection also haunt many who undertake an adoption search.

FACT

The adoption triad represents the three major parties to an adoption— the birth parents, adoptive parents, and adoptee. In most cases, mutual consent from all members of the adoption triad is required for adoption information to be released or a reunion to be arranged.

Adoption records in the United States are usually sealed by court order and inaccessible to the public. Guaranteed confidentiality has been a part of most adoptions in this country since the 1930s, and the courts feel the need to uphold these promises. In recent years, however, great debate and public interest have swirled around the legal right of adopted children to know who their birth parents were. Increasingly, states are opening at least some adoption records or passing laws granting adoptees the right to a copy of the original birth certificate, which lists the biological parents' names. Even in states with stricter adoption statutes, those adoptees who have medical problems linked to their heredity are increasingly gaining sympathy from the courts and becoming exceptions to the guaranteed privacy laws. If you fit that category, you should talk with an attorney who can explore with you your state's laws regarding an adoptee's right to be provided with needed hereditary and health-related information about his or her birth parents.

Researching Contemporary Adoptions

To begin an adoption search, write down everything you know about your adoption, no matter how insignificant. Ask your adoptive parents for any documents they may hold, such as an amended birth certificate, petition for adoption, or the final adoption decree.

Next, familiarize yourself with the laws of the state in which your adoption took place. A few states, including Alaska, Hawaii, and Kansas, allow adults full access to their adoption files. Most, however, restrict access to original birth certificates. In this case, contact the state or agency that handled your adoption to obtain nonidentifying information. Governed by state law, the information released may include medical details, health history, ethnic origins, religion, and other facts that are considered appropriate, yet still protect the privacy of the birth parents.

Because most state laws make it difficult to access adoption records, alternatives have been established to help arrange reunions between adoptees and birth parents when all parties of the adoption triad consent. Many states provide an adoption registry, usually operated through the department that handles vital records (see Chapter 6). For a fee, that department will add your search details into its database. If both a birth parent and an adoptee register for information, the department will help arrange a contact. For a more substantial fee, some states also offer Confidential Intermediary (CI) services. The CI is given access to the complete adoption file and, using that information, attempts to locate and contact the individuals involved. If the other parties are located, they are given the right to refuse contact, or to permit release of their names and current addresses.

The Internet provides access to numerous adoption registries, as well as support groups and mailing lists for those searching for birth parents or adoptees, and information about current laws affecting access to adoption records. See Chapter 14: Special Situations in Family Trees in Appendix A for suggested resources.

The International Soundex Reunion Registry (P.O. Box 2312, Carson City, NV 89702, ✐*www.isrr.org*) is the world's largest free adoption registry. It provides a system for matching individuals who desire contact with their next-of-kin by birth. The registry is committed to privacy, and only arranges contact between registrants if all parties are agreeable to a reunion.

Researching Historic Adoptions

What about an adoption that occurred a few generations back? Genealogy research often strikes a dead end when the adoptee involved is long deceased. Adoptions prior to the mid-nineteenth century were usually informal and rarely officially recorded. Abandoned and orphaned children were usually taken in by relatives or placed with families that were willing to share their home in return for the extra labor. Children old enough to learn a trade may have been bound as apprentices when no one else could be found to support them.

FACT

Between 1854 and the mid-1930s, social agencies sent hundreds of thousands of orphaned and abandoned children by train across the United States to find new homes with families in the Midwest. The Orphan Train Heritage Society of America serves as a volunteer clearing-house for individuals interested in researching the "orphan train" experience.

If genealogical answers about parenthood are to be found for long-ago adoptees, they will generally come from pursuing clues regarding date and place of birth or adoption. Search for birth records for that time period to find out which mothers delivered around the birthdate of the adoptee. Church baptism or christening records may help with this.

Also, you can make educated guesses about the adoptive parents' distant relatives—often a family arranged for a very distant relative to adopt the child, especially if that family was having trouble bearing children of their own. Tracing families through census records can sometimes pick up the addition of a child who was not born into the family. Probate records will occasionally include a reference to an "adopted" child. County court records may also reveal clues, such as fathers ordered to pay support for their illegitimate children, and apprenticeship records for children taken in to learn a trade.

Researching African-American Roots

Tracing African-American ancestry can be uniquely challenging, especially when researching the pre–Civil War era. The majority of Americans with African ancestry are descendants of slaves forcibly brought to the United States, West Indies, and Caribbean during the eighteenth and nineteenth centuries. These slaves had no legal rights, leaving few signs of their existence in the traditional records of the time period. Adding to the complexity of the research, many of today's African-Americans have racially mixed backgrounds, encompassing African, Caucasian, and Native American ancestry.

Find assistance and inspiration by connecting with other African-American researchers online. AfriGeneas (*www.afrigeneas.com*) features a mailing list, message boards, and weekly chats related to black genealogy, plus slave data, and a beginner's guide.

Despite the obstacles, an African-American genealogy project begins like any other—at home. Interview all family members, especially the eldest ones (see Chapter 2), learning everything you can about their parents, grandparents, and traditions regarding the family's distant past. Black genealogy depends heavily on oral tradition, and your relatives may know more than they realize. Much is to be learned from Alex Haley's *Roots*, and his celebration of the stories of the family being passed orally to the next generation.

Pre-Civil War Records

The vast majority of African-Americans in the United States prior to the Civil War were slaves, and slavery severely inhibits tracing African-American family connections. Public records reflect the appalling reality that under the institution of slavery, African-Americans were legally classified as property. For genealogists, this means that the search must focus on learning the name of the slave owner and locating records relating to the slave-owner's "property."

Owners gave slaves first names in place of their African names, robbing them of their identity. In order to help keep track of their relatives and lineages, some slaves chose a surname that represented or identified the family's first slave owner. This surname was often kept secret from the slave owners, but passed down orally from generation to generation. After the end of slavery, those who already possessed surnames revealed them, while others chose a surname for the first time.

FACT

Former slaves were faced with choosing a surname following the Civil War in order to enroll in many government programs. Some studies of former slaves have concluded that as many as 71 percent chose the name of their most recent owner. Other studies, including one done by African-American genealogist Tony Burroughs, put that number closer to 15 to 20 percent.

Identifying the Slave Owner

U.S. federal censuses did not list the majority of African-Americans by name until 1870. To conduct census research for black ancestors prior to 1870, look for slave owners with the same name as your family surname, or one that is similar. By checking the age and sex of the owners' slaves, perhaps you can find circumstantial evidence that your ancestor was in that group.

When searching for a slaveholding family based on surname yields no result, turn to the surrounding community for clues. Check the 1870 census for white families living in the same area as your African-American ancestors, especially ones with larger real estate values. Land records and other records of property may also provide clues to the former slaveholder. Bills of sale for slaves were recorded. The buyer received a copy, and a copy was usually filed in the county's deed books. Tax collectors assessed the individual taxable value of residents' personal and real property, including the value of their slaves. Plantations, being farm businesses, also produced business records. Those that survive include financial ledgers with entries regarding slaves bought and sold, and who died. Check for plantation records with reference librarians in the state historical society where your relative was a slave.

Wills can be excellent sources for finding names and ages of slaves. In their wills, slaveholders often mentioned slaves by name and indicated to which white relative or associate they were leaving the slaves, or whether the slaves were to be sold or, occasionally, freed. If a slaveholder died intestate, the probate court most likely handled the estate. If so, the court had to make an appraisal of the estate, including the slaves by name and their market value. This appraisal, or return, was filed with the court records, so look for the returns as well as the probate records themselves.

Not all African-Americans living in the United States prior to the Civil War were slaves. The 1860 federal census and slave schedules reported 4,441,830 African-Americans, of whom 488,070 were free. The majority of the 3,953,760 slaves and more than half of the free blacks were living in the Southern states.

Military Records

African-Americans who served in the U.S. military and in state militias can be found in military records, including military pension records. Slaves fought in the American Revolution and in the War of 1812. Many were granted their freedom in return for their service. African-American also fought in the Civil War, many in the North, which had several all-black units. See Chapter 8 for further discussion of military records.

Religious Sources

Some slaveholders were religious and cared about the salvation of all human souls. They therefore allowed ministers to perform baptisms, marriages, and other church ordinances for their slaves, and some records of the religious rites name the slaves who received them. Blacks who attended church services did so at a church fairly close to their home. Some white churches kept records of their slave members.

Oral Histories and Slave Narratives

Law forbade slaves from learning to read or write, so life stories and history were oral, passed from one generation to the next by tellings and retellings from memory. Some of this early family history has been preserved in published slave narratives. The largest known collection is *The American Slave Narratives*, a collection of more than 2,300 published interviews conducted with former slaves by Work Projects Administration workers in the 1930s. Many slave narratives can be found online, and in collections at major libraries.

Manumitted Slaves and Runaways

When slaves became runaways, owners posted notices and obtained warrants for arrests, naming the slaves being sought. Some of those documents can be used to trace ancestors. Freed, or manumitted, slaves had to be legally certified as such in order to prove they were freedmen. This was a property transaction, so the manumission record was typically recorded in the county deed book.

Post–Civil War Records

The years 1865 to 1870 are pivotal when researching African-Americans who were in the United States prior to the Civil War. The end of the war in 1865 brought the emancipation of thousands of slaves, and the 1870 federal census was the first national census to list these recently freed slaves by name. You should use traditional genealogy resources, including wills, probate records, land records, census records, and military records, to trace African-American families back to this date.

Before, during, and after the Civil War, black churches sprang up in order to serve free blacks, in both the North and South. The African Methodist

Episcopal Church became the most popular. You can contact its church headquarters in Williamstown, Massachusetts, to find out how to access its records. Two other churches to contact are the National Baptist Convention, USA, in St. Petersburg, Florida, and the Christian Methodist Episcopal Church in Memphis, Tennessee.

ALERT!

African-Americans were included in vital records compiled by the states by the turn of the twentieth century. However, through the first quarter of the century, midwives rather than doctors delivered many African-American children. In many of these cases, no birth certificates were issued. Look for delayed certificates of birth, or for clues in family and church records.

After the Civil War, former slaves had to find ways to earn a living. Many became sharecroppers; that is, they farmed on someone else's land, paying in return a share of their produce to the landowner. Some of these sharecropping account books survive. To find them, check in local records and in the small collection in the National Archives.

At the end of the Civil War, the federal government established the Bureau of Refugees, Freedmen, and Abandoned Lands, commonly referred to as the "Freedmen's Bureau," to assist former slaves and indigent whites. Field offices were set up in the former Confederate states, as well as in Kentucky, the District of Columbia, and Maryland. The Freedmen's Bureau helped to establish schools; provide food, clothing, and medical help; assist former slaves to get married; help black war veterans to apply for pensions; and set up employment programs. The surviving records of the Freedmen's Bureau were collected and are now housed in the National Archives.

In 1865 the federal government established a banking system for freedmen throughout the South, which lasted a decade. The Freedman's Bank Savings and Trust Company ledgers include two kinds of records of interest to genealogists: indexes to deposit ledgers, and registers of signatures of depositors. These bank records may contain individual and family information, including the name of the account holder, age and birth information, occupation, and the names of spouses, children, parents, and even siblings. Some provide the former slaveholder's names. Microfilm copies of the Freedman's Bank depositor records are available at various national, state, and local libraries. A variety of indexes, abstracts, and digitized copies of the Freedman's Bank records are available online through HeritageQuest Online (available free to members of participating libraries and genealogical societies), Ancestry.com (subscription only), and on CD-ROM from the Family History Library.

FACT

A portion of the Freedmen's Bureau records has been microfilmed, and can be accessed at major genealogical libraries, including Family History Center branches of the Family History Library. Transcriptions of some of these records, especially the marriage registers, can also be found online at ⌁*www.freedmensbureau.com*.

Back to Africa

Because most tribal history in Africa was recorded by oral tradition rather than written down, actually tracing one's roots in Africa can be an extremely difficult task. For more than two centuries the slave trade between Africa and North America was big business.

Enslaved men, women, and children came from many different African nations and tribes, and were transported to numerous locations along America's east coast and in the West Indies. While extremely difficult, the best chance of tracing an ancestry back through slavery to people and villages in Africa comes from educating yourself about slave trade in the area in which your ancestors lived, including how, when, and why slaves were transported to that state. Slave advertisements, bills of sale, and slave ship manifests may provide a clue to slave origins in Africa.

Canada and the Caribbean

Many people of African ancestry have immigrated to the United States from the Caribbean since the end of World War II. Some slaves were first transported to the Caribbean prior to being sent to the United States, which for some happened after a generation or more. Search for records indicating origins in the Caribbean, and familiarize yourself with the migrations of enslaved Africans from Africa to the Caribbean to America. Runaway slaves who escaped via the Underground Railroad to Canada may have re-entered the United States following the Civil War, so transit to and from Canada should also be explored.

Jewish Genealogy

The search for Jewish ancestors is unique. Unlike many ethnic cultures, no single country serves as a place of origin for Jewish people because Jews live all over the world. Centuries of religious persecution and forced migration have scattered Jewish records and instigated name changes that make Jewish research challenging, but there are many research options available.

As with all other family trees, Jewish genealogy begins with the basics. Use a variety of home sources and public and private records to trace your Jewish family tree back to the immigrant ancestor. Use immigration and naturalization records, as well as passport records, Social Security records, family letters, and other sources to determine the family's town or village of origin in the old country. Once a name has been found, consult a gazetteer to help you pinpoint the town's exact location. Because spellings often aren't accurate, the online JewishGen ShtetlSeeker (✑*www.jewishgen.org/ShtetlSeeker*), a database of more than 500,000 places in Central and Eastern Europe, allows you to search for towns by exact spelling or the Daitch-Mokotoff Soundex system.

ALERT!

When a census or other record refers to a place of origin in "Russia" it most likely does not mean the modern nation of Russia that we recognize today. Most Jews listing Russia as a place of origin lived in the outer provinces of the pre–World War I Russian Empire, areas that today are part of Poland, Lithuania, Belarus, Latvia, Moldova, and Ukraine.

Large collections of Jewish records exist in a number of libraries and archives, such as the American Jewish Archives at Hebrew Union College in Cincinnati, Ohio, and the American Jewish Historical Society in New York

City. Dozens of Jewish historical societies also maintain Jewish collections. Some of the largest include the Jewish Historical Society of Southern California in Los Angeles, the Chicago Jewish Archives, the Jewish Historical Society of New York in New York City (which is separate from the American Jewish Historical Society), and the National Museum of American Jewish History in Philadelphia. Jewish genealogical societies are another good resource. Most can be found under the umbrella of the International Association of Jewish Genealogical Societies (🖉*www.iajgs.org*).

On the Internet, the two largest Jewish genealogy resources include Avotaynu.com and JewishGen.org. Avotaynu is the Internet home of the widely regarded Jewish genealogical quarterly, *Avotaynu*, which was first published in 1985. The site features a wide variety of resources for Jewish genealogists, including a free, biweekly electronic newsletter, *Nu, What's New*, and the Consolidated Surname Index, a gateway to about 700,000 surnames, mostly Jewish, that appear in a variety of databases. JewishGen, probably the most popular site for Jewish genealogy, features a lively discussion group in which more than 5,000 Jewish genealogists participate. The site also supports the JewishGen Family Finder, a list of surnames and towns being researched by more than 55,000 Jewish genealogists throughout the world; the Family Tree of the Jewish People, a large database of family trees that have been submitted by Jewish genealogists; and the International Jewish Cemetery Project.

FACT

A basic source of information about Jewish families in the United States prior to 1840 is Malcolm H. Stern's *First American Jewish Families: 600 Genealogies, 1654–1988*. This milestone work in early American Jewish genealogy is available online as part of the American Jewish Archives at 🖉*www.americanjewisharchives.org/aja/FAJF/intro.html*, and in major genealogical libraries.

Native American Genealogy

It is possible in most cases to trace Native American genealogy back several generations. As with any ethnic group, however, the researcher faces several unique problems. Forced migrations and removals scattered the records and members of many Native American tribes. Traditions, naming customs, and kinship systems varied widely among the many Native American tribes a researcher may encounter.

Begin your search for Native American ancestry by attempting to sort out family legends from truth—not all stories of Native American ancestry are accurate. If you're not sure, the U.S. federal censuses from 1870 and later ask about Indian ancestry. A negative response doesn't mean a lack of Native American ancestry, however. Due to fear of prejudice, many Native Americans chose not to disclose their heritage. If they were of mixed race, they may also have listed whatever race was predominant.

Locating the Tribe

If the name of the tribe is known, you will be able to jump directly to the tribal records. In most cases, however, you'll need to do some research to determine the tribe to which your elusive Native American relatives belonged. It sounds simple, but in many cases the only clue is an ancestor "who appeared Indian" or a family legend of a great-grandmother who was "an Indian princess."

To narrow down tribal possibilities, educate yourself about the Native American tribes that are historically known to have resided in the geographical area where your ancestor was born, as well as those tribes who now reside in those areas. Consult *The Indian Tribes of North America* by John R. Swanton for information about more than 600 Indian tribes, subtribes, and bands. The U.S. Bureau of Indian Affairs (BIA) also publishes the Tribal Leaders Directory (*www.doi.gov/Leaders.pdf*), a list of all 562 federally recognized Native American Tribes and Alaska Natives.

ALERT!

The majority of federal records relating to Native Americans only document people who were recognized as tribal members by the federal or tribal government, and who resided with the bulk of the tribe. If your ancestor moved away from the reservation or recognized tribal boundaries, essentially ending her affiliation with the tribe, you aren't likely to find her in federal records relating to Native American tribes and nations.

Native Americans in Federal Records

The basic genealogy sources about Native Americans through 1830 are church and land records. The federal government became vigorous in transferring Native Americans to reservations between 1850 and 1887. Census records are sometimes helpful for this reservation period. The establishment of reservations necessitated government paperwork involving Native Americans by name. These records include school documents, censuses, and annuity rolls. The period between 1887 and about 1930 was what is termed the allotment period, when land was allotted to individual Native Americans. These government land grants generated allotment and family registers. Government files also contain vital facts, health records, court claims, and wills from this time.

The National Archives has many records relating to Native Americans who maintained their ties to federally recognized tribes. Most of the records, arranged by tribe, are dated 1830–1940. For historical reasons, these records are basically divided into two categories: 1) the Five Civilized Tribes, which were self-governing nations until 1906, and 2) other tribes living on reservations, who were wards of the federal government.

The term "Five Civilized Nations" is the current preferred term for the group of Native Americans composed of the Cherokee, Chickasaw, Choctaw, Muskogee Confederation (Creek), and the Seminole nations, but most older records refer to the group as the "Five Civilized Tribes." This is also the name the records are found under in the National Archives.

Records of the Five Civilized Tribes

The Five Civilized Tribes were the five major Native American tribes of the southeastern United States: the Cherokee, Chickasaw, Choctaw, Muskogee Confederation (Creek), and the Seminole. Between 1816 and 1840, these tribes signed more than forty treaties ceding their land east of the Mississippi to the federal government, and agreeing to move to "Indian Territory," a section of land set aside for these tribes in what is now the eastern portion of the state of Oklahoma. The tribes remained as self-governing nations until 1906, when the federal government reneged on its initial promises, and forced them to move to other reservations.

The first resource that should be checked for membership in one of these five Native American tribes is the *Dawes Roll*, a list of people accepted between 1898 and 1914 by the Dawes Commission as members of the Cherokee, Choctaw, Chickasaw, Creek, or Seminole tribes. Also called the "Final Rolls," this list is available on microfilm at most major genealogical libraries, and online through the National Archives (see Chapter 14: Special Situations in Family Trees in Appendix A). Another important resource is the *Guion Miller Rolls*, also available on microfilm and online. This resource includes over 45,000 applications for compensation arising from a judgment of the U.S. Court of Claims on May 28, 1906, which ruled in favor of the Eastern Cherokee tribe.

The majority of other records relating to the Five Civilized Tribes are held at the National Archives in Washington, D.C., the National Archives Federal Records Center in Fort Worth, Texas, and at the Oklahoma Historical Society. These include a variety of census records, tax lists, school records, payment rolls, enrollment records, and land allotment records (1899–1914).

QUESTION?

What is the "Trail of Tears?"
In 1838, approximately 17,000 Cherokee who refused to comply with the Indian Removal Act of 1830 (which mandated the removal of all Native American tribes east of the Mississippi) were forced at gunpoint to leave their homes and travel to what is now Oklahoma, most on foot. Many died of famine, disease, and harsh conditions along the trail—thus the term "Trail of Tears."

Records of Reservation Indians

The National Archives holds a wide variety of records relating to Indian reservations and their inhabitants. The majority of these pertain to non-Eastern Indians. Of special notice are the annual Indian censuses. Beginning in 1885 and continuing until 1940, regular censuses (usually annual) were taken by agents or superintendents in charge of Indian reservations.

Information gathered varies by year and jurisdiction, but typically the Indian census includes English and/or Native American name, tribal roll number, age or date of birth, sex, and relationship to head of household. Beginning in 1930, the censuses also shows degree of Native American blood, marital status, and place of residence.

The census was not conducted for every reservation or group of Native Americans every year. The census rolls that do exist, compiled by the Bureau of Indian Affairs, are available on microfilm from the National Archives, and in some state and local historical and genealogy libraries.

Records from the Bureau of Indian Affairs (BIA) in the collection of the National Archives include school records, land records, special censuses, and documents relating to government payments to reservation Indians as required by treaty or legislation. Annuity payrolls include lists of annual payments made to tribal members by the federal government. Allotment records, based on the General Allotment Act of 1887, detail government allotment of reservation land to individual tribe members. Arranged by tribe, these records usually include applications, lists of allottees, plat maps, and improvements made to the land.

Other Ethnic Groups

Special research aids have been written to help people find ancestors of pretty much all ethnic backgrounds, including Acadian, French-Canadian, Polish, German, Hispanic, Irish, Scottish, Italian, Asian, Scandinavian, and Eastern European. *The Source: A Guidebook of American Genealogy* includes chapters and bibliographies of helpful books and articles for a variety of ethnic groups.

Joining an ethnic genealogical society provides access to genealogists who have an interest in ethnic research. Many such societies provide access to unique research libraries, collections, workshops, conferences, newsletters, and publications specific to the ethnic group.

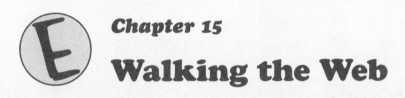

Chapter 15

Walking the Web

The Internet doesn't change history—it just presents it with whistles and bells. The explosion of online genealogy has affected the way most genealogists do research. Online access to digitized records, the ability to make immediate connections with distant relatives and fellow researchers, and the ease of searching electronic databases compared to reeling through microfilm entice new genealogists to the computer each day. Though the Internet doesn't replace traditional genealogy research, it is a powerful tool that can help bring the past into the present.

Finding a Tree in the Forest

Great-grandma's obituary, the 1880 U.S. census, cemetery transcriptions, county histories, your ancestor's land records—the Internet boasts millions of pages of genealogical content in the form of digitized records, electronic databases, and family Web sites devoted to genealogy research. The sheer volume of genealogy data available online means you have to know how to find things, to locate the information that pertains to your individual ancestors in the haystack of family tree records.

Search Strategies

The key to locating information about your family tree online is to search efficiently with several different search engines. Each search engine works slightly differently from the others and they will not all return the same results, even when the same search terms are entered. That's because different search engines index different Web pages, and no search engine will find every page on the Internet. Some search engines search only titles or portions of the content, while others claim to search every word on every page. Some will only return results that include all of your search terms, assuming an *and* between the words. Some ignore common words—known as stop words—such as *the*, *a*, and *how*. Many require that you enclose a phrase in quotes to search for that specific phrase. Others allow you to limit your search to a particular domain, country, language, or Web site. Make it a habit to read the help section or frequently asked questions (FAQ) of the search engines you use to familiarize yourself with their specific search features.

ALERT!

If you find a link to a promising Web site that no longer exists, try entering the URL in the Wayback Machine (✎*www.archive.org*), an archived collection of more than 10 billion Web pages. Google (✎*www.google. com*) also maintains cached old pages. Just click on the word "cached" after the URL listing in the search engine results.

Boolean operators, search phrases, and other tricks can help you craft an effective search engine query. They help you limit and fine-tune your results to something manageable and, hopefully, relevant to what you are looking for. For example, a plain search for *william pitt* in Google returns 2,200,000 pages. If, however, the search is crafted as *william pitt −county −university* (with minus signs preceding words you want omitted from the search), the results are down to 802,000 pages. This search helps eliminate the many Web pages that reference Pitt County in North Carolina, and the University of Pittsburgh, affectionately called "Pitt." Enclosing the name in quotes as *"william pitt"* limits the search even further, to just 192,000 pages.

Boolean Logic—And, Or, Not

Don't let your eyes glaze over; you don't need to be a math whiz to understand the basics of Boolean logic. Basically, all it means is that you'll be using the terms *and*, *or*, and *not* to help explain to a search engine what you're trying to find. To make it even easier, the majority of search engines allow you to use a plus sign (+) for *and* and a minus sign (–) for *not*.

+ Used as an equivalent to the Boolean operator *and*, the plus symbol (+) requires the search engine to find Web pages that contain the word that follows the plus sign. There should not be a space between the plus sign and the word. Searching for *+crisp +family +tree* will bring up pages that contain all three words. You may, however, get a page discussing someone eating apple *crisp* under a *tree* at a *family* picnic. Use of the plus sign doesn't guarantee that the words will appear adjacent to each other, or in any particular order. Most search engines assume an *and* between search terms, whether you include the plus sign or not. The plus sign also forces a search engine to include stop words, such as *a*, *an*, *the*, *how*, and *where* in its searches.

– Used to represent the Boolean operator *not*, the minus symbol (–) lets you exclude specific words from your search. This is especially useful when searching for surnames with a common usage, such as rice (*rice –food –cook*); place names that exist in more than one locality (*charleston –wv*); or an ancestor who shares one name in common with a famous celebrity (*ford –harrison*).

OR The Web page must contain at least one of the search terms. Remember that most search engines default to searching for *all* of your terms rather than *any* of them, so this search is particularly useful when your search term includes synonyms (*ireland OR eire*; *cemetery OR gravestone OR tombstone*). Include the OR in capital letters.

Phrase Searching

Many genealogy searches bring back too many results, even when using "+" and "–" symbols to limit your search. This is especially true for databases, transcriptions, and the wealth of other genealogy pages that contain long lists of names. A search for *+william +crisp* will return pages with names such as "William Powell" and "Sam Crisp," with no trace of a "William Crisp." This is where phrase searching becomes powerful.

FACT

Before the birth of the Internet as we know it, a computer network called Usenet connected genealogists via e-mail, newsgroups, and file transfers. The first genealogy newsgroup, net.roots, was formed on October 31, 1983. By 1990 the World Wide Web had still not arrived, but genealogy was already in full swing on the Internet through various online services and bulletin boards.

Phrase searching uses quotes to force the search engine to search for a particular phrase. This will return only pages that have all the words in the exact order shown. When using quotes to search for proper names, phrase your search in both the FIRST NAME, LAST and LAST NAME, FIRST formats ("William Powell" and "Powell, William"). Genealogy databases and transcriptions may include names in either format.

Wildcard Searching

Most search engines and large genealogy databases support wildcard searching. This allows you to enter a specific wildcard character—usually an asterisk (*)—in place of one or more letters in the word. This is especially useful for searching for plurals of a word, or variations in spelling. A search for *owen**, for example, would bring back OWEN and OWENS, while a search for *pat** would also return sites with Patrick, Patricia, Patterson, and so on.

In most cases search queries should be entered in all lowercase, even when searching for proper names, because some search engines are case sensitive. If you enter a search term in all lowercase letters, all search engines will match both upper and lower case letters on the Web page (a search for *smith* will return smith, Smith, and SMITH).

Keep in mind, however, that the more general the wildcard, the more cluttered your search results will be with unrelated pages. For example, your search for *pat** will also return sites containing words such as *patent*, *patio*, and *pâté*. This is why wildcard searches are generally most effective in large genealogy databases, where the search engine already knows that you're entering a name or location. In that case, the wildcard can help locate alternate spellings.

Don't Just Search for Surnames

Unless you're searching for a very unusual surname, your search results will contain Web pages about everyone who shares the same last name. You'll get better results if you use another relevant search term in conjunction with the surname. One of the best to start with is the word "genealogy." Search for *+your surname +genealogy* or *+your surname +family* to bring up pages that are more likely to relate to family history. You can also try similar searches such as *+your surname "family tree"* or *+your surname +ancestry*.

Why wade through SMITH pages from Zimbabwe when your SMITH ancestors lived in Louisiana? Another excellent qualifier for a surname search is to add a place name, usually the name of the town, village, county, or state where your family lived, such as *+smith +virginia*. If the place name is more than one word long, include it in quotes (*"north carolina" +smith*).

Another useful search technique is to combine the primary surname with other family names. Pairing the surname with a given name is the most obvious, but you can also combine it with other more uncommon surnames in the same family. If your SMITH married a SNAGGLEPUSS, then a search for *+smith +snagglepuss* may help locate relevant Web pages.

Connecting with Cousins

There was a time, way back when, when several generations of a family lived close together, rarely moving to a new area unless they went as a family group. People knew their great-aunts, second cousins, and even third cousins. Today, however, many families have drifted apart, finding themselves scattered around the country, out of touch with their roots. Locating relatives with whom you've lost touch or exchanging e-mails with a distant cousin that you never knew existed is a very rewarding part of family tree research. It can lead to the discovery of old family photos, stories, and documents that were passed down another branch of the family tree, as well as the discovery of some potential new kin who are as excited about family history as you are! Fortunately, the Internet offers a variety of means for tracking down and communicating with long-lost relatives, bringing people together in a way never before possible.

Mailing Lists

Genealogy mailing lists offer an easy way for family history enthusiasts to connect with others working on the same lines, or pursuing similar research interests.

Because mailing lists come to you via e-mail, they make it easy to stay in touch. There are a few ways to go about finding the right mailing list to suit your searching needs:

- **Searching for Surnames**—Unless you are researching an extremely unusual last name, there is probably a mailing list with your name on it. These surname-focused lists offer one of the best ways to connect with other researchers who may have information about your family, as well as potential cousins.
- **Look by Location**—Focused on research in a particular country, state, county, parish, or other location, these lists are a good way to find relatives who may still be living in the area, as well as exchanging information and records with others also doing research there.
- **Need a Helping Hand?**—Even expert genealogists need help every now and then, and dozens of mailing lists revolve around the exchange of help, advice, and ideas. As sounding boards for genealogy questions and concerns, there are mailing lists for all levels of family historians wanting to improve their research skills.
- **What's Your Interest?**—Hundreds of genealogy mailing lists cover specialized topics, such as Jewish genealogy, Civil War research, witch trials, DNA, royalty, or Ellis Island immigration. Hundreds more connect people with similar interests or backgrounds, including RVing genealogists, disabled genealogists, teens, and seniors.

Thousands of mailing lists and newsgroups have been established, each with a primary focus. The majority deal with specific surnames and geographic locations, but there are also mailing lists for specialized research topics ranging from newbie genealogy to the Andersonville Civil War Prison.

How Mailing Lists Work
Begin by selecting one or two mailing lists that tie into your research interests. If you're researching the Butler family, for example, subscribe to

the Butler genealogy mailing list. Introduce yourself to the other list members and share details about the Butler family you are researching. Since everyone else on the list is also researching the Butler surname, you may find others with information about your family, or who are interested in collaborating on research.

Generally, subscribing to a mailing list just requires sending an e-mail to an administration address with the word *subscribe* in the subject line. This will automatically add you to a list of subscribers. When you subscribe, you'll have the option of receiving the e-mails in list mode or digest mode. In list mode, sometimes called mail mode, you'll receive each message posted to the list individually, as they are sent. For smaller lists, this may be as few as two or three e-mails per week. Some larger lists, however, generate several dozen e-mails per day. For these, digest mode may be the better option, as it batches individual e-mails together and sends them as one large e-mail. Digest mode means you'll have less e-mail cluttering your inbox, but can make it harder to follow the thread of a conversation.

FACT

When you subscribe to a genealogy mailing list, be sure you have turned off your signature file and removed any additional words in the message body. Your subscribe request will be read by a computer that is designed to look for a certain format. If you do not follow that format, you won't be successfully subscribed to the list.

Finding the Lists

The best place to start is RootsWeb (*http://lists.rootsweb.com*), which sponsors more than 28,000 genealogy-related mailing lists. Locality-specific mailing lists are offered for most areas through USGenWeb.com and WorldGenWeb.com, although the majority of these are sponsored through RootsWeb and can also be found there. Genealogical societies, family tree software publishers, and a variety of independent genealogy groups also sponsor their own mailing lists.

I've Joined a Mailing List—Now What?

Genealogy mailing lists are a type of community. Much like the differences between city neighborhoods and rural villages, these discussion groups reflect the varied interests and personalities of their members. Some lists are chatty and sociable, a great place for forming friendships as well as pursuing research interests. Others are very focused, and allow no "off-topic" or personal discussion. It's really a matter of personal preference.

The mailing list moderator should make it clear in the welcome letter what the rules are, but it also helps to "lurk" for a few days to get a feel for the list's community before you post your first message. Many mailing lists also save an archive of their past messages online. Browsing through these can also provide a good feel for the members, frequency, and types of discussions.

"Read Only" Mailing Lists

These read-only lists are actually electronic newsletters, sometimes called e-zines, which you can subscribe to and receive on a daily, weekly, or monthly basis, depending on the publication schedule. These differ from conventional mailing lists in that their sole purpose is to distribute the newsletter or e-zine, and there is no back-and-forth discussion. Refer to Appendix A for a list of major electronic genealogy newsletters.

ALERT!

When you hit "Reply" to respond to a mailing list message, be sure to look at where your reply is going. For some lists, any replies automatically go to the sender. Other mailing lists default to send responses to everyone. If you're sharing something personal or potentially embarrassing, be sure the mailing list address isn't in your "Reply To" field!

Message Boards and Forums

Similar to mailing lists, free genealogy message boards and forums have sprung up around pretty much every surname and research topic imaginable. The major difference is that mailing lists use e-mail for communication, while message boards require you to visit to read and post messages. One distinct advantage of message boards, however, is that many are indexed by the search engines, providing the potential for your posts and queries to reach a larger audience.

Some message boards provide the option for you to have a notification sent to your e-mail address when someone responds to any posts you have made. Selecting this option ensures that you won't miss important replies. You should also keep a running list of the message boards where you have left queries, so you can check back on a periodic basis.

Message boards also allow you to search or browse through past posts, providing yet another avenue for connecting with others researching your family. Visit message boards for your primary surnames of interest and try some searches on the given names or locations for your particular family. Then stop by the forums that focus on the localities where your ancestors lived and search for the names in your family tree. Don't neglect to search beyond the immediate family for spouses, neighbors, and other related individuals. It's possible that people searching for those surnames may have information about your family as well.

If you find a post that relates to your family, take the time to reply with the reasons you think you are connected, what you have to share, and any questions you may have about the post.

Online genealogists tend to be generous, but no one likes to feel used. If you're free with sharing your information, you will receive more in return.

Message boards and forums can be found on many genealogy Web sites. The largest, most frequented boards are those at GenForum.com and Ancestry. com. Both of these sites include thousands of message boards focused on surnames, localities, and a wide variety of genealogy research interests.

Although not a true message board, CousinConnect.com is another popular place for connecting with other researchers. It's dedicated solely to queries, and responses go directly to your e-mail instead of being posted to the site.

More Ways to Locate Living Relatives

Posting queries on genealogy message boards and mailing lists will locate most living relatives who are also interested in the family tree. But what about the ones who aren't? There are many cousins out there who aren't actively visiting genealogy Web sites, and some who may not even have Internet access. How can you connect with them?

The Internet offers a wealth of resources for tracking down living people, including telephone and business directories, databases of personal information, and access to organizations such as business associations and veteran's groups. Living relatives may also be found through personal family Web pages, class reunion sites such as Classmates.com, and online people search services, including KnowX.com, InteliUS.com, and USsearch.com.

Mining Electronic Databases

Lineage-linked databases, indexed databases, and digitized records are where the Web is really starting to shine in terms of tracking down the people in your family tree. When you visit a major online genealogy site, you'll typically find collections of transcribed records and compiled family histories organized into large databases. More and more are also scanning original images into digital format, and creating indexes to facilitate searching.

Lineage-Linked Databases

While it's not really true that everyone's family tree is on the Web, chances are good that you'll find at least some portion of your family tree listed in a lineage-linked database. These databases combine family information submitted by various researchers into large collections of linked family trees. Almost all are available for free online searching, and the largest contain millions of names. A few lineage-linked databases are only available on CD-ROM or through an online subscription.

Lineage-linked databases and similar family tree sites allow you to view and print family trees, or download them as GEDCOM files for importing into your own family tree software. (See Chapter 17 to learn how to read, create, and share GEDCOM files.) Most also allow you to contact the submitter of the file.

FamilySearch Databases

The FamilySearch Web site sponsored by the Church of Jesus Christ of Latter-day Saints (LDS) offers two different family tree databases for searching. Ancestral File, which contains more than 35 million names, is the older of the two lineage-linked databases. It was created primarily from records and pedigree charts submitted to the Family History Department of the LDS Church since 1979. Duplicate individuals from various contributors have been merged, which has led to some errors, and source information other than the name of the submitter is not included.

The Pedigree Resource File also contains family trees submitted by individuals to the LDS Church. It differs from the Ancestral File in that the information appears as it was originally submitted, and is not merged with information submitted by others. It also contains notes and sources when provided by the contributor. The index to the Pedigree Resource File can be searched online, but you'll have to purchase the set of CD-ROMs that contains that particular family for access to the full GEDCOM file, including source citations. These are sold at cost by the Family History Library, generally in sets of five with a combined 1.1 million names.

www.familysearch.org/Eng/Search/frameset_search.asp

If you find what you think is your family in a lineage-linked database, don't succumb to the temptation to download the file and add it directly to your own research. You first need to be sure that *all* the information fits, and that you've checked the accuracy of any original documents listed in the sources.

Ancestry World Tree / RootsWeb World Connect

This huge pedigree database contains more than 385,000 million names from family trees submitted to the RootsWeb World Connect Project, begun in 1996, and Ancestry World Tree, begun in 1997. The two databases are now merged into Ancestry World Tree, which provides advanced search options, submitter contact information, and the ability to add electronic "Post-it" notes with comments, updates, additions, or corrections to any family tree.

http://worldconnect.rootsweb.com

GenCircles Global Tree

Another popular database of lineage-linked family trees, GenCircles Global Tree contains information about more than 90 million individuals, contributed by users of the site. If you've submitted your own GEDCOM file to GenCircles, you can take advantage of its "matching technology" to pair the people in your family tree file with others in the database.

www.gencircles.com/globaltree

GeneaNet.org

This pedigree database boasts more international family trees than most, and can be accessed in many languages as well. Because it was founded in France, GeneaNet is especially useful for tracing French and other European family trees. There is a cost to upgrade to a Privilege Club membership, but you can access many of the site's useful features free of charge. A handy e-mail alert can even notify you when new trees are added that match the criteria you set.

www.geneanet.org

Family Trees by Subscription

Subscription or CD-based lineage-linked databases include MyTrees. com, Genealogy.com's *World Family Tree* series, Millisecond Publishing Company's *Family Forest*, and Everton's *Bureau of Missing Ancestors*. Like the databases already discussed, these also contain millions of individuals linked together into family trees.

Compiled Databases and Digitized Records

Once you've explored the family research previously done by others, it's time to turn to actual data—in the form of indexes, transcriptions, and even digitized copies of original records. These types of genealogy resources, ranging from transcribed passenger lists to scanned images of original land patents, can be found in numerous places online.

USGenWeb

This massive volunteer project includes Web sites for every county in the United States, each maintained by volunteers. Researchers have submitted a wide variety of genealogy-related records for each county, from transcribed cemetery lists to census indexes and marriage bonds. In addition, there are links to Web sites with more county-specific information, and mailing lists and message boards for interaction with other genealogists doing research in the area. Best of all, everything is free.

When citing a source from the Internet, you should record the following: the author, person or agency who wrote the content or sponsors the Web site; the name of the Web site or subject line of the e-mail; the Web site address (URL); and the date you found the information, or the date of the e-mail.

Pay as You Go

Free is great, but there may come a time when you want more than the free genealogy resources can offer. Several large commercial sites offer access to numerous published genealogical databases and indexes for a monthly or annual subscription fee. The largest of these are Ancestry.com and Genealogy.com, both owned by the same parent company. Generally, subscription genealogy sites offer a free trial so you can check out their offerings, but will charge your credit card for a subscription if you don't cancel before the trial period expires. Many libraries also offer AncestryPlus, a library version of Ancestry.com, to their patrons—but this resource cannot be accessed via the Internet.

HeritageQuest Online, free to members of subscribing libraries, societies, and institutions, provides searchable indexes to several large collections of digitized census records, historical newspapers, and family and local histories. Check with your local library or genealogical society to find out whether it subscribes. If not, some societies and libraries will allow anyone to join as a member, no matter where they live. The Godfrey Scholar program at Godfrey Memorial Library in Middletown, Connecticut, is touted by many as one of the best such deals (*www.godfrey.org*).

Sharing Your Success

Once your family tree has started to take shape, it's fun to share the success with others. The Internet is perfect for this, allowing you to send an electronic newsletter (see Chapter 21), build a family Web site, create a research group, or exchange photos or GEDCOM files (see Chapter 17) with other interested researchers.

FACT

Facts, such as names and dates, cannot be protected by copyright. This means that anyone can use these details from your family tree. What is protected, however, is creative expression—the way in which you present your data. Your words, designs, and compilations are your own, so post a note that this information cannot be used without your permission.

Creating a family Web site is your best chance for collaborating with other researchers around the world. By posting your family tree data on the Internet, you create a means for others who are researching those same individuals to find you.

If you're already Web savvy, you can create and host a Web site at one of several existing domains, such as RootsWeb.com, that offer free or low-cost space for genealogy sites. Or register your own domain name and start from scratch.

If thoughts of HTML and FTP make your head spin, check out the low-cost family sites offered by MyFamily.com. This site offers predesigned lay-outs, plenty of space for sharing photos and other family files, and e-mail addresses for each of your family members. The Web site you create is also password-protected, so you can share addresses, phone numbers, and other personal information without worrying about posting it in a public place.

Chapter 16

Shelves of Possibilities

Given the current trend toward making historical records available online, it can take just a few minutes at a keyboard to uncover a branch of your family tree. For every cemetery transcription and census record found on the Internet, however, there are thousands of other genealogical records waiting to be discovered in courthouses, libraries, and other repositories around the country. Once you've used the Internet to compile initial facts and identify possible ancestors, it's time to take your family tree research on the road—exploring the genealogy resources found on a bookshelf.

Published Indexes and Compilations

Whether collected, transcribed, abstracted, or indexed from other records, published sources are a valuable tool in the family tree adventure. Indexes, databases, and other compiled records can help you quickly determine which original record sources are most likely to include information about your ancestors, allowing you to benefit from the work already done by others.

From published family and county histories to census indexes and cemetery transcriptions, published sources can help you quickly fill in the branches of your family tree. Traditional print sources include family genealogies, county histories, cemetery transcriptions, and indexed or abstracted original records such as census enumerations, military records, passenger lists, and estate records. Digital and online compilations run the gamut from larger databases such as the SSDI (Social Security Death Index) and Ellis Island passenger arrivals database to smaller, more specialized resources including local cemetery transcriptions, abstracted court records, military rosters, and indexed marriage bonds.

Printed Records

When looking for published family history information, begin with the card catalog of a major genealogy library or a public library that serves the area in which your ancestors lived. Search by surname and location to compile a list of resources that may include information about your family.

For more obscure family or local histories, you should also consult the Library of Congress (✐www.loc.gov) and Family History Library (✐www. familysearch.org) catalogs, both of which can be searched online.

The state and county genealogy Web sites of the USGenWeb Project (✐www.usgenweb.com) are another good place to find lists of published sources for a particular locality, along with volunteers who may be able to check these sources for information about your ancestor. Be sure that you don't overlook local genealogical or historical societies; they often include unpublished family genealogies among their holdings, along with the more traditional printed indexes, abstracts, and compilations.

Check the Facts

Remember the telephone game you played as a kid? You would whisper a short sentence into someone's ear. By the time the message had passed through a dozen people it was so different from the original that it had everyone laughing hysterically. Similarly, the accuracy and completeness of published sources, which are one or more steps removed from the original records, vary as widely as their content. Some online databases may have content that is three steps or more removed from the original records, greatly increasing the likelihood of errors and omissions (an example might be a digital database compiled from a published county history that contains facts and stories collected by various authors from a variety of original and published sources).

It may be tempting to immediately add the new clues found in such compiled works to your family tree, but the limitations of a published source should first be taken into account. Examine the source citations for their quality and completeness and spot-check several of the facts through examination of the original sources.

ALERT!

Published sources are extremely useful for providing a foundation for your research and leads to other sources, but they are only as good as their authors or compilers.

Libraries and Archives

Access to a tremendous variety of published books, indexes, and original and microfilmed records is available through numerous archives and libraries around the country. Some of these facilities maintain large genealogy collections of a national scope, while others serve as repositories for state, regional, or local records. Aside from the books and records, the staff at most libraries and archives are also a treasure. Many are genealogists themselves, with a broad knowledge of family history research techniques and records. Even those who know little about genealogy are trained researchers, able to quickly locate and access information of all types.

Archives Versus Library

There are many exceptions to the rule, but in general, archives focus primarily on microfilmed and original copies of genealogical and historical records pertinent to their covered area, including vital, census, military, land, estate, and court records. Libraries, on the other hand, typically concentrate on records of more social significance, including local histories, family genealogies, biographies, diaries, newspapers, census records, maps, and published abstracts and compiled records. Archives are usually found at the regional or state level. Libraries, however, run the gamut from the massive Family History Library in Salt Lake City to public and private libraries located at the state, county, or local level. Some churches, ethnic groups, genealogical societies, and colleges and universities also maintain libraries with rich genealogical holdings.

Although there is obviously quite a bit of overlap among the collections of various types of repositories, researchers typically start at the library for a review of published sources, and then follow up with original records at the archives or similar historical repository. Alternatively, you can just begin at the repository that is the most convenient to visit in person.

FACT

The National Archives and Records Administration (NARA) oversees the management of all federal government records, including census records, military service records, passenger arrival lists, and post-1906 naturalization records. It operates main archive centers in Washington, D.C. and College Park, Maryland, and regional research centers in Anchorage; Atlanta; Boston; Chicago; Denver; Fort Worth; Kansas City, Missouri; Laguna Niguel, California; New York; Philadelphia; San Francisco; and Seattle.

Libraries with Major Genealogical Collections

Several large libraries contain genealogical departments with records of a national or international scope. They all make their library catalogs available on the Internet, and most also offer some type of online access to a small portion of their collections.

FamilySearch, the online arm of the Family History Library, is in the process of digitizing their entire collection of microfilmed family history records, with plans to eventually make them available online. That's more than 2.3 million rolls of microfilm, the equivalent of about six million 300-page printed volumes.

The Family History Library

Discussed in greater detail later in this chapter, the Family History Library, in Salt Lake City, contains the world's largest collection of genealogical records. If you can't travel to Utah, you can access the same records at any one of a network of local Family History Centers. Online, you can access the Family History Library Catalog, as well as the International Genealogical Index, Pedigree Resource File, 1880 U.S. Census, 1881 Canadian Census, 1881 British Isles Census, and a Vital Records Index for Mexico and Scandinavia.

✑*www.familysearch.org*

Library of Congress

The Local History and Genealogy Reading Room at the Library of Congress includes published genealogies and Civil War regimental histories, and the Geography and Map Division maintains an extensive collection of historical maps. The American Memory Collection offers online access to historic maps, photos, documents, audio, and video that document the American experience.

✑*www.loc.gov*

New England Historic Genealogical Society Library

A must-stop library for individuals with ancestors from the New England states or eastern Canada, the New England Historic Genealogical Society (NEHGS) Research Library offers a comprehensive collection of books, periodicals, microfilmed materials, and manuscripts. A circulating library offers members at-home access to certain items from the library's collection. Numerous online genealogical databases and articles also are available to members.

✍*www.newenglandancestors.org*

FACT

The New England Historic Genealogical Society is the oldest genealogical society in the entire country. It was founded in 1845 and voted to allow women to join in 1898. It now boasts over 20,000 members from all over the world.

Allen County Public Library

This public library, which is located in Fort Wayne, Indiana, is the second largest genealogical library in the United States. Its genealogy-related holdings include more than 600,000 items, in the form of books, microfilm, and microfiche. Primary areas of interest include the United States, Canada, and Europe. You can search the library's catalog and surname file online.

✍*www.acpl.lib.in.us/genealogy*

DAR Library

Established in 1900, the library of the National Society Daughters of the American Revolution is a treasure for individuals researching early American ancestors. The collection boasts several hundred thousand books, files, manuscripts, and microforms, as well as unpublished genealogical records. The organization's Web site provides access to the library catalog and the DAR Patriot Lookup Service.

✍*www.dar.org*

Newberry Library

This independent Chicago library provides access to more than 17,000 genealogies, many from Colonial America, as well as census records, city directories, and numerous other genealogy resources from the United States, Canada, Great Britain, and Ireland. You can access guides to specific collections and a portion of the library catalog online.

www.newberry.org/genealogy

New York Public Library

The Local History and Genealogy Department of the New York Public Library maintains one of the nation's largest publicly accessible genealogical collections, including extensive holdings of local, state, national, and international scope. The NYPL Digital Gallery offers free viewing and downloading of more than 337,000 digital images from primary sources including rare prints, historical maps, illustrated manuscripts and books, vintage posters, rare photographs, and printed ephemera.

www.nypl.org/research/chss/lhg/research.html

Clayton Library

Another of the top genealogy libraries in the United States, this center, located in Houston, Texas, is visited by thousands of researchers from all over the country each month. Texas residents with a library card can access several online genealogical databases.

www.hpl.lib.tx.us/clayton

Genealogical Repositories Online

Every state in the United States maintains a Web site for its library and archives. These Web sites usually include helpful information such as hours and directions, finding aids, and answers to frequently asked questions. Some even include Internet access to compiled indexes or digitized copies of original records.

LDS Family History Center

Owned and operated by the Church of Jesus Christ of Latter-day Saints (LDS), more commonly known as the Mormons, the Family History Library in Salt Lake City provides access to the world's largest collection of genealogical records. More than three million records have been gathered, abstracted, or microfilmed by the church since 1894, in an effort to assist members in tracing their family histories.

While there is almost nothing as exciting to a genealogist as a visit to this great library, a trek to Salt Lake City isn't necessary to make use of its resources. The Family History Library is just the cornerstone of a vast system of more than 4,000 branch libraries known as Family History Centers. Usually located inside church buildings, these genealogy research centers operate in more than eighty-eight countries.

FACT

More than 100,000 rolls of microfilm, including court, vital, census, land, church, and probate records from all over the world, are circulated to the Family History Centers each month in response to genealogy requests by researchers.

You don't need to be a member of the Latter-day Saints to utilize the resources and services of any Family History Center. These library branches are open free to the public, and are staffed on a nonprofit basis by local church and community volunteers. Although the libraries are funded by the Latter-day Saints church, you don't need to worry about religion being an issue. Family History Centers are focused on genealogy, nothing else.

What to Expect

Each Family History Center (FHC) is different. Some centers are large and complex, much like a public library, while others consist of one small room with a single computer and microfilm reader. Whatever its size, each FHC will offer Internet, CD-ROM, and/or microfiche access to the Church's various databases, including the *International Genealogical Index* (IGI),

Pedigree Resource File, and Family History Library Catalog. A number of books, microfilms, and microfiche, typically focused on the research interests of members and resources from the local area, will also be available as part of the permanent collection.

The Family History Library Catalog

Available at all FHCs as well as online at FamilySearch.org, the Family History Library Catalog is a finding aid to the vast genealogical holdings of the Family History Library. Search by surname to locate published family histories or by locality to learn which original and published records are available on microfilm for your research area. Once you've located an item of interest, click on "View Film Notes" for details and the FHL call number for each individual microfilm or microfiche.

Microfilm is a roll of film containing reduced images of documents. It is widely used to preserve records of genealogical value, because of its durability and is viewed on a microfilm reader that enlarges the images. *Microfiche* are single sheets or cards of photographic film containing reduced images, and are also read with a special viewer.

Requesting Records from Salt Lake City

The most valuable use of the Family History Centers is to request copies of most of the records available at the Family History Library in Salt Lake City. These records, catalogued in the Family History Library Catalog, are available on either microfilm or microfiche. A small fee is charged by the Family History Center for each requested item. This covers the costs of making a copy of the original microfilm stored at the Family History Library and mailing it to your local FHC.

Temporary, Indefinite, and Permanent Loans

When the microfilm or microfiche arrives at the FHC, it will be available for you and other patrons to use until the loan period has expired. Microfiche are available for indefinite loan, generally becoming a part of the FHC's permanent collection. Microfilmed records, however, offer three different loan options. The initial loan period is thirty days, allowing enough time for the researcher to evaluate the record and make a few notes or copies. If more research time is needed, you can renew the microfilm for an additional period of sixty days. If the record covers an area in which you have numerous ancestors and is one that you find yourself consulting frequently, you can place a third renewal order. This places the item on indefinite loan to your Family History Center, making it available to you for as long as you want. Each additional loan renewal term, including indefinite loan, will usually require an additional fee.

QUESTION?

May I immediately request an item for indefinite loan?
If you know up-front that you want a specific record placed on indefinite loan, the FHC volunteer can set this up for you, avoiding the necessity of remembering to renew the rental before the film is returned to the Family History Library.

Visiting the Courthouse

A place almost every genealogist visits eventually, the local courthouse is the cornerstone of family tree research. From the birth of their children to their first purchase of land, the joys and hardships of your ancestors' lives can often be found documented among the numerous original records of the local court. Divisions of estates, land deeds, marriage certificates, naturalizations, and other transactions that required the court's intervention are tucked away in folders, boxes, and books—a wealth of information just waiting to be discovered.

Planning Ahead

The first, and most important, step in courthouse research is determining which courthouse most likely had jurisdiction over the area in which your ancestors lived during the time they lived there. In most of the United States, this is the county courthouse. In Louisiana, parishes are the county equivalent.

Some states, such as Alaska and many of the New England states, do not operate on a county system. Instead, records in these localities may be found housed in town halls, probate districts, or other jurisdictional authorities.

FACT

In a few states, most notably Virginia, independent cities are another exception to the general county jurisdiction rule, each operating with its own independent court system and courthouse.

Remember, ancestors who lived in one county in the mid-1800s may have actually purchased their land decades earlier under the jurisdiction of the parent county. Records for counties that no longer exist may be stored in the courthouse that presently serves the area, or in the state archives or other facility.

Several published resources can be valuable for determining when each county was created, verifying the existence and location of some of the most valuable records, and providing contact information for each courthouse. The most widely used include the Everton's *Handy Book for Genealogists,* Ancestry's *Redbook*, and the *Family Tree Resource Book for Genealogists* edited by Sharon DeBartolo Carmack. Local county Web sites may also include quite a bit of helpful information.

If this is your first visit to a courthouse, there are a number of practical considerations that you might not have thought about. You can usually obtain the information you need by visiting the Web site for the courthouse or the local genealogical society, or by calling the courthouse itself.

QUESTION?

When is the best time to go to the courthouse?
Try to avoid visiting the courthouse on Mondays, Fridays, and the last week of the month, as these are usually the busiest times. Courthouses are often cramped enough without having to compete with busy clerks and attorneys for record books and research space.

Are the Records Available?

In some states, many of the original county records may have been transferred to the state archives or another repository. In many cases, these records will still be available on microfilm at the courthouse. In other situations, the indexes may be located at the courthouse proper, while the record books themselves are stored in another, off-site facility. In cases such as these, you'll often need to provide at least twenty-four hours' advance notice in order to have the record books brought to the courthouse for your examination. You may be allowed to visit the off-site storage facility yourself, but you still need to allow time for the back-and-forth travel when preparing for your visit. Occasionally, certain record books may also be temporarily unavailable due to repair or preservation work.

ALERT!

If someone tells you that the courthouse records were destroyed by fire, flood, or other disaster, keep in mind that this may not mean all of the records. Some may have been stored in another location or survived partially intact. Other records—especially land records—may have also been re-created after the tragedy as people brought in their original records to be re-recorded.

What to Take to the Courthouse

Courthouse offices are often small and cramped, so it is best to keep your belongings to a minimum. Pack a single bag or briefcase with a pad of lined paper or a notebook; pens and pencils; coins for the photocopier and parking; a list of your research goals; a brief summary of what you already know about the family; and a camera (if allowed). Some courthouses only allow access to members of a state or local genealogical or historical society. If this is the case, don't forget to take your membership card! If you plan to take a laptop computer, make sure that you have a charged battery, because many courthouses will not provide electrical access.

FACT

Using a digital camera to photograph documents can provide a cost- and time-saving alternative to traditional photocopies. For best results, you'll need at least a 3-megapixel camera with optical (not digital) zoom, and a flash that can be switched off. Just be sure to ask in advance whether cameras are permitted, and take good notes just in case.

Types of Records

From land patents to guardianship petitions, the type and variety of records found at the courthouse will differ greatly depending upon the area and time period you're researching. In general, your first visits to the courthouse are likely to involve searching one or more of the following record groups.

Land Records

The Recorder of Deeds or similar courthouse department will house the county's recorded deeds, mortgages, plats, survey books, and other land-related records. In some cases the records may also include copies of original land grants and patents, although these are more often found in more central, statewide facilities.

Vital Records

Early births, deaths, and marriages may be found among the records of the county courthouse, although more modern vital records are usually housed at the state level—such as in the Department of Health. In many cases, the county also holds copies of these more recent records.

Wills and Estates

Typically found in the court department designated as the Register of Wills, Probate Department, or Surrogate's Court, estate records include wills, administrations, estate inventories and accounts, guardianships, bonds, and other estate-related records.

Civil Court Records

Civil court proceedings may detail a variety of matters of genealogical interest, including adoptions, divorce, custody, bastardry (children born out of wedlock), property disputes and, sometimes, naturalizations. In Pennsylvania, they're located in the prothonotary's office.

Deciphering the Indexes

Depending upon the type of record and location of the courthouse, you may face a variety of different indexing systems in the record books. Some of the more complicated, but most widely used, indexing systems include the Russell Index, the Cott Index, and the Campbell Index. Several other indexing systems are also in use around the country.

ALERT!

If you find an index that you don't feel comfortable with, don't be afraid to ask the clerk for assistance. It's definitely preferable to overlooking your ancestor's records because you're using the index incorrectly!

The Russell Index

The Russell Index is a popular indexing system used in many courthouses around the country. It is similar to the Soundex system, in that it groups surnames based on certain key letters. The index includes a chart in which you choose a column based on the surname's key letter and a row based on the first initial of the given name to determine the page number on which the individual is indexed.

The Cott Index

There are a number of variations on the Cott Index, but in general they use some type of index system to divide surnames into groups and then organize given names within the surname grouping in alphabetical order. Given names with more than one entry are typically displayed in chronological order. One of the more common variations of the Cott Index is to break down the surname by its first two or three letters. In this example,

Tom Jones might be found listed among the surnames that begin with the letters *JO*, under given names that begin with the letter *T*.

The Campbell Index

Often referred to as a "first name" index, the Campbell system groups individuals by the first initial of their surname, and then further indexes the individuals by the first letter of their given name. Thus all people whose last name starts with a *P* would be in one book, but organized semi-alphabetically by first name rather than last name. If you're looking for Tom Jones, for example, you'll find him listed in the *J* book among other individuals whose first name begins with *T*. Therefore, Tom Jones may be located on the same page with Terrance Jackson, Thomas Jewart, and Timothy James. Sometimes several different first-name letters are combined in a section, so Tom Jones' section may also include first names beginning with *S*, or *U–V*.

Long-Distance Courthouse Research

While personal visits to a courthouse are definitely the most rewarding, they aren't always possible given time, monetary, or physical limitations. In many cases, courthouse personnel are happy to provide photocopies of certain records in response to written requests. In some cases they will be able to check index entries for you, while in others they may only be able to provide copies if you give them an exact citation for a record.

Contact the courthouse for information about what services they can provide via mail, as well as details about copying fees, postage, and expected turnaround time.

If you plan to do a lot of research by mail, it is worthwhile to copy relevant indexes at the library or FHC for your surnames and locations of interest. Then, when you discover a new ancestor, you only need to check the indexes for any relevant entries and you'll have the exact citations needed to order the records from the county courthouse.

Genealogical and Historical Societies

Genealogical and historical societies exist in many towns and counties across America. These volunteer, nonprofit groups hold regular meetings, share information, and compile genealogical data about families who have lived in the area since settlement began. The members create registers, indexes, transcriptions, and other finding aids for local records containing genealogy information. America's leading genealogy organization is the National Genealogical Society (NGS), which includes a national membership of more than 17,000, publishes the highly acclaimed *National Genealogical Society Quarterly*, maintains a large circulating genealogy collection, and hosts several annual conferences, research trips, and tours.

FACT

Among the better-known specialized societies are the New England Historic Genealogical Society (NEHGS), the Mayflower Society, and the National Society Daughters of the American Revolution (NSDAR, commonly shortened to DAR).

Even if you don't live close enough to attend meetings or avail yourself of the genealogical collection, membership in a local genealogical society can greatly enhance your family tree research. Individuals belonging to these societies typically can provide a wealth of knowledge about genealogical resources specific to the area, and may also be willing to help members who live outside of the area with record lookups or cemetery photos. A society's published newsletters or quarterlies will provide you with information about genealogical research in the area, and may also include transcripts of actual records. Joining a genealogical society can also put you in contact with others who may be researching your family.

You can find the names and addresses of most genealogical societies in Elizabeth Petty Bentley's *The Genealogist's Address Book, 5th edition* and on the Internet at Society Hill (*www.daddezio.com/society/hill/index.html*).

Chapter 17

Tools for Taming the Family Tree

The sheer amount of information required to dig deeply into your family tree and document the journey can quickly lead to bulging folders and ever-mounting piles of materials. This onslaught of papers, books, family photographs, maps, magazines, and computer printouts can easily overwhelm even the most experienced genealogist unless steps are taken to organize, store, and protect the research. Genealogy software, filing systems, and other tools can help you reduce this clutter, so you can spend less time looking for stuff on your desk and more time looking for your ancestors.

Making Sense Out of Chaos

Most family trees begin with a single genealogy chart and a sharpened pencil. No problem there. It doesn't take long, however, for that single piece of paper to multiply into a stack or two. Next thing you know, there are disorganized piles of documents, notes, and other papers taking over the guest room, sitting on top of the washing machine, and even hiding out in the back seat of the family car. You can't even find your desk, much less the letter you received from your grandmother last week full of family information.

This doesn't mean you need to give up genealogy in favor of another hobby. Take charge of the chaos with a few simple steps.

1. **Seek some space**—If you're lucky, you can devote an entire room to your family history. Otherwise, try to clean out a corner, desk, or closet where you can store your important records and research. Even a storage container under the bed is a good start.
2. **Stock up on supplies**—Head to the office supply store and stock up on binders, binder dividers, file folders, archival-quality page protectors, labels, acid-free pens, and highlighters.
3. **Sort the stuff**—Go through each paper and document, dividing them into groups by surname, family group, or location.

If you're looking at an organizational nightmare, don't let procrastination or perfectionism overwhelm you to the point that you never begin. Select one stack, or box, or closet, and begin with that.

The mess didn't happen overnight, so you can't expect the organization to happen that quickly either. Learn to tackle small chunks at a time—maybe fifteen to thirty minutes per week—and you will be able to make progress.

Choosing a Filing System

The filing system you decide upon isn't really important, as long as it is easy for you to create and maintain. It needs to match the way you work and think if it's going to stand a chance of being used. There are a number of popular systems used by genealogists, including binders, file folders, notebooks, and various combinations of these.

Whatever storage system you choose, you need to decide how you want to organize your files. The choice will depend largely upon the way you do your research:

- By surname
- By couple or family
- By family line
- By geographic location
- By type of document (event)

The way you choose to organize may easily change as your research progresses. Many people begin organizing by family line—one folder/binder for each of their grandparents. As the research progresses, and the folders start to bulge, the filing system can be adapted with separate folders or binders for each surname or each family group. Alternatively, you may decide to subdivide as your research progresses. Files organized by surname, for example, can be broken down further by geographic location or record type.

Next, you need to decide on the basic physical form for your filing— binders, notebooks, or file folders. You can accomplish the same basic things with each. Many genealogists recommend notebooks or binders because the papers aren't as easily lost or disorganized as they might be with file folders. Proponents of folders tout their affordability, portability, and ability to handle different sizes and shapes of paper.

Most genealogists end up using a combination of storage methods. Some people, for example, use binders to organize the research about their primary families, and file folders for unproven connections or secondary families. Others may use a notebook to organize the research project, including discussion of their progress and copies of correspondence, but keep copies of documents and records in folders.

Some genealogists recommend color-coding your files or binder tabs if you are tracing the lineages of more than one grandparent. Basically, this is just another means of subdividing your files. The files for each grandparent and his or her ancestors are assigned a specific color.

Don't feel that you have to be perfect to keep your genealogy research organized. Organization is, and always will be, a work in progress. Try a few different methods and see what works best for you.

FACT

A common color scheme assigns blue to the paternal grandfather, green to the paternal grandmother, red to the maternal grandfather and yellow to the maternal grandmother. For each grandparent's lineage, you may choose to create folders of the same color for individual surnames or record types.

Family Tree Software

If you own a computer, you'll most likely want to invest in a family tree software program for recording, organizing, and storing the information that you find. Even if you are a big fan of notebooks and paper charts, genealogy software helps you reorganize things in new ways as well as print out your charts and reports in a variety of different formats. A good program can keep your research project organized right along with the family tree, allowing you to create and maintain research logs and "to-do" lists and to attach digital copies of your records directly to your source information. Software also takes the work out of sharing your family tree—enabling you to create a GEDCOM file (explained later in this chapter) or print out a new family group sheet with just a few clicks of the mouse.

ALERT!

The more features the software offers, the steeper the learning curve. If you're easily frustrated and hate to read instruction manuals, you may want to forgo the fancy software with the whiz-bang features in favor of a simpler program you can become comfortable with quickly.

Dozens of genealogy software titles are available, with a wide range of prices and options. Most programs do a pretty respectable job of letting you enter your family data and view it in a variety of formats. They differ in their look and feel, as well as in the way they format data, the types of reports and charts they produce, and their bells and whistles such as photo editing or family history book capabilities. The prices vary too, ranging from free to almost $100.

The majority of family tree software programs are designed for Windows, including Ancestral Quest, Ancestry Family Tree, Family Tree Legends, Family Tree Maker, Genbox Family History, Heredis, Legacy Family Tree, Personal Ancestral File (PAF), RootsMagic, and the Master Genealogist. Options for Macintosh users are a lot more limited; Reunion is the program used by most. The newer Heredis Mac X is also an option. Some of these are available from major chains; others can only be purchased and/or downloaded from the software companies' Web sites.

Interface and Organization

Most important is the way the program handles data. How intuitive is the data entry? Can you navigate quickly through your family tree? Are there multiple ways to look at your information, including individual view, family view, and pedigree view? Does it automatically check for duplicates when you add new people? Does it allow you to enter multiple dates and locations for an individual event, so that you can enter the birth date of your grandmother from both her tombstone and from her death certificate when the two conflict? One nifty feature offered by some genealogy programs is the ability to open and view multiple databases at once, and even drag and drop information from one to another.

QUESTION?

Which program is right for me?
Start with a list of your requirements and then try on a few programs for size. Most offer free trial versions that give you a chance to try before you buy. The few that don't offer trials are sold with money-back guarantees. In a nutshell, look for a program that is easy to use, provides the options and features you most want, and fits into your budget.

Documentation

Genealogy software should include the ability to record citations that link a name, date, place, or event to the source of the information, and to record the repository where the source was obtained. Does the program offer flexible source citation options? Are there templates that help you input details for different types of sources? Can you create custom source templates? Can you enter a source once and use it over and over? Can you add unlimited notes and facts to individuals and events? Can you add a global citation to a group of individuals? Can you customize the way that source citations appear in footnotes, endnotes, and bibliographies?

GEDCOM Compatibility

All popular genealogy software programs let you import and export family information in GEDCOM format. Some, however, handle GEDCOM transfers better than others do, with minimal to no loss of important data. A few programs can also directly import the files created by other genealogy programs—something to consider if you're thinking about switching from one program to another.

Reports and Charts

How many different reports and charts can the program generate? Are they fully customizable in terms of how much information you can include? Do you need to purchase an add-on program to get fancy charts and other options? At a minimum a good genealogy program should be able to generate quality family group sheets, pedigree charts, and narrative ancestor and descendant reports from your genealogy data. It's also nice if it can generate blank versions of the charts and forms, in case you want to fill them out by hand.

FACT

Some programs can present your family tree in fancy formats, such as hourglass and fan shapes, or even help you design wall charts for framing or family reunions.

Publishing

If you plan to write and publish a family history, you may want genealogy software that supports this goal. Does the software provide book publishing tools? If so, is it capable of creating a table of contents, index, footnotes or endnotes, and a bibliography? Can the book be exported to the word processor of your choice for final editing? Can you save it in Portable Document Format (PDF) and other formats?

Web Capabilities

Can the program produce reports or Web sites in HTML format for uploading to your own personal genealogy site, or will the company only publish online if you host a site with it? Can you mark people's information as private to keep it out of published reports? Does the program offer an automatic online backup option? Not all people want this option, but for those who do, some programs also offer Internet integration, which compares names in your file with names in specific online databases.

GEDCOM 101

Genealogy software programs each have their own specialized file format, making it difficult to share data with other programs and researchers. To facilitate the exchange of genealogical data, GEDCOM was created in 1985 by the Family History Department of the Church of Jesus Christ of Latter-day Saints. GEDCOM, short for GEnealogical Data COMmunications, is a data format standard that allows the data—names, dates, places, and other information—from one genealogy program to be easily read and converted by other genealogy software programs. All genealogy software programs allow you to export your family information as a GEDCOM file to easily share with others.

How to Open and Read GEDCOM Files

Spend a few weeks researching your family tree on the Internet, and you're likely to run across GEDCOM files. Most lineage-linked databases (discussed in Chapter 15) store information in GEDCOM format. You may also have received a GEDCOM file from a researcher who uses different genealogy software than you do.

Always look at the GEDCOM file by itself first, before merging it directly into your own family tree database. Chances are there are a few errors or unrelated people you're going to want to remove first. It is often easier to add the good information manually than it is to figure out how to remove the unwanted information after the fact.

That means you now have a great family tree that may contain vital clues to your ancestors, but your computer can't seem to read it. What to do?

1. Check to be sure it is a GEDCOM file. These files have the .ged extension. If the file has a .zip extension, you'll need to unzip it first.
2. Save the GEDCOM file to your computer. Scan the file for viruses before saving. Some people create a special folder for imported GEDCOM files.
3. Make a backup of your current genealogy database. This ensures that you can revert back to your original file in case something goes wrong when opening and/or importing the new GEDCOM file.
4. Use your genealogy software to open the GEDCOM file. Close any open family tree projects. Then follow the software's instructions for opening/importing a GEDCOM file. Generally, the command will be located under the File menu, as "Open," "Import," or "Import GEDCOM."

How to Create and Share GEDCOM Files

GEDCOM files are a great way to share your family tree with family, friends, and fellow researchers. GEDCOM is also the preferred format for submitting your family tree to online lineage-linked databases. It's easy to save your family tree as a GEDCOM file; the software does all the work.

1. Open your genealogy file. Don't worry, the GEDCOM process will create a new file, not overwrite your working family tree.

2. Choose the "export" or "save as" option. This is usually found under the File menu. If several file types are listed, choose "GEDCOM" or ".ged."

3. Remove names of living individuals. Most genealogy programs allow you to identify living relatives and remove their private information from the GEDCOM file.

4. Choose a name and location for your GEDCOM file. The name should be something that describes the contents of the file (perhaps your last name, or the primary surname). The location should be someplace that's easy to remember.

FACT

Many beginners try to read a GEDCOM file with a word processor. Because they are basically just a list of information and tags, GEDCOM files are difficult to read this way. They are designed to be opened with a family tree software program. If you don't own such a program, you can download a free GEDCOM viewer from the Internet.

Once you've created a GEDCOM file, it is ready to share with others. You can send it to family or friends as an e-mail attachment, upload it to a genealogy Web site that accepts GEDCOM submissions, or burn a copy onto CD-ROM to send to someone via postal mail.

Pass It On—Preserving Family Records

Lucky is the person who possesses treasured photographs or heirlooms important to the family's heritage. As family generations branch and treasures are passed down, many important pieces of family history are lost, discarded, or even destroyed. It's not uncommon to find old family albums moldering away at antiques shops, military medals hidden in a pile of junk at a garage sale, or photos succumbing to the hazards of heat and humidity in an old cardboard box in the back of an attic. Searching out important family records, photos, and heirlooms, and seeing that they are stored properly and preserved for future generations, is a big part of your family tree project.

Collecting Family Materials

In some families there is an unofficial "record keeper" who collects and keeps all important family possessions, from naturalization certificates to the family Bible. In most families, however, different branches of the family tree end up with different bits of the family's history. As a genealogist, you can perform a great service to your family by finding and preserving these family heritage materials.

You will most likely run across at least one family member who is unwilling to let you keep, borrow, or copy records and family keepsakes. When this happens, try one of these suggestions for persuading the reluctant person to share:

- Offer to make a copy for your relative when you make a copy for yourself. For example, you can scan photographs from multiple family members and then burn them all onto a CD to present to each of them.
- Design a family project, such as a family history book or photo collection, for which you need to copy and use a family member's materials. This links your request to a family cause rather than having it seem to be just personal.
- If the person's reluctance to share is because of the monetary value of the items, consider offering to buy the material from them.
- It is entirely understandable that a relative may be reluctant to allow a valuable family heirloom, such as an old locket or Civil War uniform, out of her possession. In such cases, offer to take pictures of the items instead. Be sure to make copies to share!

While a torn photograph or broken vase may seem easy to fix, they aren't. Consult a professional conservator for advice about repairing valuable items. Conservators spend years learning their craft and will know how to best preserve or restore your precious heirlooms. Check with museums, historical societies, and libraries in your area for recommendations about conservators working in your area.

Enemies of the Past

Not many family records survive. Most people have few if any items that once belonged to a grandparent or great-grandparent. Rarely is a descendant lucky enough to have inherited a ring or comb or watch or Bible or lock of hair, let alone any old letters, diaries, or photographs. What happens to all of those items that belonged to people living three or more generations ago? Almost all of it probably was thrown away because things break or become otherwise unusable or unwanted.

ALERT!

"Magnetic" photo albums, popular in the 1970s, are very bad for photographs and scrapbook items. The glue used for the sticky pages was very acidic, and the clear-plastic press-down pages were sometimes made of polyvinyl chloride (PVC), which further accelerates deterioration. If you can't remove photos from old albums, make copies of the photos right from the album page.

Preserving Family Documents, Photos, and Heirlooms

Though you may not have the money, skills, products, equipment, and space of a professional archivist, there are several simple steps you can take to help preserve family records and heirlooms.

Location, Location, Location

Collections of family materials deserve to be housed responsibly. You will need some drawers, a file cabinet, shelves, or closet space that provide a stable, clean environment. A temperature between 40 and 72 degrees Fahrenheit is ideal, with a humidity level between 45 and 55 percent. Avoid damp areas such as kitchens and basements, and places with wide swings in temperature such as garages and attics. Also stay away from sunlight and fluorescent lights—the ultraviolet rays will cause photographs to fade and paper to become yellow and brittle. Keep an eye out for pests, too!

Heirloom Allergies

Photos, documents, and keepsakes need to be stored responsibly in acid-free, PVC-free, lignin-free boxes or containers. Shoeboxes just don't cut it! You can purchase archival-quality materials in many stationery, craft, book, and scrapbooking stores, as well as online. Store important photographs and papers in plastic sleeves made of Mylar, polyester, polypropylene, polyethylene, or Tyvek. Remove pins, staples, paper clips, adhesive tape, and cardboard when possible. Isolate acidic items, such as newspaper clippings, to avoid damaging other items.

FACT

There are no standards attached to the terms "acid-free," "archival," or "photo safe." If a product says "acid-free," it means it has a pH of 7.0 or higher. It may still be too alkaline, or contain components harmful to photos and documents. Look for items that state they comply with American National Standards Institute (ANSI) and/or National Information Standards Organization (NISO) standards.

Write It Down

Papers, photos, and other heirloom objects will continue to deteriorate with time—even if you care for them properly. To keep them from disappearing forever, take time to identify and maintain records of your treasures. Photographs, papers, and many objects can be digitally scanned into your computer. Take photographs of items that are too bulky to scan. Keep a written record of the history and condition of each object, including who made, purchased, or used the item, and what it means to your family.

Chapter 18

Assembling the Pieces

O nce you have collected a number of facts about your ancestors, it's time to create a family tree. Just as with a puzzle, each piece, or fact, needs to be evaluated to determine its appropriate placement in the big picture. A small mistake in judgment may seem inconsequential, but the implications of that mistake will compound and could lead you to ancestors who aren't yours. To lessen the chance of false trails, you must understand the different types of sources and evidence and how to use them to "prove" your family connections.

Sources, Information, and Evidence

When you were taught in school how to conduct a research project, your teacher most likely introduced you to two categories of sources: primary and secondary. Modern genealogists have taken this a step further, evaluating the reliability of a source separately from the reliability of the specific information provided by the source. This is because a single source could conceivably provide information based on both primary and secondary knowledge. A death certificate, for example, supplies primary information about the date of death, but the date of birth on the certificate is most likely secondhand information, provided long after the actual birth by someone who likely wasn't in attendance. It's entirely possible that the information on the certificate was given by a neighbor or family acquaintance who knew that your great-grandmother's birthday was March 13, but wasn't sure of the year (great-grandmas don't always like to brag about their age, after all). For these reasons, the date of death on the death certificate is much more likely to be accurate than is the date of birth.

To help distinguish between a source and the information it offers, genealogists have developed three types of criteria by which all sources and information are evaluated:

- Original versus derivative sources
- Primary versus secondary information
- Direct versus indirect evidence

Original Versus Derivative Sources

As it pertains to genealogy, a source is anything that provides information about an ancestor or the history of an ancestral family. Sources can be civil records, books, databases, microfilm, photos, interviews, tombstones, or even a piece of jewelry with a name and date inscribed on the back. A source is a tangible item or person that holds the information you seek.

Original Sources

Original sources are sources of information created at or near the time of the actual event; the information was provided or recorded by someone who was present at the event. Sometimes referred to as primary sources, original sources generally provide unedited, firsthand information. Most birth records, wills, land deeds, journals, diaries, and photographs are original sources.

ALERT!

Photocopies and digital images made from original records, when created by a reputable agency, can generally be treated as original sources. Copies made and distributed by individuals, however, do not usually carry as much weight as the originals due to the possibility of tampering.

Derivative Sources

Records or other sources either created significantly after the event occurred, or that contain information provided by a person who was not present at the event, are considered to be derivative sources. They generally provide secondhand information, which has been extracted, transcribed, or otherwise derived from original, primary sources. Most indexes, compilations, databases, books, and published family histories fall into this category, as does the majority of the information found on the Internet.

Primary Versus Secondary Information

Now that you've determined whether your source is original or derivative, it's time to evaluate the information it provides. As discussed previously in the death certificate example, any single source or record may contain information based on both primary and secondary knowledge.

Primary Information

Primary information consists of facts or knowledge, either written or oral, provided by someone who was present at the event recorded in a source—a birth, death, marriage, military skirmish, and so on. Because the individual was a witness to or participant in the event, the information is more likely to be correct, but this may not always be the case.

As an example of primary information that is not necessarily accurate, consider the experience of a group of people who witnessed a car accident firsthand. Though they all witnessed the same event, they may still tell very different stories.

Secondary Information

Facts or accounts given by people who were not participants in or eyewitnesses to an event are considered by genealogists to be secondary information. Family stories and legends, abstracts of original records, and transcribed databases are all examples of secondary information. Similar to statements given in a courtroom, such hearsay information is given less weight than is primary information.

Direct Versus Indirect Evidence

Names, dates, places, descriptions, relationships, and other relevant facts that can be extracted from a source are referred to by genealogists as evidence. As with sources, there are differing qualities or levels of evidence.

Direct Evidence

Evidence that provides the answer to a question without the need for additional corroborating facts or explanation is referred to as direct evidence. A birth date found on your grandfather's birth certificate, for example, would offer direct evidence of when he was born. Direct evidence refers only to the answers given by the information, not the quality of the information. Evidence can be direct without being true.

Indirect Evidence

Sometimes referred to as circumstantial evidence, indirect evidence requires additional facts, thought, or explanation to reach a reliable conclusion. It doesn't provide an exact answer to the question you seek, but it may provide enough information to allow you to form a hypothesis and, when combined with other evidence, reach a conclusion. If you're unable to locate a birth certificate to document your grandfather's birth, for example, you could look at census records to determine his age as given at the time of the census. This is indirect evidence because it doesn't provide you with the exact date of birth, but it does provide an approximate year of birth. The indirect evidence could then be combined with other indirect evidence—census records from other years, for example—to reach a reliable conclusion as to his probable date of birth.

Evaluating the Evidence

Now that you've assembled your evidence—names, dates, relationships, places, and so forth—it is time to evaluate its relevance and reliability. The classifications of original, derivative, primary, secondary, direct, and indirect provide a good framework, but genealogists soon learn that even first-hand information from an original source can be inaccurate if the informant had reason to misrepresent the information or just remembered it wrong. On the other hand, a derivative transcription, when diligently prepared, can often provide reliable information. Each piece of evidence you've collected needs to be weighed and examined on its own merit, much the way a jury would when considering a court case.

If at all possible, look at the original version of anything that you find. If you find your ancestor listed in a published book of extracted deeds, try to find a copy of the original deed at the courthouse or on microfilm to see if it was extracted correctly, and to see if it contains clues that weren't included in the extraction.

Is This the Right Person?

One of the most difficult problems in genealogy is being sure that the right record is attached to the right person. A source may refer to an individual of the same name as the ancestor you seek, but that doesn't necessarily mean that it really is your ancestor. If both name and age are given in the document, and they correspond with the name and age of your ancestor, then there is a greater likelihood that the record applies, but it still isn't a certainty. To make a convincing case, it is best to use a combination of several of these pieces of information to identify the individual as your ancestor:

- Name and date of birth
- Location of upbringing or settlement
- Names of spouse, parents, children, siblings, or other relatives
- Place of birth
- Occupation
- Handwriting or signature

ALERT!

A handwritten signature is a good way to distinguish the records of two individuals by the same name living in the same area, but many official records were not actually written in the applicant's own hand. Early courthouse records, including handwritten copies of deeds and wills, are actually in the handwriting of the court clerk. Even the signatures are copies.

Consider the author Laura Ingalls Wilder. Though there are at least nineteen individuals named Laura Ingalls listed in the 1880 U.S. Census, it is easy to distinguish the Laura of "Little House" fame as the thirteen-year-old living in De Smet, South Dakota (the place to which they moved after leaving Walnut Grove, Minnesota), with father Charles P., mother Caroline L., and sisters Mary, Caroline (Carrie), and Grace. The names of her family members are fairly distinctive, but for even further verification, her parents' occupations and places of birth also match the family history. Charles is listed as a farmer who was born in New York, and Caroline is listed as being born in Wisconsin. Without checking for these additional facts, it might be easy for a researcher to mistakenly identify the 10-year-old Laura Ingalls living in Walnut Grove, Illinois, with father Charles as the person being sought instead.

While original records of primary information are usually considered the most credible, evidence gathered from derivative records and/or secondary information can be used to reach a reliable conclusion as long as you feel confident that the evidence is trustworthy and reflects what really happened.

Is the Information Trustworthy?

Whether or not the evidence appears to support your theory, you need to consider its credibility. For each individual piece of evidence, you need to consider both the quality of the source and the reliability of the information it provides:

- Is the source original or derivative? Original records are generally given more weight than are derivative.
- Is the information primary or secondary? Primary information is usually considered more reliable than is secondary.
- Is the evidence direct or indirect? Direct evidence is generally preferred to indirect because it typically takes less corroborating evidence to reach a reliable conclusion.

Notice the use of the words *generally* and *usually*. Like most guidelines, there are exceptions. While original records containing primary information are usually the first choice in terms of credibility, they may not always exist or be readily available. The information they contain may also be questionable due to such factors as faded or illegible handwriting, or an informant who was biased or had other reason to misrepresent the facts.

Proving Your Argument

Proof is very rarely an absolute. No matter how much evidence you collect, you can really only call it proof if you and others find it convincing. A census record, for example, that lists a woman living on her own as a widow provides evidence that her husband is dead. It certainly isn't proof, however.

The census taker could have made a mistake or the woman could have told the census taker that she was a widow for any number of personal reasons. The evidence is there, but it isn't convincing when considered on its own.

What Constitutes Proof?

Genealogists define proof as the evidence and reasoning that supports a conclusion. Evidence alone doesn't constitute proof. There are occasions when a single document can provide enough evidence to present a reasonable conclusion, assuming that no other evidence can be found that either supports or contradicts the conclusion. Even then, however, the "proof" exists not only in the document itself, but also in the fact that no conflicting evidence was found. Your proof argument needs to present not only the evidence that you found and why you believe it to be true, but also all other sources and information that you researched and evaluated in the pursuit of an answer.

There will also be occasions where no individual piece of evidence is enough to support a conclusion. In this case, the "proof" comes from analyzing each piece of evidence and creating a logical argument from the collected evidence that carries enough weight to convince others of your conclusion.

Applying the Genealogical Proof Standard

To assist genealogists in deciding whether their evidence and reasoning is sufficient, the Board for Certification of Genealogists has defined a series of five elements that need to be met before a conclusion can be considered satisfactorily credible or "proven." Known collectively as the "Genealogical Proof Standard," the steps are:

1. Conduct a reasonably thorough search for relevant records and information.
2. Include a complete, accurate citation to the source for each piece of evidence.
3. Analyze the evidence that has been collected for relevance and credibility.
4. Resolve all conflicting evidence.
5. Arrive at an articulate, reasonable conclusion that is supported by the evidence.

A conclusion that meets this standard can be considered convincing, or "proved." This doesn't necessarily mean that it is true, just that it is the most logical conclusion given the presented evidence.

FACT

Theories or conclusions that can't be supported by enough quality evidence to meet the genealogical proof standard can still be included in your family history. Use limiting words such as *possible* or *probable* to reflect your level of confidence in the reported evidence or conclusion.

Resolving Discrepancies

In an ideal world, all evidence that you collect about your ancestors would support your conclusions. Unfortunately, we don't live in an ideal world. So what do you do when you uncover a piece of evidence that conflicts with or contradicts the other collected evidence? This is where your confidence in the reliability of the evidence becomes very important.

Who, When, and Why

To best resolve conflicting evidence, weigh the relative reliability of each piece of evidence that supports your theory. Begin by asking yourself who, when, and why—who provided the information, when did they give it, and why did they give it? Look at how close the source is to the actual event; the credibility of the person who created or provided information for the record; the reason the record was created in the first place; and how well the evidence corroborates other evidence. If the evidence came from a published source, what do you know about its reliability from your own examination and the experiences of other researchers?

Surmising the Truth

As a simple example, consider a case in which several conflicting dates of birth have been found for an individual. In general, you should give the most weight to the primary sources, which were created closest to the actual birth. A birth certificate filed soon after the birth is more likely to be accurate than is the birth date provided by an uncle on the individual's death certificate, or even the birth date as carved into the tombstone.

ALERT!

Consider your own experience and familiarity with the record and locality. Perhaps you misinterpreted something because you couldn't interpret the handwriting, didn't understand local customs, misread an abbreviation, or were unfamiliar with the exact meaning of a term. When arriving at a conclusion, give greater weight to the evidence that is most likely to represent the facts correctly.

But what happens when the date on the birth certificate conflicts with the date of the family Bible? Both were created close to the time of the birth by people who were probably present at the birth, weren't they? Not necessarily. Check both sources carefully for inconsistencies. When was the birth certificate actually issued? Perhaps it is a delayed birth certificate issued years after the actual birth. This could mean that the birth date was remembered inaccurately or even purposefully given incorrectly for some reason.

If the Bible was printed after the date of birth, then it's likely that the entries were added at some time removed from the actual event. Are all entries written in the same handwriting and ink? This also presents a suspicion that the entries weren't made at the time of the actual events.

Once you've determined the likely accuracy of a source, you still need to examine the information it contains compared to other collected evidence. When the birth certificate gives a birth date of January 1881 and you find the individual listed in the 1880 census, then the validity of the information provided in the birth certificate comes into question, no matter how accurate the birth record appears on the surface. At this point you'll need to look again at all other supporting evidence, and also do some further research to confirm the actual date that the census was taken, as well as take another look at the likelihood of the birth certificate's accuracy.

When evaluating sources, determine whether a certificate is a copy of the original, or a transcription. It's easy to transpose a number or misread a date when copying information from an original record. Is it clear and easy to read? If not, perhaps some of the information could be interpreted in more than one way.

Why Does It Matter?

Many new genealogists may wonder why there is so much fuss over sources and evidence. Who's really going to care whether Grandpa was born in 1921 or 1922? Or whether Great-Great-Grandmother died in Alabama or Georgia? Genealogy is just a hobby, after all. Like anything else, however, it's really only worth doing if you're interested in doing it well. Would you knit a sweater full of holes? Bake a cake without baking powder? Probably not. As you assemble your family history, take the time to thoroughly evaluate all evidence, prioritizing quality over quantity. The best way to honor your ancestors is to represent them correctly and take pride in your work.

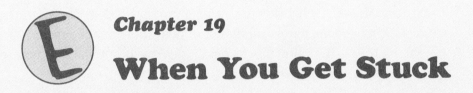

Chapter 19

When You Get Stuck

We've all have them—genealogical research problems that just don't seem to have a solution. Perhaps the last name you're researching is too common, and you just can't seem to sort out all of the "John Smiths." Or maybe you're unable to locate the maiden name of your great-grandmother, known only as Henrietta. Perhaps you've followed your ancestors back to the point at which they "crossed the pond," only to have their trail sink into the Atlantic. Where can you find the answers you seek?

I Can't Find Them!

Believe it or not, there is a solution to just about every genealogical research problem. Your ancestor did not step off a spaceship in rural Tennessee, even if that seems like the only answer. Some problems, however, can be difficult to overcome. Records are lost or destroyed. Families disappear between one census and the next. Ship records for your immigrant ancestor don't appear to exist. Or maybe the clues you have found just don't make sense. You don't have to let these stumbling blocks get in the way, however. Try these strategies for getting around or over them instead.

Retrace Your Steps

Begin your search by going over the information you already have. Most likely it has been a while since you first started your family tree project, and now you can look at it with fresh eyes and many hours of experience under your belt. Look over each document and photo, as well as your research notes. There may be names that had no significance when you first found these records, or you may be able to read the old handwriting more clearly now that you've had some practice.

ALERT!

One helpful approach when you get stuck is to check your research log to see if there are any obvious gaps in your research, or any records that you requested from a library or archives that you never received.

Branch Out Sideways

Our ancestors did not live in isolation, although we often research them as if they did. They were part of a family—husbands, wives, children, parents, aunts, uncles, and cousins. They were also part of a community, with friends and neighbors, classmates and coworkers. When the records of your ancestor reach a dead end, expand your research to the records of these other individuals with whom your ancestor had a connection—a research technique referred to as cluster genealogy.

Cluster genealogy can be an especially powerful research strategy for locating ancestors who seem to have disappeared. Because family, friends, and neighbors often moved together, you may find a clue to their former home in the records of someone else in the group. When you can't locate an ancestor in the census, look for the neighbors instead. Your ancestor's name may have been garbled or even missed in the index. You can use this trick on passenger lists, too.

Check Your Facts

Are you looking for the right name? Are you looking in the right place? Are you even looking for the right person? Many brick walls are built from incorrect assumptions. If you have used a lot of published sources in your research, go back and check them against the original documents. Also check the geography of the area. Is it possible that the family farm was under the jurisdiction of a different county at the time? Investigate all name variations as well, both last names and given names. Many people think to check for surname spelling variations, but forget that their ancestor may appear under her initials, middle name, or a nickname.

Get Creative

If you've only researched online and in a library or two, then you likely have not seen all there is to see. It's rare to have really exhausted all of your options. Spend some time familiarizing yourself with unique records and special collections that exist for the area in which your family lived. Visit the Web site for the state archives to see if the contents of its collection are listed online. Explore the Family History Library Catalog to see what records they have microfilmed. Check with the local genealogical society to see what other, less-usual record sources might be available.

In some cases, checking more unusual or unique record sources will require a trip to the location of the resource. If that's not an option, look into interlibrary loan or write a letter. You may also be able to find a volunteer willing to help with a lookup or two.

Maybe your ancestors landed in jail? The Federal Bureau of Prisons maintains an online database (✑*www.bop.gov/iloc2/LocateInmate.jsp*) to help you find inmates who served time in a federal correctional facility. If your ancestor was released prior to 1982, you'll have to send your request in writing. States and counties also maintain their own prison records, usually found in the appropriate courthouse.

Sorting Out the Smiths

Locating information about an ancestor is difficult enough. But when your ancestor shares the same name with several others in the community, the challenge intensifies. Which of those records actually refer to your ancestor? How do you pick him out of the crowd?

Smith, Jones, Butler, Brown. The sheer volume of possible records and clues available for common surnames can be overwhelming. To determine which John Smith is yours, you need to learn as much about him as you can. Remember to search for family members, occupation, and place of residence, and examine your ancestor's signature.

When you are sorting out individuals with the same name, it helps to collect at least some information about each one of them. This will make it easier for you to figure out which one's the likely candidate when you run across them again in the records.

It Says What?

The old-fashioned handwriting in your ancestor's letters and documents may be charming, but is also likely to be hard to decipher. Handwriting styles have changed a lot through the years, making it difficult for beginners to interpret older records. This is especially true when you also take into account the poor spelling, lack of punctuation, and strange words. Learning to read old handwriting is a skill that will prove invaluable in your research.

When trying to read old handwriting, use a magnifying glass so that you can closely inspect the lines and loops. When a letter in a word is hard to decipher, look for other words in the document containing the same letter. This can help you determine what the letter might be. Census records are a good place to practice this technique, where there are usually many other recognizable names starting with or containing the same letter. If you aren't sure whether a particular name starts with an *S* or an *L*, look for someone with a last name like Smith or Lewis living nearby to see how the first letter is formed in that case. Because each county usually had many different census takers, you need to make sure that you choose names written by the same individual. Letters that are used to write out the month, day, and year—often present in genealogical documents—are another good place to familiarize yourself with a writer's style.

FACT

Paleography is the study and interpretation of early handwriting, derived from the Greek *palaios* (old) and *graphein* (to write). A paleographer studies every aspect of handwriting and script, from the type of paper and density of the ink to the angle of the strokes and general style as compared to other handwriting. This allows her to differentiate between different writers and, possibly, date a manuscript.

Early spelling was primarily phonetic. Sometimes the same word might be spelled different ways in the same document—wagon, wagin, or waggen. Noah Webster produced his first dictionary in 1806, but it wasn't until the late nineteenth century that spelling really became standardized. When you find a strange word, try saying it out loud in several different ways until you find one that makes sense.

Similar Letters

A number of capital letters often look the same in early American handwriting: I and J, L and S, L and T, M and N, T and F, and U and V. Sometimes the writer may have embellished a letter with an extra curl, stroke, squiggle, or loop, which also can change the appearance of a letter or word. When a letter doesn't appear the way you expect, look at the line above where you are reading, to see if perhaps an extra swirl or loop has intruded from a word above the one you are reading.

ALERT!

One of the most misread letters in old handwriting is the *s*. As late as the 1870s, writers were using the "double S," in which the first *s* in a pair was written to look like a cursive lower case *f*, otherwise known as the "long s" or "leading s." Words like Missouri and Mississippi, written using the "double S," will look like Mifsouri and Mifsifsippi.

Common Abbreviations

Writing longhand was a lot of work, so shortcuts were often taken. Ja^{s} for James, Jn or Jno for John, and M^{y} for Mary are just some of many commonly seen name abbreviations. Commonly used words were often abbreviated too—s^{d} for said, dec^{d} for deceased, p^{o} for pole, and so on. Double letters were often written as single letters with a line or tilde above the letter. Most abbreviations are recognizable by the raised last letter.

Educating Yourself Further

This book covers most of the basics you need for growing your family tree, but like most topics, there is always more to learn. Researching your family tree can be a lifelong adventure—a never-ending quest for information. Even professional genealogists continue to learn through self-study, conferences, classes, tutorials, and journals. Numerous educational opportunities exist to help you increase your knowledge and dig deeper into your family's past.

Tuition Courses and Certificate Programs

In-depth lessons that you can do at your own pace attract many genealogists to home study courses. They allow you to choose what you want to learn, and fit the education into your time and budget. The tuition-based genealogy classes discussed here are only a few of the many that are available.

The National Genealogical Society

The National Genealogical Society offers two courses, both accredited by the Distance Education and Training Council. American Genealogy: A Basic Course is a sixteen-lesson home study course that introduces each major record group used in American research and requires some "hands-on" practice. Assignments are graded and a certificate of completion is awarded. The society also offers a shorter, less-intensive online class—Introduction to Genealogy: An Online Course.

There are numerous adult education genealogy classes taught at local community colleges and universities across the United States. Check with your local library or genealogical society to learn about classes offered near you.

Brigham Young University

Brigham Young University (BYU) offers a certificate program in family history through independent study. College credit is granted for each course successfully completed to fulfill the certificate program requirements, but the certificate itself is not a degree. BYU also offers a number of individual independent-study classes on genealogy topics. Some are available by mail for a fee, and most can be accessed online at no charge.

The National Institute for Genealogical Studies

The National Institute for Genealogical Studies, administered through the University of Toronto, offers dozens of fee-based Internet genealogy courses, on topics ranging from paleography and methodology to country-specific research. You can select courses individually based on your needs or interests, or you can work toward a Certificate in Genealogical Studies.

The International Internet Genealogical Society University offers free lessons and tutorials from a number of different instructors. Class topics range from beginning genealogy to land records to South African research.

Free Online Classes and Tutorials

The Internet is also a great source for ongoing education. You can find tutorials and classes dealing with almost every aspect of genealogy research. The vast majority are even free of charge.

The genealogy section of About.com offers a free Introduction to Genealogy class with lessons, assignments, and online quizzes, as well as tutorials on records, organization, and research methodologies. The Online University at Genealogy.com offers courses on beginning genealogy, Internet genealogy, and tracing immigrant origins. Numerous other Web sites also offer genealogy lessons and tutorials.

National Conferences and Institutes

Some of the best educational opportunities can be found at national and regional genealogical conferences and institutes. These provide the opportunity to interact with and learn from some of the top names in the field through lectures and hands-on workshops on a variety of introductory and advanced topics.

Genealogical conferences are generally two- to four-day events sponsored by genealogical societies. The two largest in the United States are the national conference that the National Genealogical Society (NGS) sponsors each spring, and the national conference held by the Federation of Genealogical Societies (FGS) each fall. Numerous state and special-interest societies also sponsor conferences.

Genealogy institutes differ from conferences in that they are more intensive and focus on a specific area of research. Think of them as weeklong training camps. The annual institutes feature topic tracks for beginner to advanced researchers, taught by professionals in the field. The small class sizes allow for a great deal of "hands-on," personalized instruction. The most well-known genealogical institutes in the United States include three held each summer: the National Institute on Genealogical Research at the

National Archives in Washington, D.C.; the Samford Institute of Genealogy and Historical Research at Samford University in Alabama; and the Genealogical Institute of Mid-America in Springfield, Illinois. If you have more free time during the winter months, you can attend the Salt Lake Institute of Genealogy, which is offered each January in Salt Lake City.

Books, Magazines, and Journals

Reading is an easy way to further your learning. It costs very little, and involves no travel. Case studies, how-to articles, research tips, and Web site links are just some of the many things you can learn from a good genealogical book, magazine, or journal.

Genealogy magazines have hit the mainstream, and several can now be found on the newsstand at your favorite bookstore. They all also have their own Web sites featuring some of the tips and articles from the print magazines. The most well known include *Ancestry*, *Everton's Genealogical Helper*, *Family Chronicle*, *Family Tree Magazine*, *Genealogical Computing*, and *Heritage Quest*.

Sources for Help

The genealogical community as a whole is a very giving bunch. Ask a question, and you'll usually get an answer. When you reach a dead end, or can't track down an essential resource, there are several places to turn for assistance. Some helpful heroes—librarians, genealogical societies, and genealogy mailing lists—have been covered elsewhere in this book. But there are also a few other notable places where you can find volunteers willing to help you with your research questions.

Books We Own

This free service, in operation since 1996, lists genealogy-related books and other published resources along with volunteers who own or have access to them and are willing to look up information about specific people.

www.rootsweb.com/~bwo

Random Acts of Genealogical Kindness

More than 4,000 genealogists from all over the world volunteer their time here to provide physical assistance with genealogy research in the area in which they live. Some of the most commonly fulfilled requests include photos of cemetery markers, copies of birth records, and obituary lookups in local newspapers.

✐*www.raogk.org*

Hiring a Professional

For even the most enthusiastic of genealogy researchers, the time often comes when time, knowledge, or travel constraints leave the family tree wilting. Perhaps you don't have time to research the records yourself, or you need specific on-site research, and just can't find the time or money to visit in person. Maybe you've done the research but want some help putting it all together into a published family history, or maybe you just don't have the necessary genealogical research skills to tackle a specific problem. It is rare not to need help at some point in your genealogy research. Seeking the assistance of a professional genealogist may be the solution.

What a Professional Genealogist Can Do for You

Most people hire a professional to trace their ancestors—to discover who an immigrant ancestor was, to prove descent from a military hero or famous individual, or to research a family line back to a specific country, time period, or individual.

FACT

Professional genealogists provide an array of services. They can track down living descendants of a particular individual, locate records in a repository, consult with you on specific research problems, decipher old handwriting, write a family history, or translate foreign records. If it has anything to do with family history, there is likely to be a professional researcher who can offer expertise.

Locating a Professional Genealogist

Anyone thinking of hiring a professional genealogist in the United States should begin with a professional association. Although no laws govern the certification of genealogists, there are several groups that work to ensure quality and ethics among professional researchers. Two provide credentials or certification to genealogists who have passed rigorous tests of their research skills: the Board for Certification of Genealogists (BCG) and the International Commission for the Accreditation of Professional Genealogists (ICAPGen). While not a credentialing body, the Association of Professional Genealogists (APG) works to support high standards in the field of genealogy and requires all of its members to adhere to a code of ethics. All three offer an online member list or database that can assist you in locating a researcher by geographical location or specialty.

ALERT!

Don't let a lack of credentials dissuade you from hiring a specific genealogist. Many highly competent researchers do not seek certification. Years of experience, specialized skills, and satisfied clients are just as important, if not more so, than is a title. Ask for a sample of the genealogist's work as well as a list of clients who can provide recommendations.

By contracting with a researcher found through the groups discussed here, you increase the chances that you have retained an individual who will handle your project in a professional manner. Should you find yourself dissatisfied with the work done by a member of one of these organizations, the group will help you rectify the situation.

Unless you specify otherwise in the contract, the genealogist doing your research owns the copyright to the material presented in the client report, and so can publish this information in the form of an article or case study. Also, you won't be able to include the information in a publication of your own, unless you rewrite it in your own words.

How Much Will It Cost?

Most genealogists charge by the hour for their time and expertise and, in addition, will bill for incurred expenses including photocopies, record fees, and travel costs. Hourly rates vary from as little as $20 to more than $100, depending upon the scope of your project and the skills and experience of the genealogist. You will usually be asked for an initial retainer to cover a predetermined amount of work, and the hours of research will then be billed against the retainer. It is important that you include in your contract what you want done when the retainer amount has been depleted, unless you happen to have the funds for unlimited research. Most reputable genealogists will ask for your approval before doing additional research beyond the retainer amount, and this should be specified in your contract.

What to Expect

The key to working effectively with a professional genealogist is to clearly define the goals of your project before you begin. This should include a review of the information you've already obtained. You don't want someone wasting their time (and your money) looking for things you already know. With the information you provide, the researcher will usually develop a research plan that outlines the research steps and objectives. This research plan can provide both of you with a general idea of how much time the project will require before you start.

If you've hired a professional for a research project, you should expect that person to analyze her findings and provide a report of her research activities. This report may include a list of the records and repositories she has searched, the information gained from each record, sources checked where nothing was found, copies or abstracts of important information, and suggestions for continued research. Bills for the work are often submitted with these reports, and should include specific details about the time spent and expenses incurred. Even if you have paid up-front, you should expect to receive an itemized bill to show how and where the money was spent.

If you do your homework, state your expectations clearly, spell out details in the contract, and communicate regularly, your experience with hiring a professional is likely to be everything you hope it will be.

Chapter 20

Uncovering Your Genetic Roots

As recently as a decade ago, DNA was a topic rarely discussed outside of science class. Modern advancements in genetic testing, however, have brought astonishing possibilities to almost every aspect of human life—our laws, our health, even our families. DNA analysis is now standard practice for determining criminal guilt or innocence, resolving paternity or maternity questions, unlocking the genetic roots of diseases, and even tracing the connections in our family tree.

What DNA Can Tell You

It's in your genes. That's how scientists explain the physical characteristics, personality traits, and behaviors that make each human unique. DNA does more than just show the differences between individuals, however; it also confirms the connections. Because DNA is inherited, there are regions of the DNA strand that can link an individual to his family, both immediate relatives and long-distant ancestors. On their own, DNA tests can't provide you with the names of your ancestors or every branch in your family tree. But as a tool added to traditional research techniques, DNA testing can help provide the "proof" that is missing in so many of our genealogical conclusions—the "gene" in our genealogy.

Ancestral DNA testing can help you determine a number of family relationships, including:

- Whether two people are related
- Whether two people descended from a common ancestor
- A relationship to others with the same surname
- Possible connection with an ethnic group

FACT

Many features, such as your height, are not determined by a single gene. They are influenced by a combination of genes acting together, along with the environment in which you grew up. The average height of Americans has increased by almost four inches over the past 200 years, a trend thought to be influenced by better food and increasingly comfortable lifestyles.

As promising as it is, DNA testing does have plenty of limitations. While it can tell you that you share a common ancestor with another individual, it can't tell you who that ancestor is. It can tell you approximately how many generations you are descended from that common ancestor, but not exactly how many. DNA tests also can't tell you much about the large portions of your family tree that don't descend directly from father to father to father, or mother to mother to mother, at least not without tracking down direct-line descendants of those other ancestors and having them tested as well. DNA testing is exciting to be sure, but don't get your hopes up beyond what science can provide.

Markers

A marker is a segment of DNA with known genetic characteristics. These markers are essentially places in the DNA where the same pattern repeats a number of times—sort of a "stutter" in the DNA. The number of repeats in a marker is known as an allele, basically a variant form of a specific gene. Because the number of repeats within these sequences is inherited, they make useful mileposts for genetic testing.

ALERT!

Because genes are carried on the paired chromosomes, humans have two copies of each gene, one from each parent. Genes, however, come in variant forms, known as alleles, which work together to express traits. This is why your hair color and blood type may not match those traits in either of your parents.

A special type of marker known as a Short Tandem Repeat (STR) is the one most often used for hereditary and forensic testing. STRs are short sequences of DNA (usually 2 to 5 base pairs) that are repeated as many as 100 times along the DNA strand. STRs are chosen for their tendencies to display variations, caused by mutations, among different people, allowing scientists to differentiate between individuals.

To determine a connection between two individuals, specific markers on the DNA strand are analyzed for the number of repetitions at each marker. Because mutations happen randomly, however, a mutation that appears at a specific marker may have begun with the current generation, or it may have been handed down through five generations. This is why a number of different markers are tested and compared. The number of markers examined varies from test to test and company to company, but most ancestry DNA tests are typically in the 12- to 40-marker range. The DNA test results provide you with the number of repetitions at each of the specific markers tested. The more locations that match, the more likely it is that the two individuals are related.

Paternal Line (Y-line) DNA Testing

The Y-chromosome is passed down in DNA from father to sons. A small portion of this chromosome has been discovered to pass down virtually unchanged from one generation to the next. Certain markers along this portion of the Y-chromosome can be tested to track descent along the direct male line of a family—from father to father's father, and so on.

When you take a Y-line DNA test, your results will come back as a string of numbers. These numbers represent the repeats found for each of the tested markers along the Y-chromosome. Matching numbers at all or most of the tested markers can indicate a shared ancestor between two men who have both taken the test. This ancestor is referred to as your Most Recent Common Ancestor (MRCA). Depending upon the number of markers tested and the number of markers that match between the two individuals, a DNA test can determine a time frame for the MRCA. A 37 marker test in which all 37 markers match another individual's test, for example, could show an MRCA within 4.7 generations with a 50 percent probability rate and within 16 generations at 90 percent probability. As you can see, the test is not exactly conclusive, but when combined with traditional genealogy research it can be quite helpful.

FACT

The Y-DNA test is only available for males because females don't carry the Y-chromosome, and is most often used by individuals with the same surname to learn whether they share a common ancestor.

Maternal Line (mtDNA) Testing

Just as Y-chromosome DNA testing can help confirm relationships in the paternal line, mitochondrial DNA, or mtDNA, can provide information about the maternal line. Most DNA is located in the nucleus of our cells, and is referred to as nuclear DNA. A small amount of DNA, however, can also be found within the cytoplasm of the cells, inside tiny structures called mitochondria. Mothers pass this mtDNA down to their children.

Unlike the long chain of base pairs found in chromosomal DNA, mtDNA exists as a closed circular loop of bases. It changes, or mutates, *very* slowly over time; on average, once every 3,000 to 12,000 years.

The mtDNA tests most commonly used for determining ancestry examine the base sequences in two specific sections of the control region, known as hypervariable region I (HVRI) and hypervariable region II (HVRII). They were chosen for ancestral and other genetic testing because they are not part of the coding region, and have the fastest rate of mutation of any region in mtDNA.

Most mtDNA tests will test one or both of the hypervariable regions and report your specific sequence. Some companies may list your entire actual sequence, but because mtDNA changes so slowly, most will only report the differences, or polymorphisms, as compared to the standard Cambridge Reference Sequence (CRS). Having both HVRs tested will generally shorten the time frame of any matches.

Because mitochondrial DNA is inherited by both males and females from their mothers, both men and women can take this test. Men can inherit mtDNA, but they cannot, with possible rare exceptions, pass it down to their children. For this reason, mtDNA can only be used to trace the direct maternal line—son or daughter to mother to mother's mother, and so on.

DNA Surname Studies

DNA testing for ancestral connections provides the most information when you have others with which to compare the results. One of the best ways is to join a DNA Surname Study, in which researchers with the same surname compare their lineages and DNA test results in an effort to prove or disprove descent from a common ancestor.

Several thousand surname projects are already under way, so it's best to start by searching you favorite search engine for "your surname DNA" to see if a project has already been started for your surname.

The Web sites of many DNA genealogy testing companies include information about the surname projects of their clients. By joining a surname project that researches individuals who have the same surname that you do (or a variant), you can find out if and how you could be related.

If you're unable to find a DNA surname study that focuses on your particular surname in the geographic region where your ancestors lived, then you can start your own. This is usually easiest if you already know of several other researchers who might be interested in joining. To set up a DNA surname project, you'll need to:

1. **Determine the goal of your project.** What do you hope to learn? Do you want to include everyone with the same surname? Try to prove descent from a specific ancestor? Prove that two families with the same name are unrelated? Discover whether family tales of famous relatives are true?
2. **Select a testing lab. Most DNA** testing companies that cater to genealogists can assist you with setting up and organizing your surname study. Many will also offer group discounts on tests. Do some background research into the company's test options, reliability, privacy assurances, and cost and payment options.
3. **Recruit participants.** This is often the hardest part of the project. You need to locate people who can help you meet your project's objective, and sometimes you must convince complete strangers to hand over their DNA—no easy task. Creating a good Web site with information about the project's goal and ongoing results can be very helpful in locating prospects.

Once you have test results coming back in from your participants, you need to interpret the findings and disseminate the results. Nothing will keep people excited about your project more than seeing possible connections to that elusive ancestor start to take shape!

Explaining the Study to Family

Confidentiality and trust are a very important part of any DNA research project. People may fear that a DNA test may uncover a genetic defect, or that the government or an insurance company could gain access to their results and use it against them in some way. You're going to have to work hard to gain the trust of project participants. This means that you're going to need a good grasp of how the DNA testing works (as discussed in the previous part of this chapter) so that you can explain it to them. Make it clear that test results are only provided to the surname project by ID number, not name. Reassure them that the portion of their DNA that is tested does not provide any information about their genetic health. In short, as the leader of a surname project you'll wear the hat of educator, cheerleader, genealogist, and analyst.

The GENEALOGY-DNA-L mailing list at RootsWeb.com is a good place to learn more about genetic genealogy and surname studies. Its participants are always full of helpful advice, inspiration, and encouragement.

One of the best ways to learn how to organize a successful DNA surname study is to spend time exploring the projects run by others. DNA surname studies can be found linked to and from genealogy testing centers, and by searching for "DNA surname" in your favorite search engine. Look over those resources' explanations of their projects, the information they provide about DNA testing, and the way they present the results.

Your Family Health History

Many, if not most, human diseases have their roots in our genes. Heart disease, cancer, diabetes, and other common diseases often run in families. So do rare diseases such as cystic fibrosis, hemophilia, and sickle cell anemia. Even health conditions such as high blood pressure and obesity can often be found in multiple generations of a family.

Tracing the health problems suffered by your parents, grandparents, and other blood relatives can help your doctor predict the disorders for which you may be at risk and help you take possible preventive action. For instance, people at increased risk for heart disease may be able to reduce their risk by not smoking, getting regular exercise, and following a healthy diet. Finding out your family health history can benefit both you and your relatives—and it can be fun, too!

Gathering Information from Relatives

Your family's health history isn't easily learned from a book. You'll need to talk to your relatives to find out about their health and the health of other family members. Try to interview relatives face-to-face, when possible. This gives you the chance to explain your project and answer their questions and concerns. If you can't interview a family member in person, then conduct the interview by phone. Send a letter or e-mail as a method of last resort. Family gatherings present an ideal opportunity for family health history interviews.

FACT

Some diseases are purely genetic. Most, however, are a mixture of genetic makeup and environmental factors. In these cases, you are not born with the condition; you only inherit a susceptibility or predisposition to developing it during your lifetime. By learning about the possible inherited risk, you can take steps to lessen your chances of acquiring the disease or condition.

Gather information about as many generations of relatives as you can, including parents, grandparents, siblings, aunts, uncles, nieces, nephews, children, and grandchildren. If you're married and have children, include your spouse's family members as well. Pay special attention to older members of the family. They may know things about long-dead family members that haven't been passed down to younger generations.

Begin the interview with an explanation of your research and why compiling the family's health history may prove valuable, both for them and for future generations. Because you will be delving into the intimate medical history of your family members, it is imperative that you stress that all information will be kept confidential, even from other family members, unless you first obtain the individual's permission.

Next, ask about the overall health of the family. Use open-ended questions that require an explanation, rather than just a "yes" or "no" response. Find out whether there were any sudden or unexplained deaths in the family. Ask about the health and cause and age of death for any deceased family members that they may know about. Remind them to include any infant deaths as well. For family members with known diseases, ask whether they smoked or were overweight, and also ask about their exercise habits.

QUESTION?

Where else can I find family health information?
Death certificates and obituaries are an excellent source for medical information. Most death certificates list the cause and age of death. Obituaries may also provide a clue as to cause of death. If the cause isn't mentioned directly, look for a request for donations to be sent to a particular medical-related charity.

When you've elicited as much as you can about other family members, ask about the personal health history of the person you are interviewing. Record the name, age, sex, and approximate height and weight. Ask about any serious illnesses or diseases he may have had, including his age at onset. For women, list the pregnancies, both successful and unsuccessful.

Draw Your Medical Family Tree

Now that you've documented significant family illnesses and health conditions, it is time to put it all into a form that can be more easily evaluated and interpreted. This is done by drawing your family's medical pedigree. This graphic description of your family's health history can help you and your doctor spot patterns of specific conditions and diseases in the family tree.

ALERT!

Remove the names in your medical family tree prior to sharing it with your physician or other health-care provider. The names aren't needed to determine genetic predispositions and links, and you never know where the tree may end up. Medical information is very personal, and you must do your part to be sure that it stays private.

A medical pedigree provides both critical medical information and biological relationships at a glance. It looks similar to a traditional family tree, except that it uses standardized symbols to depict medical conditions and family relationships. If you're interested in learning to draw a medical family pedigree on your own, there are a few software programs that can help you. GeneWeaver, by Genes & Things, Inc., offers questionnaires and forms for collecting family data, and produces a variety of medical pedigree charts and reports.

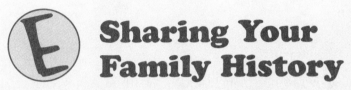

Chapter 21

Sharing Your Family History

It's not history until you write it down. The stories of your ancestors need to be told, and the family history that you've spent months, years, or even decades on deserves to be shared. To get the attention of your children, cousins, and other genealogists, you have to present your research in a pleasing, easy-to-understand format, such as a family history book, autobiography, or family newsletter. Now, on to the writing!

Writing Your Own Life Story

You cherish life stories written by a grandparent or other ancestor. You can read them, however, only because those people took some time to write an account of their lives. Many people write their own life stories. By seeing how others have done it, you can gain some useful ideas about how to write your own.

Why Bother?

People fail to write personal histories for three main reasons: lack of interest, lack of know-how, and discouragement caused by the amount of work such a project requires. If you are reluctant, is it because you don't think your experiences are important enough to write about? Why not leave some accounting of your life as a way, perhaps, of crediting those who helped shape who you are? Are there not some insights and lessons of life you can pass along to the next generation?

QUESTION?

My life is boring. What can I possibly write about?
While you might not find your life interesting, your descendants probably will. Potential topics include emotional highs or lows, friends, work, home improvement projects, romantic interests, major purchases, pets, your neighborhood, weather, religious beliefs, good deeds, historic happenings, favorite movies and music, talents, sports, deaths, weddings, vacations, major decisions, and goals.

In the process of reviewing your memories, you can learn a great deal about yourself. Also, if you record your history yourself it will be more accurate than will the accounts that others might later write about you. You can save your life story from errors that may be inflicted upon it by well-meaning descendants who will try to write your history.

Starting to Write

Writing your life story is a very personal enterprise. Only you can decide what to tell and how to tell it. Just as for any good story, you should begin your life history with an outline of what you want to write. In most cases, this will be a timeline of the major events in your life, complete with dates. This outline will become more detailed as you further explore your life story.

Next, create a very simple filing system in which you can organize the bits of information that you collect. Whether you use binders, file folders, or your computer, the keys to a successful filing system are the categories or sections of your life into which you divide the pages. Generally, people choose to divide up their life into stages, each of which could later be the subject of a separate section or chapter of the final history. Life stages could include:

- Roots and family heritage
- Childhood
- Youth or adolescence
- Early adulthood
- Middle or prime adulthood
- Later years

Some people file information by geographic location, which is extremely useful if you have moved a few times within a decade or two. You can also create files for special topics that cut across the chronological or geographical periods. Such topics could include work experiences, parenting, influential people, or humorous experiences.

Rounding Up Information

With a filing system in place, you can start gathering information about your life—from your memory and from other sources. Jot down brief notes whenever important memories come to mind. Some people keep index cards or a notepad with them at all times for this purpose.

Devote short blocks of time to brainstorming for memories on a particular topic—while driving to work, just before falling asleep, while doing dishes, or while mowing the lawn.

Putting the History Together

When writing a life story, it is easiest to do one section at a time. Select one of the topic files and thumb through all the notes you have collected there. Organize and group them. Develop a tentative outline to follow when writing or tape-recording your remembrances about the subject.

To make your story alive and interesting, give details about what you did. Don't just say that you worked at a drugstore. Share some of your experiences while working there as well. It is important that you not only tell what occurred, but also how you felt about it, including some explanation as to how and why things happened.

Avoid the temptation to leave out problems or unpleasant events. Deal with them if they are important in your life's development. To sugarcoat your history is to be dishonest. Everyone has problems, and your history should show that you did, too. Treat sensitive matters with great empathy for the subjects of the history and with tact, however.

ALERT!

Never try to make the first version of your written history the only and final version. That's way too much pressure to put on yourself! Start with a working draft and use it to get your facts and details straight, with the basic information told adequately rather than perfectly. Polish comes later.

Writing a Family History

Writing a biographical history about your relatives is one of life's most rewarding—but also most challenging—projects. As a genealogist, you are a finder and compiler of facts; this project, however, requires that you put on the historian's hat and become not just a collector but a narrator of the family story or a relative's biography. Good history happens when you combine solid records and a good explanation of what the records say.

Therefore, your task as a family biographer is twofold. First, you must search diligently and locate records that contain information about the history of individuals. Second, you must study those records, decide what they tell you, and then write well the story that your findings provide.

Decide What the Project Will Be

It pays to visit a larger library, browse through its genealogy and family history shelves, and study the family histories and biographies that appeal to you. They may help you decide how you want to do yours. Some key questions whose answers will help shape your family history project are:

- Do you want to write an essay or book?
- How many people or generations should you include?
- Who is your intended audience?

Starting Your Story

You can't know what your history will be about unless you can summarize what it is you intend to do with it. Before writing, or at least while working on the first draft, you need to tell yourself and future readers what your history deals with. This introduction or preface should include:

- Who the history deals with
- What the main developments are
- Where the history takes place
- When or what time period it covers
- Why you've chosen to write about this person or family

First Draft and Working Drafts

Once you've done a reasonable job of finding records and source materials, you need to start writing. Whether it's a chapter or an entire book, it will take a few drafts to make the narrative respectable. The first draft should begin with an outline of your family history. Then, when your outline seems workable, enlarge it by making it into a sentence outline. That is, instead of saying "Dad's childhood in Butte," you say "Dad's childhood in Butte was a rough experience for him and his parents." To move from a topic into a sentence is to begin the writing process.

You may encounter skeletons in the family's closet, and wonder how to handle them. Genealogists' most common approach is "tell, don't dwell"—meaning don't whitewash history by glossing over the facts, but don't embellish it or make it the focus of your family history either. If the telling will hurt a living family member, you may wish to omit the information.

The first draft should be an attempt at giving the information in your files organizational structure—to present a factual running account of the individual or family. This lets you see the gaps, imbalances, contradictions, and problems in the story. Here you really find out what your sources seem to be telling you, as well as what they are not telling you.

The first draft is a major threshold. Finishing the first draft should produce a great sense of accomplishment. At last you can see the shape that the next versions of the history will take.

Revising

Once you have the workings of a first draft, you follow by doing more research to fill in gaps and make better sense of your story, and you start revising.

The key to good writing is simple: revise, revise, revise. It's like sanding rough wood or polishing a stone. Rewriting and revising produces better organization, better paragraphs, and better sentences and word choices. If you are using a word processor to revise, be sure to save a copy of the first draft—don't revise it out of existence.

Effective Writing Techniques

While revising, you need to move into a stage in which you work on writing the narration well. During this stage, you move beyond your earlier concerns about the organization and factual content of your story. Several good writing techniques make all the difference in the world between a ho-hum narrative and a compelling family history:

- **Use Details and Good Description**—Details will make your family history more enjoyable to read and easier to understand. Include physical descriptions of the people in your story, give good descriptions of the places where they lived, and so forth. It's hard to visualize "a puppy," but if you say "a black and tan Cocker Spaniel puppy," your readers will be able to see the puppy as they read your words.
- **Use Short Quotes Instead of Long Ones**—Quotations are one of the best "seasonings" you can sprinkle into your family history. Long passages, however, tend to be skipped over by readers. Keep quoted material to a one- or two-paragraph maximum.
- **Use Words That Appeal to the Five Senses**—Homemade bread baking in Grandma's oven. A church bell tolling eleven o'clock on a dark, moonless night. Writing that deals with sensory matters—seeing, hearing, touching, tasting, and smelling—carries instant appeal for readers.
- **Capitalize on Feelings and Emotional Situations**—Readers most enjoy and best remember writing that makes them feel something. A major failing in many family histories is that they are all facts. But human beings feel. Histories about real people should show how they felt, so include situations and events that convey or trigger emotion.

The most important paragraphs of your family history are the first and last. The first paragraph of your family history needs to grab the reader's attention. If you begin with "James Owens was born in North Carolina in 1876," your readers will be yawning before they reach the end of the first paragraph. Instead, the opening paragraph should leave the reader curious. Is there a story or episode you can use to attract the reader? Can you start out with a statement that makes the reader curious? Why not begin with an interesting question that makes the reader want to know the answer?

One tactic often used by family history writers is to start with an interesting event that actually occurs in the middle of the story, and then use flashbacks to tell readers how the family got to that point. Look for the most interesting event or aspect of your ancestors' lives—the first time they stepped foot on American soil, the marriage of two young people in love, a family's struggle to rebuild after the Civil War—and open your narrative with it.

The last paragraph of a good family history should leave the reader wanting to know a bit more. In other words, don't end with "and they all lived happily ever after." You shouldn't necessarily end your family history with the death of the main characters, either. You can end the story of your grandparents with the marriage of your parents. Or you can conclude with a humorous story, interesting event, or reminiscence. The ending should be as compelling as the beginning.

ALERT!

Most genealogical software programs can help you create and print a family history book. The narration that these programs generate leaves a lot to be desired, however. The software is useful for creating the table of contents and index, as well as charts and pedigrees, but it's best to replace the narrative portion with your own personally written story.

Finishing Touches

One major mistake many family historians make is to clutter up their narration with charts, documents, and pictures. Instead of constantly interrupting the flow of your story with these materials, it sometimes makes sense to include supporting documents such as detailed genealogy charts, certificates, detailed maps, and copies of letters in an appendix at the back of the book. If one of these items easily illustrates your story, it's fine to use it in the narrative, but otherwise put it in the appendix instead and include a reference to it in your narrative.

Readers need a list of all the sources you consulted while you were doing research for the biography. Source citations leave a trail for your family members to follow, and show that you're supported by facts. These can be presented in the form of a biography or end notes. If you really want your story to be read and used, be sure to include a table of contents and index as well.

FACT

Your family history is automatically protected by copyright—you should include a notice of copyright on the back of the title page. You can also register the copyright through the Library of Congress. Copyright registration requires a completed application, payment of a filing fee, and two complete published copies of your book to be included in the Library of Congress.

People usually look at photographs in books before they read a word, so adding pictures is another nice touch. Photographs can be scattered throughout the text, or put in a picture section in the middle or back of the book. If scattered, however, photos should be used to illustrate the narration, not detract from it. Balance your selection of pictures to give equitable coverage to each family. Also, be sure you include short but adequate captions that identify each picture—people, place, and approximate date.

Publishing Your Family History

It's important to share with other relatives what you discover about your family heritage. You can do this through videotapes, audiotapes, sets of family photographs, and by creating books and booklets that you self-publish.

Today's technology makes self-publishing a fairly easy process, and families and individuals are self-publishing history and genealogy books in record numbers. Once you've written your family history, why not take the time to bind and print copies for your relatives?

Connecting with Kin—Family Newsletters

One of the best ways to connect far-flung family members is to keep everyone up-to-date with a family newsletter. The family newsletter can focus on current events, helping family members scattered across the country to stay in touch with the details of each other's lives. Alternatively, you can develop a newsletter around a family tree research project—sharing documents, stories, photos, and newly discovered facts with all interested researchers. Many people choose to incorporate a mix of both the present and the past.

A family newsletter makes a great vehicle for interesting family in your family tree project and gathering information from distant relatives. The more they feel a part of the project, and the more they see what results you are getting, the more they are willing to share.

Family newsletters make a great alternative to the traditional holiday card or letter. The newsletter format, with feature stories and photos, is easy to read and packs a lot of information into a small space. The collection of back issues is also sure to be appreciated by any future family genealogists!

Family newsletters don't have to be complicated, but there are a few things that you need to consider: what it will contain, who you will send it to, and how it will be delivered.

What to Include

Deciding what to write about is the first step in producing a family newsletter. If you're focusing on current events, include the everyday things that folks are up to—vacations, work, hobbies, school and sport updates, and announcements of major events such as births, weddings, reunions, and graduations.

If your focus is the past, your own research will provide a lot of the content. A research update can keep people in touch with what you've learned about the family. Feature at least one family photo, letter, or document per newsletter—this will encourage a lot of new submissions from your family members. You can also use the newsletter as a way to share family recipes and stories.

Who to Send It To

Once the news goes out, you're going to have people coming out of the woodwork asking to get the family newsletter. There will be family members who aren't interested, however. To make it easy, you can start by sending the first edition out to your immediate family and close relatives and let word-of-mouth build up your mailing list. Alternatively, you can send out a copy of the newsletter to everyone you think will be interested, asking them to respond if they'd like to continue to receive future editions.

ALERT!

Set aside a section of your newsletter for a "call to action"—requesting submissions, photos, documents, stories, and other useful content to include in future editions. Making your request specific and focused on a particular topic, such as weddings, photos, immigrant ancestors, and so on, will help encourage a positive response.

Delivery Options

You can print and distribute family newsletters by postal mail, or send them in electronic format. Your choice will be dependent upon family preferences and your budget. If you send out an e-newsletter periodically, you will save money on printing and postage and are more likely to hear back from your relatives. People will more readily dash off an e-mail than sit down and write a letter these days. If there are a lot of family members without computers and e-mail, a printed newsletter may be more appreciated. Many family newsletters offer both options—an electronic format for those who prefer it, and a printed newsletter for the rest of the folks.

Appendix A

For Further Information

Chapter 1: Family Tree Basics

Free Genealogy Charts and Forms
http://genealogy.about.com/od/free_charts

Family Tree Magazine—Download Forms
www.familytreemagazine.com/forms/download.html

Ancestry.com—Charts and Forms
www.ancestry.com/trees/charts/ancchart.aspx

Misbach Enterprises—Genealogy Charts
www.misbach.org/pdfcharts/index.html

Calendar Converter Tool
www.fourmilab.ch/documents/calendar

Curran, Joan F., Madilyn Coen Crane, and John H. Wray. *Numbering Your Genealogy: Basic Systems, Complex Families, and International Kin.* (Arlington, VA: National Genealogical Society, 1999).

Chicago Manual of Style, 15th ed. (Chicago: University of Chicago Press, 2003).

Mills, Elizabeth Shown. *Evidence! Citation and Analysis for the Family Historian* (Baltimore: Genealogical Publishing Co., 1997).

Chapter 2: The Journey Begins at Home

Family and Home Information Sources Checklist
www.pbs.org/kbyu/ancestors/charts/old-pdf/checklist1.pdf

50 Questions for Family History Interviews
http://genealogy.about.com/cs/oralhistory/a/interview.htm

StoryCorps—Interview Your Loved Ones
www.storycorps.net

Veterans History Project
www.loc.gov/vets

Taylor, Maureen. *Uncovering Your Ancestry Through Family Photographs*, Rev. ed. (Cincinnati, OH: Family Tree Books, 2005).

Severa, Joan. *Dressed for the Photographer: Ordinary Americans and Fashion, 1840–1900.* (Kent, OH: Kent State University Press, 1995).

Chapter 3: Growing the Family Tree

Library of Congress Online Catalog
http://catalog.loc.gov

Allen County Public Library—PERSI
⌨*www.acpl.lib.in.us/genealogy/persi.html*

FamilySearch.org—Research Outlines
⌨*www.familysearch.org/Eng/Search/RG/
frameset_rg.asp*

Family History Library Catalog
⌨*www.familysearch.org/Eng/Library/FHLC/
frameset_fhlc.asp*

U.S. Geological Survey (USGS) Maps
⌨*http://store.usgs.gov*

American Memory Map Collections: 1500–2004
⌨*http://memory.loc.gov/ammem/gmdhtml/
gmdhome.html*

Perry-Castañeda Map Collection—
University of Texas
⌨*www.lib.utexas.edu/maps/historical*

The Gold Bug—Historic Map Reproductions
⌨*www.goldbug.com*

About Geography
⌨*http://geography.about.com*

Thorndale, William, and William Dollarhide. *Map
Guide to the U.S. Federal Censuses, 1790–1920.*
(Baltimore: Genealogical Publishing Co., 1987).

Genealogical Correspondence Log
⌨*www.cs.williams.edu/~bailey/genealogy/
CorrespondenceRecordSheet.pdf*

Research Calendar
⌨*www.familytreemagazine.com/forms/
research/calendar.pdf*

Chapter 4: The Name of the Game

Glossary of Last Name Meanings and Origins
⌨*http://genealogy.about.com/library/
surnames/bl_meaning.htm*

Last Name Meanings Dictionary
⌨*www.last-names.net*

Hanks, Patrick, and Flavia Hodges. *A Dictionary of
Surnames.* (Oxford and New York: Oxford University Press, 1988).

Smith, Elsdon C. *American Surnames.* Reprint.
(Baltimore: Genealogical Publishing Co., 2003).

College of Arms
⌨*www.college-of-arms.gov.uk*

Court of the Lord Lyon
⌨*www.lyon-court.com*

American College of Heraldry
⌨*www.americancollegeofheraldry.org*

Chapter 6: Vital Records

Eichholz, Alice, ed. *Ancestry's Red Book: American State, County and Town Sources.* Rev. ed. (Salt
Lake City: Ancestry, Inc., 1992).

Kemp, Thomas Jay. *International Vital Records Handbook*, 4th ed. (Baltimore: Genealogical Publishing Co., 2000).

United States Vital Record Information
 www.vitalrec.com

Where to Find U.S. Vital Records
 http://genealogy.about.com/library/blvitalus.htm

Vitalchek Network, Inc.
 www.vitalchek.com

Online Searchable Death Indexes and Records
 www.deathindexes.com

GenWed—Free Public Marriage Records Online
 www.genwed.com

Chapter 7: Clues in the Census

Soundex Code Generator
 http://genealogy.about.com/library/bl_soundex_tool.htm

Soundex Converter
 resources.rootsweb.com/cgi-bin/soundexconverter

FamilySearch.org—Search Census Records
 www.familysearch.org/Eng/Search/frameset_search.asp?PAGE=census/search_census.asp

Ancestry.com—U.S. Census Records (subscription)
 ancestry.com/search/rectype/census/usfedcen/default.aspx

Genealogy.com—U.S. Census Collection (subscription)
 www.genealogy.com/uscensussub.html

HeritageQuest Online—U.S. Census (available through participating libraries)
 www.heritagequestonline.com

Census Online
 www.census-online.com

Where to Find U.S. Census Indexes—
A Comparison Chart
 http://genealogy.about.com/od/us_census/f/census_indexes.htm

Dakota Territory 1885 Census
 www.lib.ndsu.nodak.edu/ndirs/databases/census.php

Hinckley, Kathleen. *Your Guide to the Federal Census: For Genealogists, Researchers, and Family Historians.* (Cincinnati, OH: Betterway Books, 2002).

Lainhart, Ann S. *State Census Records.* (Baltimore: Genealogical Publishing Co., 1992).

Szucs, Loretto Dennis, and Matthew Wright. *Finding Answers in U.S. Census Records.* (Orem, UT: Ancestry Publishing, 2002).

Chapter 8: Marching Papers

National Archives—Request Military Service Records
✍ *www.archives.gov/veterans/military-service-records/get-service-records.html*

DAR—Patriot Index Lookup Service
✍*www.dar.org/natsociety/pi_lookup.cfm*

American Civil War Research Database
✍*www.civilwardata.com* (subscription)

Civil War Soldiers and Sailors System
✍*www.itd.nps.gov/cwss*

World War I Draft Registrations (partial)
✍*www.rootsweb.com/~rwguide/WWIdraft.html*

World War I Draft Registration Card Request Form
✍*friendsnas.org/pdf_files/WWIDraftRequest.pdf*

Selective Service System Records
✍*www.sss.gov/records2.htm*

National Archives—WWII Enlistment Records
✍*www.archives.gov/aad*

Sons of Confederate Veterans
✍*www.scv.org*

General Society of the War of 1812
✍*www.societyofthewarof1812.org*

Chapter 9: A Nation of Immigrants

Strassburger, Ralph B., compiler. *Pennsylvania German Pioneers—A Publication of the Original Lists of Arrivals in the Port of Philadelphia from 1727 to 1808, 1934*, 3 vols. Reprint. (Camden, ME: Picton Press, 1992).

Filby, P. William. *Passenger and Immigration Lists Index—A Guide to Published Arrival Records of 300,000 Passengers Who Came to the United States and Canada in the Seventeenth, Eighteenth, and Nineteenth Centuries.* (Detroit: Gale Research Co., 1980).

Filby, P. William, and Ira A. Glazier. eds. *Germans to America: Lists of Passengers Arriving at U.S. Ports.* (Wilmington, DE: Scholarly Resources, 1997).

Ellis Island Passenger Arrivals Database
✍*www.ellisislandrecords.org*

Castle Garden, NY—Immigrant Database
✍*www.castlegarden.org*

Texas Seaport Museum—Galveston Immigration Database
✍*www.tsm-elissa.org/immigration-main.htm*

Bremen Passenger Lists, 1920–1939
✍*www.schiffslisten.de/index_en.html*

Hamburg Emigration Lists
✍*www.linktoyourroots.hamburg.de*

U.S. Citizenship and Immigration Services
http://uscis.gov/graphics/aboutus/history/index.htm

Early American Roads and Trails
http://freepages.genealogy.rootsweb.com/~gentutor/trails.html

Migrations.org
www.migrations.org

Chapter 10: Clues in the Cemetery

Find a Grave
www.findagrave.com

Interment.net—Cemetery Transcription Library
www.interment.net

The Political Graveyard
www.politicalgraveyard.com

Saving Graves—Preserving Historic Cemeteries
www.savinggraves.org

USGenWeb Tombstone Transcription Project
www.rootsweb.com/~cemetery

Tombstone Art and Symbols
www.tales.ndirect.co.uk/A_ZINDEX.HTML

American Battle Monuments Commission
www.abmc.gov

Commonwealth War Graves Commission
www.cwgc.org/cwgcinternet/search.aspx

U.S. Geographic Names Information System
http://geonames.usgs.gov

Topozone
www.topozone.com

Carmack, Sharon DeBartolo. *Your Guide to Cemetery Research*. (Cincinnati, OH: Betterway Books, 2002).

Keister, Douglas. *Stories in Stone: A Field Guide to Cemetery Symbolism and Iconography*. (Salt Lake City: Gibbs Smith, Publisher, 2004).

Chapter 11: Following in Their Footsteps

Bureau of Land Management—Search Land Patents
www.glorecords.blm.gov

Virginia Land Office Patents and Grants
www.lva.lib.va.us/whatwehave/land/index.htm

Deed Platter—Online Platting Tool
www.genealogytools.net/deeds/

Deed Mapper Software
http://users.rcn.com/deeds/factsht.htm

Deed Plotter Software
www.greenbriergraphics.com

Hatcher, Patricia Law. *Locating Your Roots: Discovering Your Ancestors Using Land Records*. (Cincinnati, OH: Betterway Books, 2003).

Hone, E. Wade. *Land and Property Research in the United States.* (Salt Lake City: Ancestry, Inc., 1997).

Chapter 12: Probate and Estate Trails

Glossary of Legal Terms
 www.mylawyer.com/glossary.htm

Index to Texas Probate Records
 http://three-legged-willie.org/texas.htm

Delaware Probate Index, 1680–1925
 www.state.de.us/sos/dpa/collections/ probate.shtml

Prerogative Court of Canterbury Wills, 1384 to 1858 (England and Wales)
 www.nationalarchives.gov.uk/ documentsonline/wills.asp

Scottish Wills and Testaments, 1513–1901
 www.scotlandspeople.gov.uk

Mitchell, Thornton W. *North Carolina Wills: A Testator Index, 1665–1900.* Reprint. (Baltimore: Genealogical Publishing Co., 2001).

Torrence, Clayton. *Virginia Wills and Administrations, 1632–1800: An Index of Wills Recorded in Local Courts of Virginia.* Reprint. (Baltimore: Genealogical Publishing Co., 2000).

Chapter 13: Branching Out

Melton, J. Gordon, ed. *Encyclopedia of American Religion*, 7th edition. (Detroit: Gale Research, 2002).

National Union Catalog of Manuscript Collections
 www.loc.gov/coll/nucmc

The National Yearbook Project
 www.rootsweb.com/~usyrbook

New York Times Digital Archive
 http://pqasb.pqarchiver.com/nytimes/ advancedsearch.html

NewspaperArchive.com
 www.newspaperarchive.com

National Digital Newspaper Program
 www.loc.gov/ndnp

The Olden Times—Historic Newspapers Online
 www.theoldentimes.com

Obituary Central
 www.obitcentral.com

ObitsArchive.com
 www.obitsarchive.com

Social Security Death Index—Search the SSDI
 www.newenglandancestors.org/research/ database/ss

Social Security—Geographical Number Assignments
www.socialsecurity.gov/foia/stateweb.html

Social Security Administration—FOIA Requests
www.socialsecurity.gov/foia

Glossary of Old Occupations and Trades
http://genealogy.about.com/library/glossary/bl_occupations.htm

Waters, Colin. *A Dictionary of Old Trades, Titles and Occupations.* (Newbury, Berkshire, England: Countryside Books, 2002).

Encyclopedia of Associations. (Detroit: Gale Research Co., published biannually).

Classmates.com
www.classmates.com

Reunion.com
www.reunion.com

Genelines Software
www.genelines.com

Cyndi's List—Timelines
www.cyndislist.com/timeline.htm

About Genealogy—Historical and Social Timelines
http://genealogy.about.com/cs/timelines/

Chapter 14: Special Situations in Family Trees

International Soundex Reunion Registry
www.isrr.org

State and National Reunion Registries
http://adoption.about.com/od/registries

Adoption Search Angels
http://adoption.about.com/od/searchangels

American Adoption Congress
www.americanadoptioncongress.org

Orphan Train Heritage Society of America
www.orphantrainriders.com/othsa11.html

The African Methodist Episcopal Church
www.amecnet.org

National Baptist Convention
www.nationalbaptist.com

Christian Methodist Episcopal Church
www.c-m-e.org

Freedmen's Bureau Online
www.freedmensbureau.com

Rawick, George P., ed. *The American Slave: A Composite Autobiography.* 41 vols. (Westport, CT: Greenwood Press, 1972–79).

American Slave Narratives Online—Selections
from *The American Slave*
    *http://xroads.virginia.edu/~HYPER/wpa/
wpahome.html*

AfriGeneas
    www.afrigeneas.com

National Underground Railroad Freedom Center
    www.freedomcenter.org

JewishGen Shtetl Seeker
    www.jewishgen.org/ShtetlSeeker

American Jewish Archives
    www.americanjewisharchives.org

American Jewish Historical Society
    www.ajhs.org

International Association of Jewish Genealogical
Societies
    www.iajgs.org

Avotaynu
    www.avotaynu.com

JewishGen
    www.jewishgen.org

Stern, Malcolm H. *First American Jewish Families:
600 Genealogies, 1654–1988.* (Baltimore: Otten-
heimer Publishers, 1991).

Swanton, John R. *The Indian Tribes of North America.* Reprint. (Washington, D.C.: Smithsonian Institute Press, 1984).

BIA Tribal Leaders Directory
    www.doi.gov/Leaders.pdf

National Archives—Native American Records Online
    *www.archives.gov/research/arc/topics/
native-americans.html*

Oklahoma Historical Society
    www.ok-history.mus.ok.us

Szucs, Loretto Dennis, and Sandra Hargreaves
Luebking. *The Source: A Guidebook of American
Genealogy,* Rev. ed. (Salt Lake City: Ancestry, Inc.,
1997).

Ryskamp, George R. *Finding Your Hispanic Roots.*
(Baltimore: Genealogical Publishing Co., 1997).

Family Tree Books—Discovering Your Ancestors
Series
    www.familytreemagazine.com/store

Chapter 15: Walking the Web

Google
    www.google.com

Yahoo! Search
    http://search.yahoo.com

MSN Search
    http://search.msn.com

Ask Jeeves
&*www.ask.com*

The Wayback Machine
&*www.archive.org*

Google Search Strategies for Genealogists
&*http://genealogy.about.com/library/weekly/ aa052902a.htm*

RootsWeb Mailing Lists
&*http://lists.rootsweb.com*

Genealogy Resources on the Internet:
Mailing Lists
&*www.rootsweb.com/~jfuller/gen_mail.html*

Yahoo! Groups—Genealogy
&*http://groups.yahoo.com/ search?query=genealogy*

Google Groups—Genealogy
&*http://groups.google.com/groups/ dir?q=genealogy*

GenForum
&*www.genforum.com*

Ancestry.com Message Boards
&*http://boards.ancestry.com*

Cousin Connect
&*www.cousinconnect.com*

About Genealogy Newsletter
&*http://genealogy.about.com/gi/pages/ mmail.htm*

Ancestry Daily News
&*http://ancestry.com/learn/library/article. aspx?article=dailynews*

Eastman's Online Genealogy Newsletter
&*www.eogn.com*

Family Tree Finders
&*http://rhondamcclure.com/newsletter.htm*

Missing Links
&*www.petuniapress.com*

RootsWeb Review
&*http://rootsweb.com/~review*

Phone Directories on the Web
&*http://genealogy.about.com/cs/phone*

KnowX
&*www.knowx.com*

InteliUS
&*www.intelius.com*

US Search
&*www.usssearch.com*

FamilySearch.org—Search for Ancestors
&*www.familysearch.org/Eng/Search/ frameset_search.asp*

Ancestry World Tree
  www.ancestry.com/trees/awt/main.htm

GenCircles Global Tree
  www.gencircles.com/globaltree

GeneaNet
  www.geneanet.com

Genealogy.com World Family Tree (subscription)
  http://familytreemaker.genealogy.com/wftonline/

Cyndi's List of Genealogy Sites on the Internet
  www.cyndislist.com

About Genealogy
  http://genealogy.about.com

USGenWeb Project
  www.usgenweb.com

MyFamily.com
  www.myfamily.com

Godfrey Scholar
  www.godfrey.org

Richley, Pat. *The Everything® Online Genealogy Book.* (Avon, MA: Adams Media, 2001).

Binder, Mark, and Beth Helman. *The Everything® Build Your Own Home Page Book.* (Avon, MA: Adams Media, 2000).

Chapter 16: Shelves of Possibilities

Library of Congress
  www.loc.gov

FamilySearch
  www.familysearch.org

National Archives and Records Administration (NARA)
  www.archives.gov

Allen County Public Library, Indiana
  www.acpl.lib.in.us/genealogy

DAR Library, Washington, D.C.
  www.dar.org

Newberry Library, Chicago
  www.newberry.org/genealogy

New York Public Library, New York City
  www.nypl.org/research/chss/lhg/research.html

Clayton Library, Houston
  www.hpl.lib.tx.us/clayton

New England Historic Genealogical Society Library
  www.newenglandancestors.org

Eichholz, Alice, ed. *Ancestry's Red Book: American State, County and Town Sources*, Rev. ed. (Salt Lake City: Ancestry, Inc., 1992).

Everton, George B., ed. *The Handy Book for Genealogists*, 10th ed. (Draper, Utah: Everton Publishers, 2002).

Bentley, Elizabeth P. *County Courthouse Book*, 2nd ed. (Baltimore: Genealogical Publishing Co., 1995).

Carmack, Sharon DeBartolo, ed. *The Family Tree Resource Book for Genealogists: The Essential Guide to American County and Town Sources.* (Cincinnati, OH: Family Tree Books, 2004).

Meyerink, Kory L. *Printed Sources: A Guide to Published Genealogical Records.* (Salt Lake City: Ancestry, Inc., 1998).

National Genealogical Society
   ✎*www.ngsgenealogy.org*

New England Historic Genealogical Society
   ✎*www.newenglandancestors.org*

The Federation of Genealogical Societies
   ✎*www.fgs.org*

Bentley, Elizabeth P. The *Genealogist's Address Book*, 5th ed. (Baltimore: Genealogical Publishing Co., 2005).

Society Hill
   ✎*www.daddezio.com/society/hill/index.html*

Chapter 17: Tools for Taming the Family Tree

Clooz—The Electronic Filing *Cabinet for Genealogical Records*
   ✎*www.clooz.com*

Family Roots Organizer
   ✎*http://123genealogy.com/organizer*

Kindred Trails—Color Track System
   ✎ *www.thefamilyhistorystore.com/index. php?cPath=22*

Carmack, Sharon DeBartolo. *Organizing Your Family History Search.* (Cincinnati, OH: Betterway Books, 1999).

Fleming, Ann Carter. *The Organized Family Historian: How to File, Manage, and Protect Your Genealogical Research and Heirlooms.* (Nashville, TN: Rutledge Hill Press, 2004).

Ancestral Quest
   ✎*www.ancestralquest.com*

Ancestry Family Tree
   ✎*www.ancestry.com/aftexec*

Family Tree Legends
   ✎*www.familytreelegends.com*

Family Tree Maker
   ✎*www.familytreemaker.com*

Genbox Family History
   ✎*www.genbox.com*

Heredis
  www.myheredis.com

Legacy Family Tree
  www.legacyfamilytree.com

Personal Ancestral File (PAF)
  www.familysearch.org/eng/paf

RootsMagic
  www.rootsmagic.com

The Master Genealogist
  www.whollygenes.com

About Genealogy—Genealogy Software Reviews
  http://genealogy.about.com/cs/genealogy-software/a/software.htm

GEDCOM Viewer
  http://users.northnet.com.au/~generic/gedcom

GEDClean—Remove living individuals
  www.raynorshyn.com/gedclean

GED2GO—Remove living individuals
  www.geocities.com/yosemite/trails/4849/evb

Scanning Tips for Genealogists
  http://genealogy.about.com/cs/digitalphoto/a/digital_photos.htm

Sturdevant, Katherine Scott. *Organizing and Preserving Your Heirloom Documents.* (Cincinnati, OH: Betterway Books, 2002).

Taylor, Maureen A. *Preserving Your Family Photographs. How to Organize, Present, and Restore Your Precious Family Images.* (Cincinnati, OH: Betterway Books, 2001).

Chapter 18: Assembling the Pieces

BCG—The Genealogical Proof Standard
  www.bcgcertification.org/resources/standard.html

NGS—Standards for Sound Genealogical Research
  www.ngsgenealogy.org/comstandsound.cfm

Board for Certification of Genealogists. *The BCG Genealogical Standards Manual.* (Salt Lake City: Ancestry, Inc., 2000).

Hatcher, Patricia Law. *Producing a Quality Family History.* (Salt Lake City: Ancestry, Inc., 1996).

Mills, Elizabeth Shown, ed. *Professional Genealogy: A Manual for Researchers, Writers, Editors, Lecturers, and Librarians.* (Baltimore: Genealogical Publishing Co., 2001).

Chapter 19: When You Get Stuck

Rising, Marsha Hoffman. *The Family Tree Problem Solver: Proven Methods for Scaling the Inevitable Brick Wall.* (Cincinnati, OH: Family Tree Books, 2005).

Pfeiffer, Laura Szucs. *Hidden Sources: Family History in Unlikely Places.* (Orem, UT: Ancestry, Inc. 2000).

Federal Bureau of Prisons Database
  www.bop.gov/iloc2/LocateInmate.jsp

Five Tips for Tracking Down Parents
  http://genealogy.about.com/od/basics/a/parents_names.htm

Sperry, Kip. *Reading Early American Handwriting.* (Baltimore: Genealogical Publishing Co., 1998).

National Genealogical Society—Education
  http://ngsgenealogy.org/edu.cfm

Brigham Young University
  www.byu.edu

National Institute for Genealogical Studies
  www.genealogicalstudies.com

International Internet Genealogical Society University
  www.iigs.org/university

About Genealogy—Classes and Tutorials
  http://genealogy.about.com/library/onestop/bl_beginner.htm

Genealogy.com—Genealogy Classes
  www.genealogy.com/university.html

NGS Conference in the States
  www.ngsgenealogy.org

Federation of Genealogical Societies Conference
  www.fgs.org/fgs-conference.htm

National Institute on Genealogical Research
  www.rootsweb.com/~natgenin

Institute of Genealogy and Historical Research
  www.samford.edu/schools/ighr/ighr.html

Salt Lake City Institute of Genealogy
  www.infouga.org/slc.aspx

Ancestry Magazine
  www.ancestry.com/learn/publications/ancmag.htm

Everton's Genealogical Helper
  www.everton.com

Family Chronicle
  www.familychronicle.com

Family Tree Magazine
  www.familytreemagazine.com

Genealogical Computing
  www.ancestry.com/learn/publications/gencomp.htm

Heritage Quest
  www.heritagequestmagazine.com

The American Genealogist (TAG)
  www.americangenealogist.com

The Genealogist (TG)
  www.fasg.org/TheGenealogist.html

The National Genealogical Society Quarterly (NGSQ)
   ✎*www.ngsgenealogy.org/pubsquarterly.cfm*

The New England Historical and Genealogical Register (NEHGR)
   ✎*www.newenglandancestors.org*

Books We Own
   ✎*www.rootsweb.com/~bwo*

Random Acts of Genealogical Kindness
   ✎*www.raogk.org*

Board for Certification of Genealogists (BCG)
   ✎*www.bcgcertification.org*

International Commission for the Accreditation of Professional Genealogists (ICAPGen)
   ✎*www.icapgen.org*

Association of Professional Genealogists
   ✎*www.apgen.org*

Chapter 20: Uncovering Your Genetic Roots

African Ancestry—Trace Your DNA
   ✎*www.africanancestry.com*

Ancestry by DNA
   ✎*www.ancestrybydna.com*

Family Tree DNA
   ✎*www.familytreedna.com*

GeneTree
   ✎*www.genetree.com*

Oxford Ancestors
   ✎*www.oxfordancestors.com*

Relative Genetics
   ✎*www.relativegenetics.com*

GENEALOGY-DNA Mailing List
   ✎*http://lists.rootsweb.com/index/other/ DNA/GENEALOGY-DNA.html*

My Family Health Portrait
   ✎*www.hhs.gov/familyhistory*

Generational Health—Chart Your Family Health History
   ✎*www.generationalhealth.com/*

GeneWeaver
   ✎*www.geneweaveronline.com*

Shawker, Thomas H. *Unlocking Your Genetic History: A Step-by-Step Guide to Discovering Your Family's Medical and Genetic Heritage.* (Nashville, TN: Rutledge Hill Press, 2004).

Smolenyak, Megan, and Ann Turner. *Trace Your Roots with DNA: Using Genetic Tests to Explore Your Family Tree.* (Emmaus, PA: Rodale Books, 2004).

Chapter 21: Sharing Your Family History

United States Copyright Office
  www.copyright.gov

Creative Continuum—Short Run Publisher
  www.creativecontinuum.com

Family Heritage Publishers
  www.familyheritagepublishers.com

Modern Memoirs
  www.modernmemoirs.com

Carmack, Sharon DeBartolo. *You Can Write Your Family History.* (Cincinnati, OH: Betterway Books, 2003).

Kempthorne, Charley. *For All Time: A Complete Guide to Writing Your Family History.* (Portsmouth, NH: Boynton/Cook Publishers, 1996).

Appendix B

Charts for Plotting Your Family Tree

Pedigree Chart

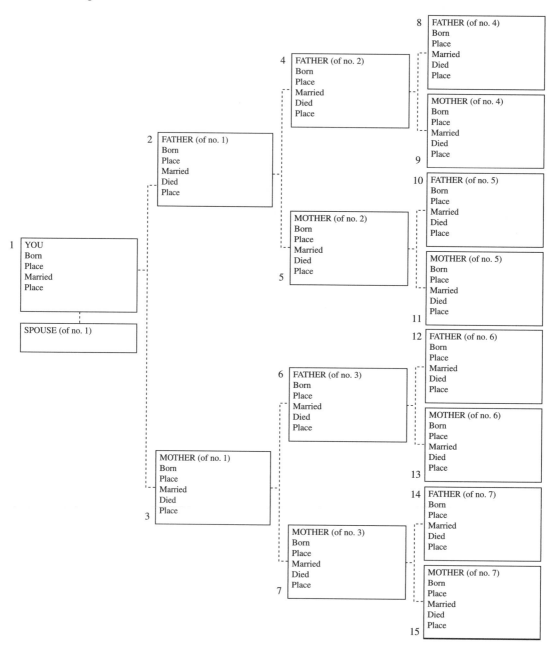

Family Group Record

Husband´s name

Born	Place
Chr.	Place
Mar.	Place
Died	Place
Bur.	Place

Father	Mother

Husband´s other wives

Wife´s name

Born	Place
Chr.	Place
Died	Place
Bur.	

Father	Mother

Wife´s other husbands

Children

1 Sex	Name		Spouse	
	B/Chr	Place	Mar.	Place
	Died	Place	Bur	Place

2 Sex	Name		Spouse	
	B/Chr	Place	Mar.	Place
	Died	Place	Bur	Place

3 Sex	Name		Spouse	
	B/Chr	Place	Mar.	Place
	Died	Place	Bur	Place

4 Sex	Name		Spouse	
	B/Chr	Place	Mar.	Place
	Died	Place	Bur	Place

5 Sex	Name		Spouse	
	B/Chr	Place	Mar.	Place
	Died	Place	Bur	Place

6 Sex	Name		Spouse	
	B/Chr	Place	Mar.	Place
	Died	Place	Bur	Place

7 Sex	Name		Spouse	
	B/Chr	Place	Mar.	Place
	Died	Place	Bur	Place

8 Sex	Name		Spouse	
	B/Chr	Place	Mar.	Place
	Died	Place	Bur	Place

Other Marriages

Index

A

Abstracts, 9

Access to Archival Databases
(AAD), 104

Adoption records, 5, 178–81

African-American roots, 181–87

AfriGeneas.com, 181

Ahnentafel system, 14–15

Allotment records, 192

American Civil War, 94, 98, 101–2,
182–84

American Jewish Archives, 187

American Jewish Historical
Society, 187–88

American Revolution, 95, 98, 100

American Slave Narratives, The, 184

Ancestors, explanation of, 3–4

Ancestors, searching for, 61–70

Ancestral File, 204

Ancestral pyramid, 2–3

Ancestry, 257

Ancestry World Tree, 205

Ancestry.com, 36, 83, 202, 207

AncestryPlus, 207

Archer, Frederick Scott, 30

Archive.org, 194

Archives, 211–15. *See also*
National Archives and Records
Administration

Autobiography, 272–74

Avotaynu, 188

B

Basics, 1–18

Bentley, Elizabeth Petty, 224

Bibles, 23, 24, 162

Birth certificates, 64, 71–76, 221

Blended families, 5

Books, 36–37, 283–97

Books We Own, 257

Boolean logic, 195–96

Brigham Young University (BYU),
255

Bureau of Land Management
(BLM), 146–48

Bureau of Missing Ancestors, 206

Burial records, 127–28

Burroughs, Tony, 182

C

Calendars, 12–14

Campbell Index, 222–23

Canadian border crossings, 117–18

Carmack, Sharon DeBartolo, 219

Cemeteries, 123–36

Census, 62, 65–66, 81–94, 112

Charts, 5–7, 230, 298

Chicago Manual of Style, The, 17

Church of Jesus Christ of Latter-day
Saints, 38, 94, 139, 157, 163, 204, 216

Church records, 162–64, 184–85,
190

Citing sources, 16–18, 206

Citizenship, 119–22

Civil court records, 221

Civil War. *See* American Civil War

Civil War Soldiers and Sailors
(CWSS), 101

Coats of arms, 57–59

Compiled Service Record (CSR), 98

*Consolidated Index to Compiled
Service Records of Confederate
Soldiers,* 101

Correspondence, 42–45

Cott Index, 222–23

Courthouse research, 78, 139–40,
218–23

Cousin relationships, 4, 198

CousinConnect.com, 203

Crane, Madilyn Coen, 15

Curran, Joan Ferris, 15

Customs Passenger Lists, 110, 111

D

Daguerre, Louis Jacques Mandé,
30

"Date brackets," 70

Dates, recording, 11–14

Daughters of the American
Revolution (DAR), 100, 105–6, 214,
224

Dawes Roll, 191

de Sosa, Jerome, 14

THE EVERYTHING SERIES!

BUSINESS & PERSONAL FINANCE

Everything® Budgeting Book
Everything® Business Planning Book
Everything® Coaching and Mentoring Book
Everything® Fundraising Book
Everything® Get Out of Debt Book
Everything® Grant Writing Book
Everything® Home-Based Business Book
Everything® Homebuying Book, 2nd Ed.
Everything® Homeselling Book, 2nd Ed.
Everything® Investing Book, 2nd Ed.
Everything® Landlording Book
Everything® Leadership Book
Everything® Managing People Book
Everything® Negotiating Book
Everything® Online Business Book
Everything® Personal Finance Book
Everything® Personal Finance in Your 20s
     and 30s Book
Everything® Project Management Book
Everything® Real Estate Investing Book
Everything® Robert's Rules Book, $7.95
Everything® Selling Book
Everything® Start Your Own Business Book
Everything® Wills & Estate Planning Book

COOKING

Everything® Barbecue Cookbook
Everything® Bartender's Book, $9.95
Everything® Chinese Cookbook
Everything® Cocktail Parties and Drinks
     Book
Everything® College Cookbook
Everything® Cookbook
Everything® Cooking for Two Cookbook
Everything® Diabetes Cookbook
Everything® Easy Gourmet Cookbook
Everything® Fondue Cookbook
Everything® Gluten-Free Cookbook

Everything® Grilling Cookbook
Everything® Healthy Meals in Minutes
     Cookbook
Everything® Holiday Cookbook
Everything® Indian Cookbook
Everything® Italian Cookbook
Everything® Low-Carb Cookbook
Everything® Low-Fat High-Flavor Cookbook
Everything® Low-Salt Cookbook
Everything® Meals for a Month Cookbook
Everything® Mediterranean Cookbook
Everything® Mexican Cookbook
Everything® One-Pot Cookbook
Everything® Pasta Cookbook
Everything® Quick Meals Cookbook
Everything® Slow Cooker Cookbook
Everything® Slow Cooking for a Crowd
     Cookbook
Everything® Soup Cookbook
Everything® Thai Cookbook
Everything® Vegetarian Cookbook
Everything® Wine Book, 2nd Ed.

CRAFT SERIES

Everything® Crafts—Baby Scrapbooking
Everything® Crafts—Bead Your Own Jewelry
Everything® Crafts—Create Your Own
     Greeting Cards
Everything® Crafts—Easy Projects
Everything® Crafts—Polymer Clay for
     Beginners
Everything® Crafts—Rubber Stamping
     Made Easy
Everything® Crafts—Wedding Decorations
     and Keepsakes

HEALTH

Everything® Alzheimer's Book
Everything® Diabetes Book
Everything® Health Guide to Controlling
     Anxiety

Everything® Hypnosis Book
Everything® Low Cholesterol Book
Everything® Massage Book
Everything® Menopause Book
Everything® Nutrition Book
Everything® Reflexology Book
Everything® Stress Management Book

HISTORY

Everything® American Government Book
Everything® American History Book
Everything® Civil War Book
Everything® Irish History & Heritage Book
Everything® Middle East Book

HOBBIES & GAMES

Everything® Blackjack Strategy Book
Everything® Brain Strain Book, $9.95
Everything® Bridge Book
Everything® Candlemaking Book
Everything® Card Games Book
Everything® Card Tricks Book, $9.95
Everything® Cartooning Book
Everything® Casino Gambling Book, 2nd Ed.
Everything® Chess Basics Book
Everything® Craps Strategy Book
Everything® Crossword and Puzzle Book
Everything® Crossword Challenge Book
Everything® Cryptograms Book, $9.95
Everything® Digital Photography Book
Everything® Drawing Book
Everything® Easy Crosswords Book
Everything® Family Tree Book, 2nd Ed.
Everything® Games Book, 2nd Ed.
Everything® Knitting Book
Everything® Knots Book
Everything® Photography Book
Everything® Poker Strategy Book
Everything® Pool & Billiards Book
Everything® Quilting Book
Everything® Scrapbooking Book

All Everything® books are priced at $12.95 or $14.95, unless otherwise stated. Prices subject to change without notice.

PETS

Everything® Cat Book
Everything® Dachshund Book
Everything® Dog Book
Everything® Dog Health Book
Everything® Dog Training and Tricks Book
Everything® German Shepherd Book
Everything® Golden Retriever Book
Everything® Horse Book
Everything® Horseback Riding Book
Everything® Labrador Retriever Book
Everything® Poodle Book
Everything® Pug Book
Everything® Puppy Book
Everything® Rottweiler Book
Everything® Small Dogs Book
Everything® Tropical Fish Book
Everything® Yorkshire Terrier Book

REFERENCE

Everything® Car Care Book
Everything® Classical Mythology Book
Everything® Computer Book
Everything® Divorce Book
Everything® Einstein Book
Everything® Etiquette Book, 2nd Ed.
Everything® Inventions and Patents Book
Everything® Mafia Book
Everything® Philosophy Book
Everything® Psychology Book
Everything® Shakespeare Book

RELIGION

Everything® Angels Book
Everything® Bible Book
Everything® Buddhism Book
Everything® Catholicism Book
Everything® Christianity Book
Everything® Jewish History & Heritage Book
Everything® Judaism Book
Everything® Koran Book
Everything® Prayer Book
Everything® Saints Book

Everything® Torah Book
Everything® Understanding Islam Book
Everything® World's Religions Book
Everything® Zen Book

SCHOOL & CAREERS

Everything® Alternative Careers Book
Everything® College Survival Book, 2nd Ed.
Everything® Cover Letter Book, 2nd Ed.
Everything® Get-a-Job Book
Everything® Guide to Starting and Running
     a Restaurant
Everything® Job Interview Book
Everything® New Teacher Book
Everything® Online Job Search Book
Everything® Paying for College Book
Everything® Practice Interview Book
Everything® Resume Book, 2nd Ed.
Everything® Study Book

SELF-HELP

Everything® Dating Book, 2nd Ed.
Everything® Great Sex Book
Everything® Kama Sutra Book
Everything® Self-Esteem Book

SPORTS & FITNESS

Everything® Fishing Book
Everything® Golf Instruction Book
Everything® Pilates Book
Everything® Running Book
Everything® Total Fitness Book
Everything® Weight Training Book
Everything® Yoga Book

TRAVEL

Everything® Family Guide to Hawaii
Everything® Family Guide to Las Vegas,
     2nd Ed.
Everything® Family Guide to New York City,
     2nd Ed.
Everything® Family Guide to RV Travel &
     Campgrounds

Everything® Family Guide to the Walt Disney
     World Resort®, Universal Studios®,
     and Greater Orlando, 4th Ed.
Everything® Family Guide to Cruise Vacations
Everything® Family Guide to the Caribbean
Everything® Family Guide to Washington
     D.C., 2nd Ed.
Everything® Guide to New England
Everything® Travel Guide to the Disneyland
     Resort®, California Adventure®,
     Universal Studios®, and the
     Anaheim Area

WEDDINGS

Everything® Bachelorette Party Book, $9.95
Everything® Bridesmaid Book, $9.95
Everything® Elopement Book, $9.95
Everything® Father of the Bride Book, $9.95
Everything® Groom Book, $9.95
Everything® Mother of the Bride Book, $9.95
Everything® Outdoor Wedding Book
Everything® Wedding Book, 3rd Ed.
Everything® Wedding Checklist, $9.95
Everything® Wedding Etiquette Book, $9.95
Everything® Wedding Organizer, $15.00
Everything® Wedding Shower Book, $9.95
Everything® Wedding Vows Book, $9.95
Everything® Weddings on a Budget Book,
     $9.95

WRITING

Everything® Creative Writing Book
Everything® Get Published Book
Everything® Grammar and Style Book
Everything® Guide to Writing a Book Proposal
Everything® Guide to Writing a Novel
Everything® Guide to Writing Children's Books
Everything® Guide to Writing Research Papers
Everything® Screenwriting Book
Everything® Writing Poetry Book
Everything® Writing Well Book

Everything® Sewing Book
Everything® Test Your IQ Book, $9.95
Everything® Travel Crosswords Book, $9.95
Everything® Woodworking Book
Everything® Word Games Challenge Book
Everything® Word Search Book

HOME IMPROVEMENT

Everything® Feng Shui Book
Everything® Feng Shui Decluttering Book,
    $9.95
Everything® Fix-It Book
Everything® Homebuilding Book
Everything® Lawn Care Book
Everything® Organize Your Home Book

EVERYTHING®
KIDS' BOOKS

All titles are $6.95

Everything® Kids' Animal Puzzle & Activity
    Book
Everything® Kids' Baseball Book, 3rd Ed.
Everything® Kids' Bible Trivia Book
Everything® Kids' Bugs Book
Everything® Kids' Christmas Puzzle
    & Activity Book
Everything® Kids' Cookbook
Everything® Kids' Crazy Puzzles Book
Everything® Kids' Dinosaurs Book
Everything® Kids' Gross Jokes Book
Everything® Kids' Gross Puzzle and
    Activity Book
Everything® Kids' Halloween Puzzle
    & Activity Book
Everything® Kids' Hidden Pictures Book
Everything® Kids' Joke Book
Everything® Kids' Knock Knock Book
Everything® Kids' Math Puzzles Book
Everything® Kids' Mazes Book
Everything® Kids' Money Book
Everything® Kids' Nature Book
Everything® Kids' Puzzle Book
Everything® Kids' Riddles & Brain Teasers Book
Everything® Kids' Science Experiments Book
Everything® Kids' Sharks Book
Everything® Kids' Soccer Book
Everything® Kids' Travel Activity Book

KIDS' STORY BOOKS

Everything® Fairy Tales Book

LANGUAGE

Everything® Conversational Japanese Book
    (with CD), $19.95
Everything® French Phrase Book, $9.95
Everything® French Verb Book, $9.95
Everything® Inglés Book
Everything® Learning French Book
Everything® Learning German Book
Everything® Learning Italian Book
Everything® Learning Latin Book
Everything® Learning Spanish Book
Everything® Sign Language Book
Everything® Spanish Grammar Book
Everything® Spanish Practice Book
    (with CD), $19.95
Everything® Spanish Phrase Book, $9.95
Everything® Spanish Verb Book, $9.95

MUSIC

Everything® Drums Book (with CD), $19.95
Everything® Guitar Book
Everything® Home Recording Book
Everything® Playing Piano and Keyboards
    Book
Everything® Reading Music Book (with CD),
    $19.95
Everything® Rock & Blues Guitar Book
    (with CD), $19.95
Everything® Songwriting Book

NEW AGE

Everything® Astrology Book, 2nd Ed.
Everything® Dreams Book, 2nd Ed.
Everything® Ghost Book
Everything® Love Signs Book, $9.95
Everything® Numerology Book
Everything® Paganism Book
Everything® Palmistry Book
Everything® Psychic Book
Everything® Reiki Book
Everything® Tarot Book
Everything® Wicca and Witchcraft Book

PARENTING

Everything® Baby Names Book
Everything® Baby Shower Book
Everything® Baby's First Food Book
Everything® Baby's First Year Book
Everything® Birthing Book
Everything® Breastfeeding Book
Everything® Father-to-Be Book
Everything® Father's First Year Book
Everything® Get Ready for Baby Book
Everything® Get Your Baby to Sleep Book,
    $9.95
Everything® Getting Pregnant Book
Everything® Homeschooling Book
Everything® Mother's First Year Book
Everything® Parent's Guide to Children
    and Divorce
Everything® Parent's Guide to Children
    with ADD/ADHD
Everything® Parent's Guide to Children
    with Asperger's Syndrome
Everything® Parent's Guide to Children
    with Autism
Everything® Parent's Guide to Children with
    Bipolar Disorder
Everything® Parent's Guide to Children
    with Dyslexia
Everything® Parent's Guide to Positive
    Discipline
Everything® Parent's Guide to Raising a
    Successful Child
Everything® Parent's Guide to Tantrums
Everything® Parent's Guide to the Overweight
    Child
Everything® Parent's Guide to the Strong-
    Willed Child
Everything® Parenting a Teenager Book
Everything® Potty Training Book, $9.95
Everything® Pregnancy Book, 2nd Ed.
Everything® Pregnancy Fitness Book
Everything® Pregnancy Nutrition Book
Everything® Pregnancy Organizer, $15.00
Everything® Toddler Book
Everything® Tween Book
Everything® Twins, Triplets, and More Book

All Everything® books are priced at $12.95 or $14.95, unless otherwise stated. Prices subject to change without notice.